Girl Left Behind

SAINT JULIAN PRESS

Praise for *Girl Left Behind*

"Such a lyrical, soul-rending, sumptuous book! It captures the heart and mind of a Hungarian girl who is sad and brave at the same time as she tries to make sense of what looks like her family's desertion. A testament to the triumph of the human spirit in the face of deep loneliness and loss, *Girl Left Behind* reminds us that one can have no home anywhere and at the same time have a special kind of home everywhere."

—Daniel Asa Rose
Author of *Hiding Places: A Father and His Sons
Retrace Their Family's Escape from the Holocaust*,
and other books

"This is a story full of heartache but also one which celebrates the strength of the human spirit and the will to survive. It is a book for anyone who has lost someone they loved, or even anyone who never has, but fears the experience. In short—this is a book for everyone."

—Elizabeth Cohen
Author of *The Family on Beartown Road:
A Memoir of Love and Courage*

"*Girl Left Behind* is a gripping, heartbreaking, and strikingly beautiful memoir of the immigrant experience that is all the more relevant and necessary in today's political climate. In a tale that is reminiscent of *The Liar's Club* and *The Glass Castle*, Judy Temes, a masterful and compassionate storyteller, captivates the reader with her charm, wit, and lyrical prose. This is a story that will stick with me, and that I will never be able to leave behind."

—William Dameron
Author of *The Lie: A Memoir of Two Marriages,
Catfishing and Coming Out*

Girl Left Behind

A Memoir

Judy Temes

SAINT JULIAN PRESS
HOUSTON

Published by

SAINT JULIAN PRESS, Inc.
2053 Cortlandt, Suite 200
Houston, Texas 77008

www.saintjulianpress.com

ISBN-13: 978-1-7330233-2-0
ISBN-10: 1-7330233-2-1

Library of Congress Control Number: 2020945800

Cover Art Credit: Nancy Nimoy
Author Photo Credit: Rick Dahms

To my parents, Piroska and Lászlo,
and my grandmother, Katalin.
To Peter, for his wisdom and love.
To my children—Katie, Leah, and Joseph—
who make everything worthwhile.

See it, the beautiful ball
Poised in the toyshop window,
Rounder than sun or moon.
Is it red? is it blue? is it violet?
It is everything we desire,
And it does not exist at all.

—Adrienne Rich
"A Ball Is for Throwing"

Girl Left Behind

One

Time to Go

It was finally dark. The moon rose over the onion-domed church, then hid behind a black cloud.

"Good," my father said.

He turned his back on the window to look at my mother, a leather suitcase opened before her.

"Finish packing. It's time to go."

"I just need a few more things." She stared at the stuffed suitcase. Skirts, some tops, three pairs of orthopedic shoes to adjust for her one short leg. What else? She scanned the room, looking for something: a book of poems, the gold jewelry case, maybe her brown wool coat.

"Hurry up. I want to get there before midnight. You have the visas?"

"They're in my bag. All three."

"Ok. Finish up. We need to go."

Supper was cleaned up, the kitchen spotless. Juliska Néni made sure. She was our housekeeper, a plump lady with gray hair and thick hands she was not afraid to use when my brother and I didn't do as she said. She woke at dawn that day to scrub the floors, strip the beds, and cover the green velvet sofa with white sheets. She didn't like dust and wouldn't have it collecting while we were gone. She got my brother and I out of bed early that day and made sure we packed our bags—enough socks and underwear to last a month. Everything was ready for summer vacation.

The way my mother explained it, we would drive to my grandmother's house near the lake. Juliska Néni would stay with me, to help my grandmother take care of me. She, my father, and Tibor would then go to Vienna. It was a beautiful city, she said, one of the most beautiful in the world, with bakeries that made delicious cakes, a zoo, and a palace with 1,000 rooms! She told Tibor all about it that summer. He was almost thirteen, old enough to go on the special trip, his second outside Hungary.

"Will it be like Split?" he asked. "The fishing was great there." Tibor lived for fishing. Every Saturday, our neighbor Gyusi Bácsi came over with a bucket and a fishing rod to take Tibor down the Danube in his wooden boat. The fish they brought back were slimy and I held my nose when they handed the batch to Juliska Néni to make into fish soup. I didn't like the fish any better cooked in soup.

"No, it won't be like Split," our father told him on days he was home that summer in 1969. "Vienna is a big city, like Budapest."

Split was last summer's vacation. It was the first time Tibor got to go along with our parents. I was left home with Juliska Néni then too. In the color slides they later showed on a white sheet hung in the living room, I saw my mother swimming in sky-blue waters, my brother fishing happily on a long pier, my father in his bathing suit by the sea, relaxed, reading the newspaper. They seemed so happy. I stared at the pictures flitting by on the white sheet, and didn't understand why I could not swim by their side in the crystal blue waters of the Adriatic Sea.

"But don't worry," our father continued. "There's plenty to do in Vienna. Wait 'till you taste the *Sachertorte!*" He held three fingers to his mouth and made a loud kissing sound.

"What's *sacher* . . . what's that?" I asked. It was a bold question. We weren't usually allowed to speak at the dinner table. We were to dress nice, sit up straight, and eat in silence. But my father was in a happy mood that day. I could tell by the way he slurped the soup and smacked his lips.

"Aah, it's the most delicious cake in the world," my father said, "even better than Juliska Néni's strudel," he said with a wink. "*Elnezést Juliska.* Yours is the second best in the world." Really happy mood.

"If you don't want mine for dessert, just tell me now. I'll give more to Juditka."

She could tell too.

"No, no. No sense missing the second-best pastry in the world."

"I want to eat *sacher* . . . *sacher* . . ." what was the word? "I want to eat cake too," I cried, pushing the fish soup away. "Why can't I go to Vienna and eat cake too?"

"You're too little," my brother pronounced, sitting taller in his chair. "Vienna is not for five-year-olds."

"You will have much more fun at Nagymama's house," my mother said. "You can swim in the lake all day. Remember the ice cream man from last year? Juliska Néni will buy you ice cream every day."

I loved my grandmother's house. But more than anything, I loved swimming in the turquoise waters of Lake Balaton. Even in summers when my parents went far away to places like Split, we spent at least a week there together. My father would grab the inflatable red and blue raft, put it on his head, and carry it to the beach, striding along the pebbled road like a king wearing a shiny gold crown. We would fall in line behind him, my brother bringing the beach ball, my mother carrying a basket of salami, red tomatoes, fresh bread, and juicy ripe peaches. At the end of the block, right before we hit the beach, we'd stop at the watermelon stand, where the vendor would slice a piece for my father to taste. "Good enough for you, Dr. Boros?" he'd ask. My father would bite into the red delicious sweetness and let it ooze down his chin. "Let's try another," he'd say, hoping to score another free slice before committing to pay for the whole thing. "Juditka, you try this one."

I'd suck the sweet juice and let it trickle down my chin just like my father. "This one is good," I'd nod, hoping he was in a happy mood and would buy the whole thing.

We'd splash in the lake until my fingers turned to prunes.

I couldn't wait to get to the lake. But I also didn't want to be left behind. I wanted to see all 1,000 rooms of the palace in Vienna and eat the cake that my father said had apricot jam and chocolate icing.

¤ ¤ ¤

I cried the day they went to the photographers for the official pictures. They needed them for the papers that would let them cross the border into Vienna, my mother said. They spent all morning getting dressed to look extra nice. Juliska Néni ironed my brother's button-down shirt and polished my father's shoes. My mother put on lipstick to match the color of her skirt.

"I want to go too," I wailed. "I want to have a picture taken too." I pouted and stomped my stiff black and white lace-up shoes on the polished floor. Big tears streamed down my cheeks. I kicked the floor hard, almost scratching it.

But my father said no; there'd be no papers for me, so there was no reason to spend money on pictures.

My mother tried reason. "Look at Tibike," she said, pointing to my brother, already sweating through his starched shirt, its collar nearly choking him. "You don't want to sit under all those hot lights."

"Yes I do," I cried. "Please take me with you, Anyuka. I want to go with you."

Such a fuss was not okay with my father. "Make her stop or I'll do it," he barked from the bathroom, straightening his tie before the mirror.

So my mother made me a deal. "All right. You can come along and have your picture taken," she finally said. "But you have to promise to stop acting up right now. It's making Apuka very upset."

Her soft voice, her hands like feathers on my head, got me to calm down. "Okay," I said. "But can I still go on the trip with you? Please Anyuka, I'll be good."

"I'm sorry, Nunush" she said, lowering herself down on the floor next to me in her white slip. Her outfit for the photographer's, matching pink skirt and jacket, were laid out on the bed. She never wore such bright colors.

"But I'll be good. I promise."

"Maybe in a few years. When you are older, like Tibike." She brushed a sweaty curl from my blotchy face. "Now, go and pick out a dress for the photographer."

I left her on the floor to find a dress, and came back with my favorite: a red flannel, sleeveless beach dress with little white fish sewn on the pockets and four white buttons down the front. I put my sleeves through the holes and fastened the white buttons all by myself the way they taught us in nursery school, and came back to my mother, proud.

She smiled when she saw me. "It's perfect," she said.

We walked along Liberty Street to the photographer's studio. My father raced ahead like he always did, never waiting for our mother, who walked slowly with the limp she'd had since she learned to walk. Even in her ugly shoes, she looked beautiful; her skin milky soft, her hair a chestnut brown. My brother fought to keep up with my father's long stride. I clung to my mother, so happy to be by her side. I imagined the whole city admiring us as we paraded down the main street. I imagined neighbors craning their necks from the windows like they did on the day of the May Day parade when everyone in our city—like every other city and village in Hungary—marched along carrying gigantic portraits of a man my father quietly called "that son-of-a-bitch Stalin."

"How beautiful you look Dr. Boros," Mrs. Farkas would call from her living room window, admiring my mother's new outfit. "That shade of pink suits you very nicely. And look at Juditka with her red dress. How it matches her cheeks!"

Inside the photographer's dark studio, I waited patiently while the men made small talk and snapped picture after picture of my father, mother, and brother. I sat on my hands to keep from fidgeting. It seemed to go on forever. But I promised to not whine, to show my father I was good, so I waited quietly for my turn. When the man with the camera finally called me, I leapt onto the chair in the spotlight. I squirmed under the hot lights as the man adjusted the camera. I sat up straight, patted my hair to try and straighten the curls, and put on my happiest smile. The photographer took a single shot, then turned off the light and covered up his camera. "You can pay the girl on your way out," he said to my father. I climbed down from the chair, confused by my short turn in the limelight. "Come," my brother grabbed my hand, "Let's go."

¤ ¤ ¤

The tourist visas with the black-and-white pictures glued inside arrived in the mail that summer. There was no visa for my small black-and-white portrait. My mother tucked it in her wallet.

I promised her to be good on the day of our departure that August, and I was true to my word. I woke early when Juliska Néni said so. I dressed myself; I even dressed my doll Zsuzsi Baba. She smelled like the rubber raft we took to the lake, her face was dirty, and most of her clothes were lost, but she had curly black hair like mine, so she was my favorite. I knew I would not be allowed to see the palaces in Vienna or eat *Sachertorte*. But at least I'd see my grandmother. I knew she would give me chocolate at bedtime, and Juliska Néni would take me to the lake every day and buy me ice cream. I didn't cry once all that day.

"I'm ready, Apuka!" I shouted to my father, dragging my small suitcase in one hand and Zsuzsi Baba in the other. "I packed all by myself. I can't wait to see Mamika and go swimming. Maybe you can stay one more day and take me to the beach in the morning . . . just one day . . . Apuka?"

But he was no longer in the room. He'd followed my mother into their bedroom, where she was now pacing the wood floor as her suitcase stared at her, wide-mouthed and hungry. She looked around the apartment—the piano, the television, the oil canvasses in their fancy frames, the Herend porcelain, my crib, tucked neatly beside their bed. My father may have been a doctor, but like his father, he had commerce in his heart. Every trip he managed across Hungary's iron border was an opportunity to bring something home. We were first in our small city to get a black-and-white television; we also had a flush toilet, pretty porcelain dishes that you could see through when you held them up to the light, art, and lots of books. We even had a car!

At first, he went only as far as Budapest. That's where he bought the green velvet sofa made of cherry trees. It reminded me of the mossy forests in the fairy tales. It was in our living room, but we weren't allowed in there or allowed to sit on the sofa, either. It was for special guests, but even the special guests had to sit on towels. Then my father figured out how to get across the border into Austria and Italy. He went once every four years, the maximum Hungarians were allowed to travel to the West, filling metal cans with gasoline for the trip. He wanted to spend the cash he had on nice things for us, not gasoline or food. Juliska Néni filled up baskets with canned food that would last most of the trip. Instead of staying in hotels, he and my mother camped. My brother and I would listen with fascination to my mother's stories of how a huge black bear broke into their tent in the middle of the night and almost ate them for supper, and how they ran out of gas in the Alps and it was lucky they were heading downhill.

Coming home under the cover of darkness, my father would unload from the car all kinds of luxuries: a handheld movie camera, soft sweaters from baby lambs, pretty Italian shoes, and for Tibor and me, polished wooden rings like the ones the gymnasts used in the Olympic games we watched for the first time on television in 1968. My father hung them between two doorposts in our apartment. Tibor and I twisted and turned on the rings, pointing our toes in the air just like the gymnasts we watched on the television station broadcasting from Mexico City. My father would hide these things in secret compartments of the car because they were all treasures, he told us, treasures no one else had.

¤ ¤ ¤

My mother stood before her open suitcase now. She had to pack but she didn't know what. I saw her pick up a book of poems by Radnóti. She read him every night and knew many of his beautiful poems by heart. Sometimes she recited them in the car on the way to my grandmother's house, or sometimes at night when she tucked me into my little bed, next to hers. Sometimes she cried before the poem was finished.

She picked up a tiny green porcelain girl sitting cross legged on an oak shelf. But she didn't pack that either. She put her back on the shelf. She walked to her closet and took out a soft brown wool coat. I laughed at her.

"That's not for summer, Anyuka," I told her. "Even I know that." I handed her the gray-and-black bathing suit she always wore to the lake. It had little fish on it, just like my red dress. "Take this."

"*Okos kislány*," she said. I liked it when she called me smart.

My father shooed me out of the room. "Go finish packing," he said. "We're leaving soon."

"At least this then," I heard my mother say, holding up a small brown album filled with color photographs taken last summer at the lake. We were all there—my brother, my four cousins, my father, mother, even my uncle, who came out to the lake to shoot the photos with the color film that my father brought back from somewhere that year. It was the newest thing. Juliska Néni packed a summer picnic. My father brought the inflatable raft; we played in the water until our lips turned blue. My uncle developed the pictures and sent them by mail to our home—the first color photos anyone had seen in our city.

"Not the whole thing," I heard my father say. "The guards will be suspicious. Pick a few pictures, but let's go already."

He was tall, handsome still, with thick black curly hair and a tan—already a tan—though the vacation had not even begun. She looked up at him, still amazed that she, a girl with a crooked nose and a limp, a girl her mother said no one would marry, would have a husband like him. She sighed and glanced at my brother and me, sitting on our bags in the foyer just outside their bedroom door, impatient to go, but knowing enough to stay out of their way.

"I don't know if I can do this," she whispered.

"Now is not the time, Piri. We've gone over this."

"I just . . . I don't know . . . ."

"Yes you do. You know the plan. We just have to do it."

"But what if . . . what it we never . . ."

"We've been through this, Piri."

"But how can we make this choice?"

"Enough," I heard him raise his voice from the hallway. "Everything is set. The diplomas are taken care of . . . the visas. Juditka will be fine. Now, close that bag."

I heard her take a deep sigh.

"Take a few photos," my father said after a moment. "It's time to go."

She pulled a handful of pictures from the album and tucked them in her handbag, leaving the rest. She took another long, slow breath, dropped the book of poems on top of her bathing suit, and snapped the suitcase shut. It was August, after all. A book and a bathing suit would work for the border guards just fine.

Tired of waiting, Tibor stuck his head in their bedroom. "What's taking so long?"

"We are ready when I say so," I heard my father say sharply.

Tibor came back into the hallway, and grabbed his fishing rod in one hand and my hand in the other. City vacation or not—the fishing rod was coming along.

"Come on." He pulled me through the front door and into the staircase with my suitcase clomping behind me down the cement steps to the courtyard below and out the large wooden gate to the car parked under the flickering streetlight. "*Anyuka siessél!*" I called behind me. "Hurry up Mommy."

Juliska Néni lumbered down the stairs behind us, carrying a suitcase and a basket of food. She squeezed in the back in between my brother and me, and we waited for my father and mother to come down. "*Gyere ide Juditkám,*" Juliska Néni said, putting a heavy arm around my waist and pulling me to her big bosom. "Sit closer to me." I rested my head on her squishy belly. It's not something she usually allowed. "Up up," she'd say when I tried to snuggle up against her. "There's work to be done." She was more cook and housekeeper than nanny, more comfortable with a broom than a bedtime book. She'd been with our family since Tibor was a baby and my mother needed help in the house to go to work. Sometimes I felt sad for her because I wasn't sure I loved her. Most days, I just wanted her to go away so I could be with my mother. She patted my head this time as we waited in the dark car.

Finally my mother came down, carrying a small purse. She got in the passenger seat and crossed herself. "In God's name," she whispered. She did this before every trip we took in the car, then spent the rest of the trip singing, and teaching my brother and I silly songs about big dogs and little dogs. But she wasn't singing this time. She was wiping tears from her face with a handkerchief.

"Why are you crying, Anyuka?" I put a hand on her shoulder. "Will you miss the babies?"

She was the baby doctor, the only one in our town. Mothers from our city and beyond came to the clinic down the street from our apartment carrying babies or dragging little children. Some ate too much, some not enough. Some had red rashes; others had broken arms. All of them needed shots. Sometimes when the mothers could not come to her, she rode her red bicycle to them, her skirt blowing behind her in the wind, to make sure the babies got their shots and the moms proper feeding and changing instructions.

"Yes, Juditka," she said. "I will miss the babies."

"Don't worry, Anyuka. We will be home soon. You will see the babies again."

She faced forward and didn't say any more.

Finally, my father came downstairs carrying two suitcases. He opened the trunk, placed the bags inside, closed the lid, and got in the driver's seat. He glanced up at the windows of our apartment and checked the rearview mirror. I could see that his eyes were also moist. But I didn't say anything. I put my head back on Juliska Néni's belly as my father started the engine.

The car sputtered and stalled several times, but finally the engine caught and my father pulled away from the curb, driving past the church with the green onion dome, the children's clinic, the hospital, the school, the kindergarten, the ferry terminal on the Danube, and finally out on country roads under a full moon, bright like a shiny gold coin, lighting up the night.

Our white Skoda was a horrible car. It stopped and started and sputtered to a halt at the worst times. Then my father would get out, circle the car and curse the engine and the year's salary that he lost buying a worthless piece of Czech junk. He once told me how on the cold December night I was born, it rolled into a muddy ditch with my pregnant mother inside. He was lucky, he said, to find four drunk peasants to free the car from the mud and get it back on the road. They made it to the hospital with barely a few minutes to spare before I came squirming into the world.

This time the car didn't roll in the ditch and the engine hummed as we drove from our city toward my grandmother's. It was a clear night, and I watched the countryside roll by as my father headed north toward the lake.

The engine and Juliska Néni's cozy belly finally lulled me to sleep. After a long time, the smooth paved roads gave way to something rough. I felt the pebbles under the tires and knew we were almost at my grandmother's. The engine came to a stop and I stirred awake. My father picked me up and quietly carried me through the front gate and into the cool house. I felt his bristly face turn moist next to mine. I snuggled closer to his chest, but he put me down on cold sheets and a rough woolen blanket. I felt my mother's soft cheeks brush up against mine, a cool hand against my sweaty head. A breeze blew through the open window. I heard some distant voices, some conversation I could not make out, and the sound of the engine kicking into gear. And they were gone.

Two

House on the Lake

My grandmother's house was a sturdy, yellow stucco near Lake Balaton. It wasn't on the north shore, where red-tiled roofs hung like rubies over the turquoise waters. It stood on the poorer south shore, where the water was a thick brown from the volcanic ash that settled there long ago, making the lake's bottom soft and spongy and shallow enough for the smallest child to feel safe. The house belonged to my uncle, but I never thought of it as his, maybe because the house itself was so much like my grandmother—old and stooped with cracked walls like the blue veins that snaked up her arms, but dependable and strong with a solid foundation and a good roof. My grandmother told me it was once a grand house owned by a lord or a baron, with a verandah and three graceful arches overlooking a sea of wildflowers, plum trees, and weeping willows that spread as far as the railroad that cut across the village. But by the summer of 1969, all three arches were plastered shut to create something more useful—rooms for paying summertime guests.

"*Zimmer Frei*"—"Rooms Vacant"—read the sign in German that hung in a street-side window.

My grandmother and aunt never seemed to stop working, weeding, washing, cooking, sweeping, and tending to these summertime guests—all with little help from my four cousins or my uncle, who also lived in the house. But it was of little use. Despite all their work, weeds choked the strawberries, mud seeped into the yard, the walls cracked. My grandmother said there was never enough time, money, or men to help fix things up.

¤ ¤ ¤

I didn't notice any of those things back then. Summer visits to my grandmother's house meant just one thing: the lake, with its warm waters, its muddy bottom, its grassy, beach, and white sailboats.

"Wake up Juliska Néni!" I shook my nanny hard the morning after we arrived. "I want to go to the lake."

"Juditka, it's not even seven o'clock." She never slept in, but it was her vacation too. On the bed next to mine, she rearranged the pillows and stuck her sweaty head back under the covers. "How about you go say hi to Mamika first."

My grandmother! I almost forgot my grandmother. Her black dress smelled like musty bread, but its magic pockets always conjured some delicious treat, a melty piece of chocolate or sucking candy. She wore a faded black kerchief over soft white hair that felt like a dove's feathers. Her back was stooped, her hands wrinkled apricots. A year's black soil seemed buried under her thick fingernails. I loved my grandmother. I loved her more than ice cream cones and cake, maybe even more than the lake.

I jumped from the guest room bed and ran to the front yard. I found her kneeling at the well, dangling a tin bucket by a frayed rope into a deep dark hole. I squatted down next to her and hugged her around the waist. She held me for a long time. "I'm glad you are here," she finally said, brushing back the curls that clung to my sweaty brow. "I brought you some fresh rolls and chocolate milk. I hope you're hungry."

We walked over to the arbor of green leaves and tiny hard grapes that never seemed to ripen. We sat down at a table covered with a red-checkered plastic tablecloth. She filled my cup with cold chocolate milk and broke the roll in half. I took a bite and chased it down with the chocolate milk, leaving a dark brown ring over my lip.

"Did they leave?"

"Yes, you were asleep. They didn't want to wake you."

"I didn't even get to kiss Anyuka goodbye."

"She kissed you. You were sleeping."

"Where do you think they are now?"

"Maybe in Austria already."

"I thought they were going to Vienna?"

"Same place, I think." She laughed. Where her teeth once were, she now had tough pink gums that could chew through last week's bread or even a chicken bone. She had deep grooves in her face, like the furrows she dug to plant strawberries every spring.

"I wanted to go with them."

"I know. But you will have more fun with us here swimming every day."

"Tibor got to go."

"He's older now."

"Can I go when I'm older?"

"Maybe, if your father and mother say you can. Now, how about we start the day?"

I remembered Juliska Néni, still sleeping in the guest room. I ran from the table to wake her. I found her in the dark room, changing into her housedress. I flung open my suitcase, found my bathing suit and changed too, ready for the best part of summer to begin.

¤ ¤ ¤

15

My grandmother's village, Balaton Mária Fürdő, was not much more than a tired old railroad crossing in the winter. But come summer, it turned into a rainbow quilt of colored bikinis, rafts, and beach balls. The narrow, pebbled street that led to my grandmother's house was filled with families from every corner of the world we knew. They came from Bucharest and Warsaw, from East Berlin and Leningrad. The Yugos had pretty clothes; the Germans ate well and it showed. The Soviets were skinny and had names no one could pronounce. They came for the lake, for the mountains, the bull's blood wine and cold beer. They came for the *lángos*, fried dough sold from tiny windows of tiny kitchens; they came for watered-down ice cream, for red paprika and fish stew. They filled the winding unpaved streets, bringing color, noise, and life. Men sold beach balls and rubber rafts by the road. Even the local hotel got in on the action, selling cigarettes and French perfume for American dollars and Deutsche marks. With the Western money that oozed in, teenagers like my big cousins bought makeup and perfume and bell-bottom jeans—things rare and precious. None of this was officially allowed, but somehow the summer's black market was tolerated and business thrived. The police winked, ate some fried dough, and drank it down with a cold beer.

Juliska Néni woke early every day to help my grandmother prepare breakfast and pack lunch, and we'd walk to the beach, where I played in the water, jumping from the docks, refusing to come out until my teeth chattered and Juliska Néni threatened. "Come out this minute, Juditka, or there'll be no ice cream today," she'd holler. We ate lunch on the grassy banks of the lake and licked chocolate ice cream cones on the walk home. We slept in a guest room, tucked under the soft goose down blankets normally reserved for paying guests. The next day we returned to the lake and did it all over again.

My grandmother stayed home to dig and rake, pick fruit, can vegetables, prepare breakfast, dinner and supper, and wash linen by hand in a tin tub in the back yard. She hugged me

goodbye every morning as I left for the beach holding Juliska
Néni's hand, and greeted us with a weary smile at the end of the
day.

"Hurry, hurry! Supper is almost ready," she'd call as we
walked through the front gate after a long day at the beach. My
grandmother was sitting under the grape arbor in her old black
dress, a bowl in her lap, peeling cucumbers for supper.

Juliska Néni put down the bags containing our towels, the
beach ball, and leftover food, and sat down with a heavy sigh.
She wiped her brow with a handkerchief. "She's a handful, I tell
you. Never stops bouncing around."

"That's how they are . . . little kids," my grandmother said.

Juliska Néni stuck a finger in the cucumber salad and
tasted it "A little more paprika wouldn't hurt."

"Thank you for the advice," my grandmother smiled.

"Was there, by any chance, mail today?" Juliska asked.
"Any news from Vienna?"

"No. No news. They must be enjoying themselves."

"Well, who wouldn't?" Juliska wiped her brow again. "The
opera house, the Belvedere, the Stephansdom . . . I wish I could
go for a vacation like that."

"I'd say."

"When did they tell you they'd be coming home?"

"I forget the exact day. Before school starts for sure," my
grandmother said, eyes fixed on the salad.

Katus Néni walked past the arbor, carrying a load of
freshly-dried sheets picked off the clothesline. "Mamika," she
called to my grandmother. "Can you help me make the beds?
We have new guests coming in the morning." She was my aunt,
my mother's only sister, but I almost never went near her.
Maybe it was her scrunched lips or tired eyes; maybe it was her
housedress whose pockets held clothespins, not chocolate treats.
Maybe it was because she smelled like laundry soap and bleach.
Except for the fact that she was small, nothing about her

reminded me of my mother. She walked right past me, hurrying toward the guest rooms in need of cleaning.

My uncle howled from inside the house. "What does a man have to do to get food around here?"

Zoli Bácsi rarely came out of his room at the end of the long linoleum hallway. He ate alone, and I didn't mind. With his smelly smoking stick, prickly mustache, bony arms, and loud voice always yelling at my aunt and grandmother, he scared me. My grandmother picked up the cucumber salad and carried it inside. "I better go and feed the beast," she said to my aunt. "Your husband needs his supper."

Juliska Néni and I ate alone under the green leaves of the arbor as the two of them went off to do all their chores.

We went back to the lake the following day, and the one after, the same routine for almost a month. But September brought changes. There were no more girls in bikinis, no more rainbow-colored rafts floating on the lake. The ice cream vendor packed up his cart and went home to Budapest or some other city. The Russians and East Germans returned to their factory jobs. The sailboats sailed away. Just the locals stuck around—a different sort. They were widows like my grandmother in long black frocks, kerchiefs covering their hair, bargaining for eggs; they were the men in dusty jackets riding in horse-drawn carts. They were the children in blue school jackets carrying satchels full of books covered in indigo wrap, a sticker with red borders plastered in the middle to indicate their names.

"When will I start school?" I asked Juliska Néni.

"Soon, Juditkám. Anyuka and Apuka should be back any day."

"Which day?"

"Soon. Any day now."

Back at my grandmother's house, Juliska Néni again asked about the mail from Vienna. The answer was the same. No mail. Not yet.

"I don't understand," Juliska said, shaking her head. A knot took root on her forehead and never went away. "It's not like Piri to not write."

¤ ¤ ¤

We packed our bags the next week. With no letter to tell her what to do, Juliska Néni decided it was best we go home to our apartment in Mohács and wait for my parents and brother to arrive there. Maybe they loved Vienna so much, they decided to skip the annual family vacation to the lake. With school starting, she figured they would probably be heading straight home.

We ate our last meal under the arbor as the frogs and crickets of summer sang their goodbyes. My grandmother made me my favorite supper—cream of wheat sprinkled with sugar crystals and coco powder. But I wasn't hungry. I twirled my spoon around and around in the bowl.

"Juditka, eat," Juliska Néni said. "We won't have time for a big breakfast in the morning. We have to catch the train early."

"But there's nothing to do at home," I whined. "And Apuka hasn't come to play in the lake. I want to play in the lake with Apuka and Tibor."

"Nursery school is starting. It's time we get back."

"But I don't want to go. I want Anyuka and Apuka to come to the lake."

"It's going to be different this year," she said. "Don't whine or your voice will get stuck like that forever."

She turned her back on me and whispered to my grandmother, who was chewing on a piece of hard bread. "Is it possible something happened to them?"

"I think they just decided to stay longer. They must be enjoying themselves. I wouldn't worry."

"I just don't understand," Juliska Néni said, shifting her weight in the chair and wiping her sweaty brow. She was always sweaty, her face red, her ankles swollen, her thighs stuffed into

19

tight stockings, even in summer. "It's not like them to be so delayed and not send word."

"You know the mail. It's always two weeks behind," my grandmother reassured her. "They are probably on their way home now."

"I guess I'm the idiot for worrying. Anyway, it will be good to get Juditka home. Her nursery school opened days ago."

"I'll get Árpád to help you to the train station tomorrow."

We started out early the next day, walking along the same rough pebbly walk that my father drove just weeks before. My cousin Árpád volunteered to carry our bags. Unlike my other three cousins, Árpád never said no when someone asked him to do something. The others would run away when my grandmother called them, disappear into the treehouse or get lost among the wildflowers and tall grass. Not Árpád. With his strawberry hair and freckles, he stood out among my black-haired cousins. He wore his red Pioneer scarf with pride. On the day of our departure, he carried our bags to the train station like the obedient scout he was. I waved goodbye to him through the smoky window, and we were off, heading back home.

¤ ¤ ¤

Mohács, our city, is an important one, my brother once explained. It was here that the Ottoman emperor Suleiman the Magnificent defeated the Hungarian army of King Lajos II. It was an awful day. Foreigners ruled our country for 500 years after that, he said. First came the Turks, then the Austrians, then the Nazis, and eventually the Soviets, who were in charge now. Mention my city and Hungarians still bow their heads in grief. "More was lost in Mohács," they say in bad times or moments of misfortune.

But to me, Mohács, where the Danube bends and heads south toward the Adriatic, was home. It was home to our apartment on Szabadság Utca, Liberty Street, the hospital where my father cured the sick, and the clinic where my mother healed babies and blew kisses from the window overlooking the tree-lined street I walked to and from nursery school. It was a small city, just 15,000 people. Many more lived here before my brother and I were born. There was Mr. Pollak, who sold books, Mr. Blum, who owned a diner, and the Rosenthal family, who manufactured bricks in a factory on the Danube. There was Dr. Schwartz, a lawyer named Levy, and Mr. Klein, a merchant. There was a synagogue too, with arched windows and doors and five stone columns reaching up to God, but this was torn down and replaced with a cement apartment building. The government called it progress. They had a harder time trying to take down the churches. The largest one had a bronze onion dome instead of a steeple. It stood at the center of the large square once named for the reformer, Szécsényi István, who, it was said, tamed the Danube and made it fit for ships and trade. It was later renamed Szabadság Tér, Liberty Square, in honor of our Soviet liberators, who according to the radio, gave us back our freedom and made our country safe, prosperous, and a happy place for all.

Everyone had a job, even the lowly man who never graduated grade school. He got to sweep the street. And if the kid who never graduated high school joined the party, he could get a big apartment, my father used to tell us. He could be the big boss and tell everyone what to do, even the doctors at the hospital. The party sounded like fun. I told my father I'd go to that party, but he just smirked and told my brother and me to stick to school. That sounded like much less fun.

My father used to say liberty was the wrong name to call the square, but I disagreed. I loved Liberty Square. It was a big, wide-open space where we could look up and see the bigness of the sky and count the stars at night. On the square, I could run and jump and spin as I held tightly to my mother's small hands, or Juliska Néni's firm, giant ones. On the square, we were free, at least for a little while.

Our apartment building was directly across from this square. A heavy wooden door led from a busy boulevard into a quiet courtyard: the heart of our world. Here, the mothers planted small gardens, beat their rugs with brooms, exchanged recipes for *palacsinta* or *húsleves* and complained about their lazy husbands. There was always someone borrowing sugar or loaning an egg. We climbed trees, and chased each other around the gardens and up and down the stairwells and narrow, tiled corridors, where my brother and his friend used to push me in a baby stroller, careening left and right, making me scream with joy.

The sound of the radio floated from one lacy-curtained open window to the next. The voices of our leaders reminded us daily that our factories were busy, our farms productive, our people happy. The Gypsy violins came on punctually at noon, heralding the dinner hour, reminding even us children to slow down, savor our food, and eat like ladies and gentlemen, napkins in our laps, fork on the left, knife on the right. I don't know who first thought of playing Gypsy violins every day at noon, but its impact was powerful, joyous, sweet. The music of the violins danced in the air, fusing with the aroma of *gulyás*, *csirke paprikás*, or poppy seed strudels. It mingled with the sound of teaspoons clanking, people talking, telling us that, despite occupiers old and new, this was, after all, still home.

It was late afternoon by the time the train pulled into the Mohács station. The ride was long and hot and I couldn't wait to get off, to see all my toys, and sleep in my own bed.

"I bet Éva didn't have as much fun as we did ... I wonder if she went anywhere for vacation? What do you think Juliska Néni? Do you think Éva went anywhere? I bet she just stayed home and played in the courtyard. Wait 'till I tell her about the red raft and my new beach ball and all the ice cream we ate."

Juliska Néni trudged slowly along, weighted down by the heavy suitcases. "Stop your chattering," she scowled. "You're making me tired just listening to all your talking." She put down the bags, and wiped her brow. I ran ahead, spotted our house, and raced for the gate, leaving her behind to struggle with the bags. I pushed open the heavy door to the courtyard. Home at last! I twirled around a tree and raced up the stairs toward our apartment door. Juliska Néni finally appeared in the stairwell.

"*Sijessél* Juliska Néni," I yelled. "Hurry up!"

At last she reached the second floor. She put down the bags, let out a long sigh, and unlocked the door. I nearly fell inside, so happy to be home. Maybe there'd be dinner on the table. Presents from Vienna! My mother walking through the bedroom door to greet me with a hug and kiss. *Nunus*, she would call, arms wide open. I missed you so much. I'm so glad you are finally home. We should never go away on vacation without you. Never, never. From now on . . .

But the apartment was silent. Everything was as before: the oil paintings, the piano, the velvet sofa covered in white sheets. Lady Herend stood in her usual spot on the piano, playing her porcelain guitar in silence, her pink lips frozen mid-song. I flew across the wooden floors of the living room, stirring up dust. I threw open the door to the kitchen, to Tibor's room, and my parents' room, calling. "Anyuka! *Hol vagy?*" "Where are you?"

No one came. The apartment was silent, guarding its secrets. The paintings were mum, the porcelain indifferent, the doors tight-lipped. They slammed behind me as I ran from room to room calling. "Anyuka? Tibike! *Hol vagytok?*" "Where are you?"

I wandered into the bathroom, which somehow still smelled of my father's aftershave, into my brother's room, where last year's schoolbooks sat untouched, and into my parents' bedroom, my crib pushed up against my parents' bed. I put my head on a white feather pillow. I could still smell my mother's lotion.

I stumbled into the kitchen. "Where are they?" I asked Juliska Néni. "Why are they not back?"

She put on her apron with its smells of *halászlé* and *csirke paprikás* and stuck her head in the pantry looking for something to cook for supper.

"Where are they?" I cried again, tugging on her apron.

"I told you on the train," she said, annoyed that I interrupted her. "It might be a few more days. Be patient."

I hung my head. "I just thought they'd be home already. They didn't come to the lake. What's taking so long?"

"Vienna is far away. It takes a long time to get back. Now, go play while I make supper." She turned her head back to the pantry, muttering to herself about needing to go shopping in the morning.

I left the kitchen pouting and went to my parents' bedroom. I found Zsuzsi Baba and sat her in my lap. I picked up a hairbrush and tried to brush her tangled nest of black hair. "Don't worry," I whispered in her ear. "Anyuka is coming home soon. Maybe she will bring you a present, maybe even new shoes or a new raincoat, or a friend. It won't be long now." She stared at me blankly, so I shook her head up and down and made her glass eyes nod. Yes, she whispered back. A new raincoat for the new school year—that would be nice.

¤ ¤ ¤

"Wash your face. We're going to the market," Juliska Néni called from the kitchen the next morning, waking me bright and early.

I peeked from the down covers with red, groggy eyes. "Are they home yet?"

She came into my parents' room. "Juditka, why are you not in your own bed? Have you been crying?"

"No."

"Well then, come! Out of bed. We're going shopping."

"I don't want to shop. I want Anyuka."

"None of that now. Up you go. Come on."

24

"I want my mother." I stuck my thumb in my mouth and slid under the covers of my mother's bed. "Where is Anyuka?"

Juliska Néni grabbed the blanket and flung it off me. She gripped me under my arms and lifted me from the bed.

Ten minutes later, we were out the door and across the street at the *piac*, where farmers came twice a week to sell produce and meat. She dragged me from one stall to the next, from the farmer selling peaches to the one selling onions. Toothless ladies in black kerchiefs like my grandmother's stopped Juliska Néni, handing her fresh peppers, the reddest strawberries. "Try these," one said, holding out a dried red paprika. "It will make a tasty *lecsó*." They all knew her, for she was a good customer, always buying fresh food for our family, and they were happy to see her home.

"How was the Balaton?" one neighbor asked, stopping her in between stalls. "I bet Juditka had a nice time." She beamed down at me and pinched my cheek. "You got so big. How old are you now, Juditka—ten?"

"No!" I yelled. "I'm just five." I held up five fingers showing her I knew how to count.

"Is the doctor and the rest of the family back?" she said, turning to Juliska Néni. "School started last week."

"Not yet," she answered, "but any day now."

"You'd think they'd be home by now." I saw her scrunch her brows the way my teachers at nursery school did when I refused to tie my shoelaces the way they wanted.

"I am sure they will be here before the week is out."

"You know, Juliska," the neighbor said, whispering now, "there were rumors while you were gone that the hospital has not been happy with the doctor lately."

"I would not pay attention to that. People gossip."

"But you know how the doctor can be. Remember May Day last year? He didn't even show up."

"There is no law that says you have to go."

"Yes, but still. For a party member to not go . . ."

"So, he didn't go. He doesn't like crowds."

"Oh, well, if you say so. In any case, I am glad you are home and Juditka had a nice vacation," she said, turning to me. "You had a nice vacation, didn't you, Juditka?"

I nodded politely.

"Such a nice little girl . . . ."

Juliska Néni said goodbye and pulled me along as she hunted for the right fruits and vegetables to fill up her mesh grocery bag. Before long, she accumulated enough to feed our entire family. Maybe this was the day.

Three

Vienna is Beautiful

Walking home from the market that day under a canopy of chestnut trees, we stopped outside the clinic where my mother worked. Every day after nursery school, Juliska Néni would let me call up to my mother on the second floor.

"Anyuka! Anyuka!" I'd call from the sidewalk, hugging my doll.

My mother would stop what she was doing and stick her head out the window.

"*Nunus*," she would call down, the wind tousling her brown hair. I liked that name, a name I made up, a name no one else called me. "Come up, angel. We'll have a snack." Angel. I liked that too.

I'd leap up the stairs, and we'd sit and talk, and she'd tell me about the babies that were brought to the clinic that day. Then and I'd tell her about the mean teachers in nursery school who made me eat green beans and use a fork and a knife at the table.

"Do you know what she did today, Anyuka? She made me tie my own shoelaces. I can't tie my shoelaces! That's why she's the teacher. She's supposed to do that. That's her job."

"Yes, she's a very mean one, that teacher," she'd whisper to me. "I don't like her either. But she's the teacher, so you know you have to listen to her." I shrugged and told her I'd try even though I didn't like her, and didn't like doing all the silly things they asked us to do. We ate tea biscuits together while the babies cried in the waiting room. I loved looking at the babies, with their chubby thighs and pudgy faces. But what I loved even more was that she stopped her day like this, just for me.

I looked up at the window now, hoping maybe she was there. Maybe they came home while we were at the market, and she had to run over to the clinic to take care of a sick baby. But she wasn't there. Instead, another woman stuck her head out the window. She looked down on Juliska Néni and me standing on the street below, frowned, and shut the window.

"Come, come!" Juliska Néni said, pulling on my arm. "Don't mind her. I have cookies at home for you. You can invite Eva over to play." Juliska Néni almost never allowed me to have a friend over or to eat cookies in the middle of the day. I put thoughts of my mother and the frowning lady out of my mind and ran home to play with my friend.

We ate alone the rest of the week, listening to the radio playing Gypsy violins. Their songs floated out the lacy curtains. In came the sounds of families laughing, talking, shouting, swearing.

I went looking for friends in the courtyard, knocking on doors. I went down the corridor to Farkas Néni's apartment. She answered the door in a flowery housedress coated with white powder.

"Juditka, what a nice surprise. How was your vacation?"

"Swimming was fun but the rest was boring. Is Lacika home?"

"No, he's already at school. Speaking of which, any news from your family? I haven't seen them."

"No . . . I don't know. I keep asking Juliska Néni. But she doesn't tell me."

"Hmm," her smile faded to a frown, just like Juliska Néni's. "Well, I was just baking. Would you like a cookie?"

I nodded my head eagerly. Farkas Néni was always baking something delicous.

I took the cookie and knocked on the next door and the next. All the children were at school. Only the Gypsy kids were home. I was not allowed to play with them, but I liked them the most. We ran up and down the back stairwell, climbed the plum trees, and dug up dirt in a makeshift sandbox in the courtyard. By the time I got home late in the afternoon my cheeks were flushed and sweaty, crusty leaves clung to my curls, and my knit stockings were torn.

Juliska Néni yelled when she saw what I had done. "Did you play with those filthy kids again?"

"I didn't," I lied. "Farkas Néni gave me a cookie. That's all."

"I don't think the cookie ripped your stockings. How many times do I have to tell you to stay away from those Gypsies! They are disgusting and only make trouble."

"I'm sorry. I won't do it again," I lied again.

"You better not or I'll tell your father."

¤ ¤ ¤

The following Monday, Juliska Néni woke me early. "No more running around with those dirty kids," she said. "You're going back to school."

We walked under the chestnut trees, past my mother's clinic. The window was closed this time; no one was there. The kindergarten teacher greeted us at the door. Her face was stern. She didn't even ask about the Balaton. She turned to Juliska Néni and spoke in a hushed voice, then like everyone else, shook her head. Finally, Juliska Néni put on her coat to leave.

"Behave yourself now," she called as she left. "We have enough problems. I don't want to hear that you were trouble."

I went into a corner of the room, stuck my thumb in my mouth, and stayed there. I didn't want to learn to tie my shoelaces, or learn how to hold the utensils properly. I didn't want to play with anyone or talk to anybody. I didn't want to eat the mush they gave us for lunch. I just sucked my thumb, the only thing that felt right.

At home, Juliska Néni did what she had always done since moving in with my parents after my brother was born. She had no family of her own, only a sister somewhere. She never married and had no children of her own. We were all she had. Before she moved in with us, my parents lived in a single room in the hospital where my father and mother worked. After my brother was born, Juliska Néni went with them to the apartment. She cleaned, she cooked, and she washed, allowing my mother to go to work and spend time doting on her new baby. We had a bigger home now, bigger because my father joined the party. Apartments were carved out and given to families according to need. Big families got more space. Our small family didn't qualify for more than two rooms, but over time my father figured out how to convince our neighbors to move and how much to give the local housing minister to allow our family to take over their homes.

So now Juliska Néni had more work to do scrubbing and cleaning three bedrooms, a living room, a big kitchen, and bathroom with its own flush toilet. She shook rugs out the window, polished silver, mended socks, and cooked huge pots of soup. My father loved her recipes, especially her fish soup. After a long day at the hospital—and later, when he went to jobs far from our city and only came home on Saturday or Sunday—he would come in, leave his shoes by the front door, and before even taking his jacket off, head straight for the kitchen, and stick a spoon in the boiling red broth. "This is the best one yet," he would announce, inhaling the aroma of garlic, paprika, and that day's fresh catch. Juliska would shoo him out of the kitchen with a wooden spoon but she beamed with pride at the dinner table. I didn't like the fish soup, but I loved her *palacsinta*, which she filled with apricot or cherry jam or sometimes even melted chocolate. She'd roll up each crepe and sprinkle it with powdered sugar. When I was done eating it with my hands, my face was smeared with chocolate and sugar, and she'd scrub my face with a rough towel.

But she didn't make *palacsinta* now. She only made that when she was happy.

She used to sleep on a cot in the kitchen, but Juliska Néni now packed that away and moved into my parent's bedroom to sleep in my mother's bed. I didn't like it. My mother smelled like baby powder and Nivea handcream. Juliska Néni smelled like onions. My mother put on a nightlight and played soft songs on the radio to help me fall asleep. Juliska Néni turned off all the lights and made the room black. My mother read books in the soft light; Juliska Néni snored like a train.

¤ ¤ ¤

On a rainy day in October, the doorbell rang.

"Mamika," I shouted, pushing past Juliska Néni to hug my grandmother around the waist. "Did you bring me chocolate?"

"Is that how you greet your grandmother?" Juliska Néni scowled.

"I'm sorry. *Kezit csókolom, Nagymama,*" I started over, using the formal greeting. "I kiss your hand, grandmother."

My grandmother smiled. I could see the pink gums where her teeth used to be. "I came to visit you, see how you are … and yes, I have chocolate." She reached into her sagging dress pocket and pulled out a bar of chocolate in green wrapping.

"*Boci Csoki!*" I shouted at the sight of my favorite milk chocolate bar. "*Ugy szeretlek Mamika.*" I love you Grandma.

She patted my head. "Did Juliska Néni take you back to the nursery school?"

"Yes. I hate it. The teachers are all mean."

"To what do we owe this surprise?" Juliska Néni nudged me out of the way.

"I finally have some news," my grandmother said to Juliska Néni. "But it's something we need to discuss alone." Then she turned to me. "Juditka, take the chocolate and go to the kitchen."

"But I want to stay with you."

"Later. Right now, in the kitchen. Go!" Juliska Néni commanded, giving me a push in the behind. In the kitchen I sat Zsuzsi Baba in my lap, opened the chocolate bar and smeared small bite-sized pieces around her mouth. What she didn't eat, I gobbled up.

"We received a postcard," my grandmother whispered slowly.

"From László and Piroska? Finally. Thank God. Are they all right?"

"They are fine. It's from Vienna."

"From Vienna? *Jaj Istenem*. They should be home already. Well show me! What do they say?"

My grandmother took the postcard from her bag, looked at it, and slowly handed it to Juliska.

Juliska took it, read it, and turned it over a few times, puzzled. On the front was a photograph of the cathedral of St. Stephen. The writing on the back said "Vienna is Beautiful. *Szeretettel*, Piroska."

"We know Vienna is beautiful. What else is there? A telegram? A phone call?"

"No. That's it."

"This means nothing. It's just a postcard. You traveled two hours on the train to give me a postcard?"

"It's a code; the code we agreed to. It means they are leaving the country. They're not coming home."

"You mean . . . defecting?"

"Not so loud," my grandmother lowered her voice. "They couldn't just come out and say they are leaving the country."

"Vienna is beautiful? A code? This is ridiculous! Mamika, what's going on?"

"I'm afraid it's true. I was the only one who knew. What could the police do to an old woman like me? Jail might be more peaceful than living with my son-in-law, that good-for-nothing tyrant."

"The whole city's been talking. Every neighbor's been whispering in my ear, asking if the doctor's defected. *Jó Istenem* . . . I didn't want to believe it."

"László was planning this a long time. You know how unhappy he was."

"Yes. But to take this risk, to give up everything . . ."

"He had some help, a Jewish group, I think. They got visas to Austria for everyone, except Juditka, of course."

"But to do this! And to not tell me . . . I've been with them for twelve years. *Istenem.* I have to sit down."

They moved to the living room. From the kitchen I saw Juliska Néni sit wearily on the green velvet couch, the couch where only company was allowed. She took off her apron and used it to wipe her brow. My grandmother moved closer to her.

"I am sorry. I know this is not easy for you to hear. They didn't tell you to protect you. It was for your good as well."

Juliska Néni shook her head vigorously. "There is nothing good in this for me."

"I know this is hard. But imagine. If you knew, the police would have questioned you. You could have been in trouble."

"Yes, I'm sure that was their main concern."

"Anyway, I'm here to talk about Juditka. I am sure you know why they left her."

"I can guess. You can't get through the border as a family. Not her father anyway. Always criticizing the government, doing things no one else dares."

"I can't argue with that."

"But what a risk to take! If they had been discovered, they would have all been arrested."

"László is a clever man. He had it all planned."

Juliska let out a long sigh. "Well, I can't say I'm totally shocked. László was in the party, but he had it out for them, and they for him. It was just a matter of time before he said something that would have landed him in prison."

"That's what Piroska feared."

"That time the neighbors reported him for listening to Voice of America. He was called in for a warning."

"I heard about that. Still, I can't say I blame him for wanting to leave," my grandmother said. "With everything that happened to his family."

"That was long ago, Mamika."

"Not that long. Can you imagine? His whole family taken away. "

"I don't want to talk about that. It was a terrible time. But why now? Why give up everything now? They both worked so hard. They had everything one could possibly want."

"Everything," my grandmother repeated, looking around the apartment.

"And Piroska, to think she went along with leaving Juditka here? This I can't understand."

"I guess she was the price they had to pay."

"How she wanted a daughter, begged him to let her keep that baby."

"I think he would have gone without her. That's why she went with him in the end," my grandmother said.

"No wonder Piroska has been so nervous lately...But what about Juditka? If this is true, what will happen to her?"

From the kitchen, I heard Juliska Néni mention my name. I got up from the table, dragging my doll. "Did you call me, Juliska Néni? We finished the chocolate. Can we have some more?"

"Oh Juditka. Look at your face! No, there is no more chocolate. Go back to the kitchen and clean your face."

I pouted, but did what she said. I took Zsuzsi Baba back to the kitchen, sat her in a chair and began scrubbing her face.

"That's why I'm here," my grandmother continued in a whisper. "I'll be taking Juditka to live with us. Piroska talked to me before they left. She asked us to take care of her. She will live with us in Balaton Mária until . . . until they are able to send for her, I guess, or the government lets her go to them. We must wait. We don't even know at this point where they plan to go. It might be America or Canada. There was even talk of Israel. She will write again."

"Wait. What? Take her with you? Mamika, you are too old to raise more children! You still have Kate's children. It's too much."

"Kate's children are almost all grown up. Árpád just started at the technical school last month. And when Ildiko is home, she will like having Juditka around. We can take care of her."

"Hmph, the way children are taken care of in that family? No! Absolutely not. You can't do this." Juliska said, shaking her head again.

"But we have to."

Juliska paused. "No, no you don't. You can leave her here. Nothing has to change. I can take care of her. I will stay here too until … until we hear from the government. We will live here as before."

"Stay here? But this is not your home. She is not your child. Besides, her mother wanted her with me—her family. She was clear."

"This is Juditka's home and my home, and we will stay here until we hear further about what to do." Having made up her mind, she came into the kitchen, leaving my grandmother alone on the velvet armchair, looking like a frail bird in a nest too big. "Didn't I tell you to clean up?" she said, turning to me.

35

"Look at the mess you made!" She grabbed a wet rag and scrubbed my face like she scrubbed a wet chicken, leaving my mouth red and raw. "Go get your shoes on." She turned to my grandmother. "I think we are done talking. I am taking Juditka to the market. This conversation is over."

"Why?" I whined. "I don't want to go. I want to stay with Mamika."

"I said get your shoes on!"

I left the kitchen moping, put on my shoes and twiddled with the shoelaces, trying to tie them like they were teaching us to do in nursery school. Make one bunny ear, then another. Tie the bunny ears together . . .

"Juliska, listen to reason," I heard my grandmother say. "For Juditka's sake."

But Juliska wasn't listening. "I don't want to talk about this anymore. You know the way out," she said to my grandmother as we left the apartment. I turned around to see her face frozen, her mouth wide open like fish on a hook. "Goodbye Mamika," I called to the small hunchback figure behind me.

We walked downstairs to the street, Juliska dragging me once again behind her. "What did Mamika say," I cried. "Why did she come? Where is Anyuka? Did Mamika tell you?"

"I told you already, she's coming soon." Juliska Néni repeated. "They'll be back any day."

"When? Why are they not here already?"

"Enough, Juditka. No more."

"Why did Mamika come?"

"I said enough."

When we returned from the market, my grandmother was gone.

I felt sick for the rest of that day. I left my soup untouched at supper. Juliska Néni tried to get me to eat, but I wasn't hungry. I swirled the soup with the spoon, letting it get cold. I didn't say anything to her for the rest of the night. I went into my mother's room. "Don't worry." I told Zsuzsi Baba. "Anyuka will be home soon. Apuka will bring us some nice presents. Maybe a friend for you. She'll have brown eyes like yours." I shook her head to make her eyelids go up and down.

Four

Stop Crying

"Open up! *Rendörség!*"

A few nights later, I was trying to sleep in my parents' room. A black shape rose across the walls again and again. Each time it came, I heard a deep growl. I told myself it was just the shadow of the church across the street and the cars outside. That's what Juliska Néni said. There are no monsters. No ghosts. No bears coming to eat us whole. Just shadows and cars.

I heard Juliska Néni shuffle to the front door. I heard the door unlock. I heard the door slam against the inside wall.

"Step aside. We're here to inspect."

"For what? It's the middle of the night."

"Step aside."

"I don't understand. What do you want here?"

"That Jewish swine and his wife. Capitalist collaborators. We're here to search the apartment for evidence of their crimes. Now!"

More voices, heavy shoes; doors opened and shut. I heard hands rummage through drawers, books fall and hit the floor; I heard paper dumped in boxes. I heard the piano . . . the sofa . . . tables dragged across the hardwood floor.

I drew the blanket over my head, stuck my thumb in my mouth, and covered my ears. The door opened. Light flooded the room.

"Don't! The child is sleeping."

The door closed. Shadows and cars.

"We'll be back tomorrow. Have this room cleared of the kid."

When my father sees the mess, he will be very mad, I thought. My father didn't like anything out of place. Shoes were to be lined up in the closet, coats neatly hung, sheets and towels folded, every book in its place on the shelf. "Where does this belong?" he would say to me or my brother, holding up an errant shoe or offending toy. Heads hanging, we would take the shoe or the toy and put it in the closet where it belonged. Sometimes, when dinner was not ready, or a cup of tea was left carelessly on the coffee table, or a newspaper was left opened on the floor, he would get raging mad, yell at my mother or at Juliska Néni and call them names. That's when I ran to my bed, hid under the feather pillows, closed my eyes, and sucked my thumb until it was over and he was nice again.

The next night, Juliska Néni tucked me in my brother's bed. "Why can't I sleep in Anyuka's room?" I cried.

"It's just for tonight."

"Who came last night?"

"I don't know," she said. "I don't know."

"Why don't you know?"

"You're too little Juditka. You wouldn't understand."

"Why not?"

"You're just too little. Enough talking." She shut the lamp but reached over to the radio and turned it on like my mother used to do when I could not fall asleep. "Go to sleep," she ordered.

Later the sounds were back: a knock on the door, heavy shoes, muffled voices, drawers opening and slamming. I heard it over the radio, through the songs and violins. I heard a note played on the piano from the living room, a short song.

"Idiot," one man said. "Who do you think you are? Liszt? Get to work."

"Higher, lift it higher."

I heard Juliska Néni. "Why the piano? How in the world is that going to help you?"

"The chief wants it."

I heard the door shut for the last time. I watched the sliver of light under the door slide across the floor until that too was gone, and all was dark again. I shut my eyes tight and held Zsuzsi Baba tight. "Don't be afraid," I told her. "There are no monsters, no ghosts, no bears. Just shadows, shadows and cars."

¤ ¤ ¤

I dreamed of my father. He wasn't yelling. He was standing over me, smelling of aftershave and the wine he made in the cellar at the vineyard on the hills overlooking the Danube. He had bought the small lot, and with the help of some men with calloused hands, built a two-story house. We slept upstairs; the cellar was downstairs. He didn't know anything about making wine, so he added sugar, barrels of sugar, to make it taste better. Going to sleep, I loved listening to my father's laugh, the neighbors stopping by, drinking, singing old Hungarian folk songs long into the night. *"Felmegy a legény a fára, a meggyfa tetejére . . ."*

In my dream, he was happy and dressed nicely for a party in the living room. From my bed, I could hear the music, grownups laughing, glasses clinking. I could smell the cigarette smoke as it slid under the door into the dark bedroom. He was standing over me, tucking me into bed. But I didn't want to sleep.

"Why can't I come to the party, Apuka?"

"This party is just for grownups," said the man in my dream who looked like my father.

"But I want to come. I want to be with you."

"Don't you want to go to your own party?"

"My own party?"

"The feather ball. That party is just for children. No grownups allowed."

"But I want to be with you and Anyuka at your party."

"But the feather ball is so much nicer."

"What's a feather ball?"

"Close your eyes," said the man in my dream. "Look at the sparkling ballroom, the chandelier twinkling like the stars, the dance floor, girls in pretty dresses, boys in suits."

My father never tucked me into bed, he never kissed me goodnight. But the story of the feather ball—this was real, as real as my doll, my small bed, my red flannel beach dress, as real as the empty apartment.

"That sounds nice," I yawned. "When can I go there?"

"You can go there now. Close your eyes. Look up at the ceiling. Can you see the feathers falling?

"Yes. It's very nice." I yawned again. I closed my eyes as the man in my dream drew the down blanket gently over me, and I fell asleep.

¤ ¤ ¤

When I woke up in the morning, the men were gone. The living room was a mess. There were gouges in the hardwood floor, the paint was chipped. Most of the books and the piano were gone; missing paintings left white spots on the bare walls.

I sat down at the kitchen table next to Juliska Néni, who was sipping a cup of tea. She had deep lines in her face and dark circles under her eyes. "Where is everything?" I asked her. "Where is the piano?"

"I guess some other people needed it."

"Don't we need it?"

"Not anymore."

"Tibike needs the piano. He has to practice."

"He won't have to practice anymore. That should make him happy."

"Why not? Why doesn't he have to practice?"

"He just won't ... that's all."

"Where is Anyuka? When is she coming home?"

"She is still in Vienna."

"For how long?"

"I don't know, Juditka. You have too many questions. Go play."

"I don't want to play. I want Anyuka."

She tried to smile but I knew it was a fake one, the kind the teachers at school give you when you really mess up the shoelaces. She placed a heavy arm around me and pulled me closer. "Don't worry, Juditka," she finally said. "I will stay here and take care of you until they are back. It will be like always."

¤ ¤ ¤

A few weeks later, my grandmother was back. This time she was not alone. Katus Néni came with her, along with Zoli Bácsi, smelling of cigarettes.

It was midafternoon and quiet. Mourning doves sang outside the window. I was playing with Zsuzsi Baba in a corner of my brother's room. Juliska Néni was putting away dishes.

I ran to the front door when I heard the knock. I wanted to hug my grandmother when I saw her at the door, but I wasn't sure it was all right after the way we left her last time. "*Kezit csókolom, Mamika,*" I greeted her the formal way. "I'm so glad you're back." I glanced at Juliska Néni to make sure what I said was all right. She gave me a stern look and I knew I should say no more. "*Jó napot, Juliska Néni,*" my aunt said, stepping out from behind. She smiled awkwardly, covering her mouth. A few of her teeth were missing and the rest were the color of dirty dishwater.

My uncle stepped inside. "Well, that didn't take long," he said looking around. "They did a good job cleaning out the place."

"They came again earlier this week. They said they needed things for evidence," Juliska Néni said.

"Yes. I'm sure they needed the piano for evidence."

Juliska Néni sighed and turned to me. "Juditka, go play in your brother's room."

"I don't . . ."

"Hush. Not a word. Go."

I grudgingly did as she said.

She turned to my uncle. "And to what do we owe the pleasure of this visit?"

"We are here to take Judit," my uncle announced, all business.

"I already told her grandmother. That won't be necessary."

"I didn't come to debate," my uncle said. "You read the newspapers. The family defected; her mother wanted us to take the kid."

"I read the newspapers," Juliska Néni said, sitting down on the living room sofa. "Those things they said about them. Capitalist traitor . . . nonsense. László was a decent man. He worked hard. He joined the party."

"One can see it differently. He joined the party, but he was no party man. I don't support the party either, but that doesn't mean I mouth off about it. Or get in a car and leave everything. Oh well. I suppose our puny country was not adequate for Dr. Boros and his grand ambitions. I tell you though, if I had it this good . . ." He scanned the large apartment, his eyes coming to rest on the velvet sofa. "In any case, what's done is done. We're here for the kid. If you don't want her to wind up in a state orphanage, you'll let her go. We are leaving tomorrow."

"Zoli, I told Nagymama last time. You don't have to take this on. I can stay here with her. What's the point of turning her life upside down?" She turned to my grandmother. "Mamika . . . You can understand, can't you? I can take care of Juditka. I've been doing it her whole life. Think of what's best for the child. There is no need to uproot . . ."

"Nonsense," my uncle interrupted her. "You've been slaving away for this family your whole life. You are a free woman. Go. Live your life," my uncle said.

"Sure. At 55. I'll move to Budapest and become an opera singer." She walked into the kitchen and sat at the table. The rest of the family followed her.

"I'm just saying that this might be your opportunity," Zoli Bácsi said.

"I think the only opportunity you care about is your own. But you're not that smart. You should have arrived days ago. You would have made out much better before they took everything."

"Oh, I don't need that much," Zoli Bácsi replied. "I'm a humble man."

"Hmph. I know why you are here and it has nothing to do with that child's welfare. Do the decent thing and go home."

"I'm afraid it's too late for that. The papers are signed. I am her legal custodian." He held out a stack of documents for Juliska Néni and dropped them on the table. She took a few pages, looked them over and sank deeper into the chair. I watched the grownups from my brother's room, confused and afraid to come between them.

"Juliska, we want what's best for Juditka too," my grandmother finally said. "What's best is for her to come with us. We are her family."

"How can you say that? How can you say that taking her from her home is best for her? No," she said after a pause. "I won't do it. I won't allow it. I don't care what those papers say."

"It's not your decision," my uncle laughed. "She's not your child. This is not your home … You are the maid. Your job here is over."

The room fell silent. Then it exploded.

"You have no right to treat me this way," Juliska Néni said, standing up. Her hands shook, her lips quivered, and her ears looked like they'd burst into flames. A big-boned woman with wide hips, I now watched from the other room as she seemed to tower 10 feet above everyone else. "Not after twelve years. Not after everything I've done."

"Juliska, please try to understand," my grandmother pleaded. "It's not just what we want. It's what her mother wanted. She asked me to take care of the child. As her grandmother."

"I don't believe you. You are trying to take away everything I have." And then without warning, she lunged at my hunchbacked grandmother and shoved her hard into the kitchen table. "Get out. Get out of here! All of you." From my brother's room, I saw my grandmother stumble and hit the floor. I would have run to her, but was I rooted to the ground, afraid of my uncle and Juliska Néni.

It was my aunt who finally helped her up. "How could you do such a thing?" she said, glaring at Juliska Néni.

My grandmother straightened up, smoothed the kerchief on her head and tucked in the loose strands of white hair. "This is no way to treat anybody. I will not forget this."

My uncle looked at me and winked. "Don't worry, Juci," he said as the three left the apartment. "We'll be back."

I hated when he called me that.

¤ ¤ ¤

Juliska Néni was shaking. "How can they treat a person this way?" she muttered long after they left. "First the family disappears without a word to the one person who took care of all of them. All those years of cooking and washing and mending, and nothing to show for it. And now these people, thinking they can just walk in here and . . ."

I stayed in my brother's room as the sun went down and the room grew dark. Eventually Juliska Néni put her apron back on and started supper. It was chicken soup. I was hungry and it smelled good.

"Juliska Néni," I said, tugging on her apron as she stirred the soup. She still seemed like a giant, but a sad giant, a broken giant. "I don't like Zoli Bácsi either."

She sighed but said nothing. She just kept stirring the soup without looking down at me. We ate the soup in silence.

¤ ¤ ¤

They were back the next day with the stamped documents. Juliska Néni let them in. Whatever fighting spirit she had the day before was now snuffed, like fire deprived of oxygen. She surrendered the kitchen to my aunt and grandmother and retreated to my parents' room, locking the door behind her. Katus Néni took over the kitchen. She rummaged through the cupboards, found a heavy pot and filled it with lard, onions, peppers, tomatoes, and eggs, sprinkling paprika and salt on top, then set the table for the noontime meal. My uncle settled into the green velvet chair in the living room, opened a newspaper, lit a cigarette, and read in anticipation of the meal. I sucked my thumb and pouted as the three relatives took over what was left of our home. Not knowing what else to do, I went into the bathroom and like Juliska Néni, locked myself away.

"I feel badly about all this. She has worked here for so long," my grandmother said.

"She does not need your pity," my uncle said with a wave of his hand. "She's just trying to get her hands on the apartment and what's left."

"You always think the worst of people. Juditka, come out of that bathroom and eat dinner," my grandmother said, knocking on the bathroom door. "Katus Néni worked hard to make a nice dinner." But I refused to come out. I thought my grandmother was on my side, but now she was with my uncle, that smoking dragon, and my aunt, the witch.

"I'm never coming out," I hollered. "That food is poisoned!"

"Juditka! How can you say such a thing!" my grandmother scolded.

"I don't care. I'm not eating her food."

I heard my grandmother return to the kitchen. "I'm worried about her."

"Ignore her. She'll eat when she's hungry."

I'll show him, I thought. I'll never eat. Not that evil witch's food. I held out all afternoon, as the smell of garlic and paprika and fresh bread wafted through the tiny keyhole of the locked bathroom door. "Don't smell it," I told Zsuzsi Baba. "They're trying to poison us and steal us away." But by suppertime my stomach was begging to be fed. Zsuzsi Baba was hungry too. We didn't sit down at the table but when my grandmother offered us peeled apples and fresh bread, I opened the door and let her in. Juliska Néni too decided eventually to come out of my parents' bedroom. She had packed my suitcase and brought it out, setting it down next to me in the kitchen.

"It's not what I wanted Juditka," she said with a sigh. "But you have to go with them. They are going to take care of you now."

I didn't understand. It wasn't summertime. It was cold by the lake. There'd be no ice cream man, no watermelon man. It was too cold to swim, or even play on the swings on the beach.

"Where is Anyuka? Where is Tibike?"

"It looks like they are not coming home."

"Why?"

"You just have to do like they say. Your grandmother will take care of you now."

"But I don't want to go with Zoli Bácsi" I cried. "I don't like him."

"Don't talk like that."

"Why can't I stay home?"

"You just can't. I don't like it either. But it's been settled."

"Why is it settled?"

"It just is."

"Where is Anyuka? Where is Apuka?"

"I don't know, Juditka. You have to stop asking so many questions and stop crying."

I buried my face in her lap and cried, but it did no good. She didn't change her mind.

The next morning Juliska Néni tied my lace-up shoes and helped me into my favorite pink sweater. Before the great wooden front door to our apartment, she bent down and hugged me tight. She felt soft and round, her big hands stroking my wet cheeks. She handed me my doll. "Take care of her. And be good to your grandmother. Listen to her and be a good girl."

Five

Back to the Lake

We walked to the Mohács train station, with Zoli Bácsi leading the way. I held my grandmother's hand and waited with her while Zoli Bácsi went to the ticket booth.

"Why are we here, Mamika?" I asked her while he was gone.

"We're going back to the lake. You like the lake, don't you?"

"But why are we going now? Why didn't Anyuka come home?"

"Shh . . . be a good girl. Zoli Bácsi is coming."

We waited in the cold silence until the enormous black engine arrived, thundering and spewing smoke. I hid behind my grandmother's dress.

"Let's go, move it," Zoli Bácsi said. "You're holding us up." Behind us was a line of people waiting to board. I didn't want to get on. Somehow, this train felt different than the one we took to come home. It rumbled like a fire-breathing dragon ready to swallow us. There was nowhere to go but straight into its mouth. I swallowed hard, took a step, and stumbled. Zoli

Bácsi caught me and pushed me forward. "Jesus Christ, you are a clumsy kid."

Inside, almost every seat was taken, some by peasants with live chickens squawking in their metal cages, some by toothless grandmothers like mine. We found seats as the engine rumbled and the train started moving.

Zoli Bácsi settled into his seat, rolled a cigarette, stuffed it in his long wooden smoking stick and lit it, taking a long puff. He opened his newspaper wide so that I could not see his face. Good, I thought. I wouldn't have to stare at his balding head and hairs inside his nose.

Katus Néni unwrapped a sandwich. "Juditka, eat a little. You must be hungry," she said, smiling through crooked teeth.

I shook my head, pulled my legs under me, and stuck my thumb in my mouth. I looked out the window so I wouldn't have to see her face either. Beyond my reflection, I watched the Danube fade into fog, the onion dome slip behind rain clouds, the trees of Mohács wither behind black soot. My throat squeezed in a tight knot, and I shut my eyes to keep from crying. Katus Néni pulled out a chocolate bar. "Maybe you'd like this better," she said.

I knew what she was up to. She wasn't going to trick me. I turned from the window and glared at her. Before my very eyes, her brown eyes turned fiery red; her crooked nose sprouted thick black warts; her spindly fingers grew piercing, spiky nails. "I don't want your food," I blurted out.

"Juditka!" my grandmother said sharply. "You know better."

I did. If my father ever heard my brother or I speak that way, he would have let us have it, my brother especially. I closed my eyes and prepared for my uncle to slap me across the face, or clip me with his cigarette holder. I hugged my legs, waiting for some response. But none came. My uncle said nothing. He just kept reading the newspaper and blowing smoke. Katus Néni turned away. She put the food and the chocolate bar back in the bag, looked out the window, and said nothing for the rest of the trip. I held Zsuzsi Baba in my lap and looked at the floor. If Katus Néni was the witch, why did I feel bad?

We got off the train and walked to the house in silence. The streets were hushed. It was past suppertime; the sun was almost down, the air cool. A few village ladies passed us and nodded hello. A horse-drawn buggy heading home kicked dust in our eyes. My uncle walked in military fashion, one shiny boot behind the other. My aunt shuffled behind him, her eyes fixed on the ground. I held onto my grandmother, clutching her hand, watching the dust collect on my shoes, dodging the poop left by the horse. We turned the corner into my grandmother's street, the street I walked so happily as I went to and from the beach just a few months before. Now, without Juliska Néni, without my family, without the ice cream vendor and the beachgoers, it was a different place—lonely and dark. We passed the hotel of the canning union whose roses bloomed popsicle colors all summer. Now all I could see was its thick iron fence. The restaurant that thumped music all night was silent. The watermelon man was nowhere to be found; the new pastel-colored vacation homes with running water and electricity were shut for the season. The village residents lived in houses with thatched roofs, dirt floors, some with electricity and running water—most without.

We arrived at my grandmother's house just as the sun set. One electric bulb dangled from the hallway ceiling, greeting us. My uncle left us without a word and shut himself up in his room at the end of the hallway. My aunt put on an apron and took up her kitchen duties, forgetting that I was there. Only my grandmother seemed to remember that my presence back here deserved some note, or at least, some instruction.

"You'll sleep here," she said, opening the door to the one bedroom besides my uncle's that was heated. There were two beds in this room, one for my aunt and one for my cousin

51

Ildikó. Under a window facing the front yard was a thin, old mattress where my grandmother slept.

Three of my older cousins were gone to schools in different cities. Ildikó, Katus Néni's youngest child, was home in the summer, but her bed was empty now. She was almost 12 and during the summer, she sometimes tagged along with Juliska Néni and me to the beach. She looked like a boy with short, stringy hair, long arms dangling by her side. She never smiled.

"Where is Ildkó?" I asked my grandmother.

"She's gone to school."

"This late?"

"She's living there now. You can sleep in her bed," my grandmother said, pointing.

I didn't understand why Ildikó had to live in a school. I thought maybe that's what happens when you get older. But I didn't want to take her bed. "Can I sleep with you?" I asked.

"If you want." My grandmother crouched down and planted herself on the smelly mattress, folding her legs under her faded black dress. I sat down next to her. She reached into her magic pockets and pulled out a chocolate bar. "I saved this for you. Look, it says 'Balaton' on the wrapper—just like the lake."

I grabbed the chocolate bar, unwrapped it, and ate the melting chocolate wafer in a flash. Having refused food all day, I was ravenous. My grandmother smiled a big toothless grin. "You will like it here," she said. "You'll see."

¤ ¤ ¤

It took some time to get used to my grandmother's house as it was now—without the summer sun, the sailboats, the beach balls, and ice cream, without my family. Things I didn't notice in the summer, I noticed now. A giant birch stood in the front yard, a towering oak in the back. That's where my older cousins had long ago built a treehouse, high enough to see over the roofs of the village and on to the lake. But with all four of them gone now, the treehouse sat empty. I stared at it through the blazing yellow crown, longing to climb that trunk, to be a part of the group that conquered the tree. In the summer when they visited, my cousins still talked about the tree—of spending nights in the tree, shooting birds from the tree, kissing girls in the tree, kissing boys. But those stories were just stories now. No one climbed the tree anymore. Even Ildikó was done with it.

The front yard was more important than the back. This was where we went to the bathroom and got our wood, coal, and water.

We had an outhouse like no other. Rather than a regular toilet—a wooden seat over a black hole—we had a real white porcelain bowl, just like we had at home in Mohács. But to flush it, you had to think ahead and bring a bucket of water with you. I almost never did and I wasn't the only one. So the poop just stayed smeared to the side of the pretty white bowl until the next person to use the toilet came in, made a face, and fetched water to flush it, all the while grumbling about the stink and mess. Toilet paper was another problem. We didn't have any. Eventually, I learned to hunt around the yard for leaves, old newspapers, or if nothing else was around, an old corncob.

Then there was the well. To drink or cook or wash required that someone, usually my grandmother, put on coat and shoes, go outside in the cold or rain or snow, get on all fours, dangle a tin bucket into the well, and lug the heavy bucket of water inside, usually without any help from anybody, even though she was old. With her hunched back, she reminded me of an ogre in fairy tales. Sometimes, I bent down alongside her, lowering my head into the well so I could see the water. I couldn't see anything, not even my own reflection. But I did hear a sound. "*Sziaaaa*," I yelled, and the person in the well would call back. "*Sziaaaaa*."

"Who's in there?" I asked my grandmother.

"*Kis buta*, silly child, that's your own voice," she said.

That was not silly. The well sounded nothing like me.

To warm up the chilly old house also required many trips in and out. My grandmother was first to wake. Her first job was to empty last night's ash from the coal-burning stove into a metal bucket, take it outside, dump it, and refill the bucket with fresh coal. Then she'd light the two stoves so that it would be warm by the time everyone else woke up, or at least not freezing. No one ever helped her with this either. Maybe this is why her back was so hunched, her fingernails so black, her face so creased, her dress so dirty. My grandmother was an old Cinderella. The prince never came for her with a shoe that fit just right.

Not only did we never help her. All day long we badgered her to fetch this and that. "Mama, bring me the cooking pot … get me water, warm up the soup, find the dustpan, empty the bedpan …" and on and on and on.

She did it all.

Zoli Bácsi was fifteen years younger than her, but he never did any of those chores. He sat in his room and issued commands. The things my grandmother could not do, like paint, or fix the frayed electrical wires, or replace broken windows, went undone. He had been an officer in the war, marching alongside the Germans, going to icy places where men's fingers and toes froze and snapped like stalactites. Fighting the Soviets went unappreciated by the new government that was led by them, so he could never find a decent job again. He eventually did find a job working for the railroad. It was not a bad job, my grandmother said; it came with a pension, and paid for Ildikó's school, where she now lived with 300 other children. But that job was over now, and he spent his days smoking, eating, coughing, smoking, reading the paper, and raging at invisible people who were wrecking the country. It was his mustache that scared me the most; that and his smoking stick, glowing like a torch threatening to set all of us on fire.

He got the house, a house that once belonged to a rich man, because of his four children. From each according to their ability, to each according to need, went the socialist maxim we learned at school. My uncle's four children bought him that house. But he never managed to upkeep it. Save for what my aunt and grandmother managed to do, it was now falling apart bit by bit.

His cave was the bathroom at the end of the linoleum-covered hallway that stretched from the front door, through a small kitchen, and ended in that room. No one ever explained why he lived in the bathroom all alone. Even I knew that parents were supposed to sleep in the same bed, or at least, the same room. Maybe my aunt was tired of hearing him spit and cough all day and all night. Maybe like me, she didn't like his prickly mustache and smoking stick.

He had staked out the bathroom with its clawfoot tub as his own many years before I came to live there. He found an old door and placed it on the tub. On top of this, he put a floppy foam mattress, and that was his bed. The mattress was much bigger than the door, so if you wanted to sit on it, you had to hoist yourself all the way up, lest you go sliding to the floor. But I didn't sit there very much, and neither did anyone else. He took his meals at the same time morning, noon, and night, and always alone. I never heard the sound of the Gypsy violins from his room when he ate, only the news. What I did hear was how he yelled whenever his meal was a minute late, or his food was a bit overcooked, or his porridge was too hot, or too cold. "Mama, where is my food?" he'd yell in his raspy cigarette voice. And my grandmother would go running, mumbling under her breath.

We all had to use the outhouse, no matter the time of day or the weather. But he refused. He had a bedpan, and by morning, it was overflowing with pee topped by a foam of spit. Then he'd holler for my grandmother and she'd go running to empty the bedpan, mumbling some more.

Once a year, usually around Christmas, the door and the mattress came off the tub so everyone could take a bath. My grandmother worked extra hard those days, pulling pail after pail of water from the well. She and my aunt made an assembly line, with my grandmother fetching the water, bending down to pull each pail from the deep well, and my aunt heating it one pot at a time on the kitchen stove. It took them a long time to draw and heat enough water to make a single bath. When it was finally ready, I'd climb in the tub and I would sit there as long as I was allowed, feeling like a princess, until the water drained out or turned cold. That was the only time I liked spending time in my uncle's room. The rest of the year, it was a smoky, stinky den. I stayed away.

I followed my aunt around as she went about her day, trying to figure out if she was really a witch, or if she might turn out like the fairy godmothers in the bedtime stories. She did have a crooked nose and even some warts on her neck and a wrinkled face like the witches in my book of fairy tales. But she didn't cackle. She had a voice like sour cream. And she didn't poison me. In fact, her food was tasty. She didn't scold; she never raised her voice or complained about my uncle behind his back like my grandmother did. But she also never hugged me or read me a bedtime story like my mother, or even talked to me. She didn't ask me questions or kiss me goodnight. She ran around the house with an apron around her hips and a kerchief on her head, cleaning, washing, and cooking. Somehow I knew to not get in her way.

My grandmother told me she was once a beautiful girl with pretty brown curls. She said lots of boys wanted to take her to dances and marry her. My grandmother bought her frilly dresses and fancy shoes so she could go to the dances with the boys. My mother couldn't go, she said, because she was born with a limp. They tried to fix it when she was little, but the operation didn't work. Instead of pretty shoes, she wore ugly shoes with uneven soles. Instead of pretty dresses, she got books and they told her to study. At 18, my aunt fell in love with a boy with yellow hair. But it was wartime, and my grandmother said the boy was killed. Many other boys died. Then the Russians came through the villages, and the girls that could run away did. She said my grandfather hid his daughters in the cellar for days, until the Russian soldiers had their fill and left. After the war, there weren't many choices for whom to marry. My uncle was one of the few men who survived. So my grandmother encouraged my aunt to marry him. If she agreed, my grandmother promised she would give the family house to my aunt, and help her take care of her children. And that had been her life ever since.

"Does she like him?" I asked my grandmother once, but she didn't answer me. I don't know when my aunt stopped sleeping next to my uncle, but she now shared a bedroom with my grandmother, me, and Ildikó, when she was home from her school. At night, after she let me watch the children's story hour on the black-and-white television, I'd watch her sit at the edge of her bed and slowly take off her clothes in front of the man giving the weather report, her fleshy white stomach spilling out of her underwear. "Looks like rain tomorrow," she'd say to my grandmother in a flat voice as she exchanged the housedress for a nightgown. "I better find the umbrella."

Just looking at her made me sad, with her housedress and hair in a bun, her gray teeth and empty eyes. Maybe there was a time when she was happy. Maybe when her children were small. Maybe she played with them, or sang them lullabies, or kissed their cheeks before they went to school or fell asleep like my mother did; maybe she laughed with them or read them fairy tales. I hope she smiled sometimes, because now she almost never did. She wasn't beautiful. Like a rag, she seemed all wrung out and used up.

As for her heart, she saved that for Jesus on Sundays. She never, ever missed the Sunday service at the village church, a big stone building with a tall spire. The inside walls were painted with Jesus and Mary, angels with chubby thighs, and saints with big sad eyes. Maybe someone there loved her, maybe one of those stony saints, or Jesus looking down from his wooden cross.

"Why don't you go to church, Mamika?" I asked my grandmother. She never went with my aunt. Sometimes on Sundays, she'd sleep a little late. But then Zoli Bácsi would get all mad because Katus Néni was gone and the bedpan smelled really bad and there was no breakfast to wake up to.

"I don't think you need to go to church to be close to God," she said.

"Is God in the church?"

"God is everywhere," she said. "You just have to listen."

"Don't you need special words to talk to God?"

"No. You can just talk to God like you'd talk to a friend. God will hear you."

I liked that. I didn't want to go to church either, where you had to sit still on the hard wooden pews for hours, then kneel, then stand and sing, and repeat it over and over again. It was boring and itchy. I liked it better sitting on my grandmother's mattress, praying with her. I'd pray for summer to come quick so we could go to the Balaton again, and buy ice cream cones; I'd pray for new clothes for Christmas; I'd pray for my family to hurry up and come home.

So I stayed away from my aunt too, and clung to my grandmother. When she went to buy eggs from the neighbors, when she fetched water, washed clothes, dusted the furniture, beat the rugs, and pulled weeds, I hung on to her dress pockets. And I saw that though her life was hard, her eyes sparkled like the lake on a sunny summer day. When she got mad at my uncle, or my cousins, or me, she'd reach into the pantry, find the apricot brandy hidden there, and take a nice long swig. She'd wipe her mouth with her dress sleeve, smile, wink, and keep going.

As my aunt's four children grew and needed beds of their own, my grandmother gave up her own to sleep on a blanket on the floor of the same dark kitchen pantry where she hid the brandy. I wondered how she fit in there, underneath the shelves. Or if she was afraid of spiders and mice. I wondered if she closed the door or kept it open. I did know that day or night, she never took off her black dress, a habit that stuck for life. Like a black beetle's shell, I think it protected her from the scary creatures in the pantry, and everything else in that house.

Now we shared the mattress on the floor. From here she could look up and see the window and through it, birds, and trees, and sky. At night, after she had me wash up in a tin basin that she filled with soapy warm water, we slept, snuggled together. I breathed in the smell of her dress filled with the day's work—of cucumbers and black soil, brown bread and purple plums, freshly-washed sheets and apricot brandy. She encircled me with her tired arms. She was no longer alone, and though I missed my mother and my brother and even my father, neither was I.

Six

Wooden Wagon

One cold winter day my grandmother went outside to the shed crawling with spiders and emerged with a dusty wooden wagon. "We are going to the kindergarten," she announced. "Get in."

Finally, someplace to go! I'd been cooped up inside the house for what seemed like forever with nothing to do but play with my doll. There were no toys, no friends, and the grownups just did what grownups do. Even Zsuzsi Baba was bored. "Can we please do something!" she whispered. But there was nothing to do at home and not much more to do in the village. There was the school, the church, and exactly two stores. One time my older cousins came home and we all went to the lake, but the waves weren't turquoise blue. They were black and angry. By now, it was probably frozen over with ice and snow.

The wagon was covered in spider webs and its wheels were rusty. I didn't want to get inside. I shook my head. "I can walk."

"It's a long walk for little legs," my grandmother said. "I'll pull you." She took an old rag and cleaned the wagon until the spider webs were gone and the wheels were almost shiny with rust. "This is the same little wagon we used to take Ildikó and Piroska and the boys to school."

I looked at the long road ahead and got inside, putting Zsuzsi Baba in my lap; my grandmother took hold of the metal handle and off we went. I crisscrossed my legs and wondered what kind of toys they'd have at this new school, if the teachers would be nicer than back home, if the kids would like me. After a half-hour walk, we reached a small house surrounded by a fence. I leaped from the wagon and ran to knock on the door. A tall woman with a blue jacket and hair combed in a beehive answered the door. Before she even said hello, she gave us directions.

"She can hang her jacket on the hooks; and make sure she takes off her shoes. I won't have her dragging mud all over the floor. She can't bring the doll inside either. I won't have it starting a fight with the others. And by the way, you are late. We start at 8 o'clock sharp. Tomorrow, make sure she is punctual."

"And good morning to you too," my grandmother said. Then turning to me, she whispered, "I guess we better do as she says. I don't think we want to cross her."

I handed Zsuzsi Baba to my grandmother and did as the teacher said, hanging up my jacket and lining up my shoes besides those of the other children, eager to please her. I wasn't sure this kindergarten would be any better than the one in Mohács. But at least there were children here, some old toys, and even a handful of picture books. Anything was better than the cold house with nothing to do.

The best part was that every room in the house was cozy warm. A huge orange ceramic tile wall heater radiated warmth into every corner. We could take off our gloves and sweaters and even run around in short sleeves. I was placed in the older group with a girl named Laura, a boy named Péter, and another named Gábor, who was loud and mean, pulling girls' braids and knocking down our wooden towers. I wondered why the teachers allowed him to get away with so much mischief. I was sure that if I did any of those things, I'd get a smack on the behind.

At noon, we sat down to small tables set with white dishes. We had to eat with utensils, just like at the nursery school in Mohács. I still didn't know my left from my right and couldn't remember where the fork went.

"The left, the left," the teacher scolded, and squeezed her hand around my left hand so hard the fork pinched the inside of my palm.

"Ow," I shrieked. "Don't do that!"

Laura, Péter, and Gábor stared at me with mouths open.

"And you don't talk back," she scolded again, and held up her right hand as if she was going to slap me.

I stared at the bowl of green mush in front of me. My cheeks burned. I didn't talk back to her after that. But she was still wrong. Using your left hand to eat didn't make sense when they tried to teach me that in Mohács, and it didn't make sense now. I used my right hand to draw and to scribble. Why use the left to eat? The teacher finally made me sit on my right hand so I wouldn't mess up.

Our main meal was usually some kind of vegetable mush. If it was green, it was either spinach or green beans. I hated green beans. It made me gag. If it was red, it was tomato. I liked tomato. Once a week, they gave us a little bit of meat to go with the mush. And there was always yummy crusty bread. I liked wiping my plate with the bread like my father used to do with Juliska Néni's fish soup.

If it wasn't too cold, the teachers let us outside to play. We didn't have any swings or seesaws, like we had at the beach, but there was a tree. We turned that tree into anything we wanted. It could be Rapunzel's castle or the mean king's dungeon; it could be the tallest mountain or the darkest jungle; it could be a one-eyed monster or a fire-breathing dragon.

In the afternoon, my grandmother came back with the wagon to take me home. Kati, who lived in a small house with a bit of land and lots of farm animals, walked with us. She had mousy brown hair and freckles and wore sweatpants with a faded cardigan. Her family raised pigs and chickens. We visited her farm a few times when my grandmother needed eggs or meat for a special dinner. I was happy to have someone to walk with us back and forth. Sometimes, when we asked her nicely, my grandmother pulled both of us in the wagon.

One day on our walk home Kati told me she was afraid because sometimes her father came home smelling funny and singing in a weird voice, then stumbled around the house and knocked things over. Her mother would yell at him and there was a fight, and sometimes they'd hit each other. On those nights, she and her little sister slept in her grandmother's bed.

"You're better off without parents," she said.

"I have parents," I said.

"Well, where are they then? Don't you live with your grandmother?"

"Yes, but they are coming back."

"Really?"

"Yes, and . . . and . . . I . . . I don't even live here. I am just visiting. I live in the city in a big apartment and we have a toilet inside the house and a television and a car."

"Oh? Then . . . why are you in school here?"

"Well . . . I . . . It's just for now . . . Until my parents come home."

"That's not what I heard."

"What did you hear?"

"That you're an orphan."

"That's not true. I'm not an orphan." I didn't know what an orphan was but it didn't sound good.

"So, where are your parents?" she asked.

"I forgot . . . V . . . Vien . . . Something like that. It has a big palace and . . . and . . . cake!"

"Oh. Well, that's good . . . Hey, you wanna play when we get to your house?"

63

We raced ahead, leaving my grandmother to pull the empty wagon. We headed straight for the giant birch in the front yard, which is where my gymnastic rings were now hung. I taught Kati how to stick her feet through the rings and hang by her ankles and twirl. We pretended to be the Olympic gymnasts on the TV last summer. Besides the car, the TV was my father's prized possession. It was built into a walnut frame and had two chunky dials and rabbit ears. My brother helped my father carry it up the stairs and into our apartment. Our whole family and Juliska Néni plus all the neighbors from the entire building crowded into our living room to watch the games from Mexico City. The men cheered when our soccer team beat Bulgaria for the gold. *Foci* was boring; it was the gymnast Vera Caslavska that I wanted to watch as she flew across the uneven bars and spun like a carousel. She was beautiful!

¤ ¤ ¤

"Mamika, where is Anyuka now?" I asked my grandmother that night after Kati had gone home and the dishes were washed and put away.

"Where is she now? Well, right now, she's in Italy, a city called Rome."

"I thought they were in that other place, the one with the big palace and the cake with jam."

"Vienna. Yes, they were there for a while. But now they are in Rome, another beautiful city."

"Do they have good cake there too?"

"Cake? Oh yes. They have lots of cake, and all kinds of other good things to eat."

"And Apuka and Tibi?"

"They are there too."

"Why?"

"Why?"

"Why are they there?"

"Well, they are visiting there for a little while. It's a beautiful city, like Vienna. Here, let me show you . . . these postcards came just a few days ago." She walked into the parlor, a big room where only guests were allowed. I followed her up two steps and through sliding doors. The room was freezing. From a drawer in a cabinet, she took two postcards. On the front of one was a huge round building, half of it missing. "They call this the Coliseum," my grandmother said.

"What happened to it?"

"It's old . . . from ancient days. They have many buildings like that in Rome . . . Here is the other."

It was a picture of a huge church. "They call this the Vatican. It's where the pope lives."

"Who is he?"

"He's an important priest. The most important."

"It looks like he lives in a palace."

"He does." She turned the card over so I could see my mother's handwriting. "Italy is warm," my grandmother read. "The people are all nice. We are having a nice time. Many kisses, Piri."

I looked at the postcards, turning them over and over, inspecting my mother's handwriting, wishing I could read her curly letters. I thought about that word Kate used—orphan. I had parents. They were just on a long vacation in a beautiful place.

"When will they be home, Mamika?"

"Soon, Juditka. Soon."

"Why couldn't I go to that place? To Rome?"

"One day you will."

"I'm too little?"

"Yes. You are still little. When you are big, like Tibike, you will get to go."

"How old is he?"

"Thirteen. Almost fourteen."

I was getting sleepy. We went back into our room. I changed into pajamas and got under the blankets on the mattress on the floor. Katus Néni came in to turn on the story-time bear on the television. I thought about the big circle building and the church where the pope lived. I thought about my mother walking on those streets. Maybe she should have taken her brown wool coat, I thought. It was warm when they left. It was cold out now, very cold.

Seven

The Other Side of the Ocean

I turned six the day before St. Nicholas Day. My two front teeth fell out. My grandmother held up a mirror. "Look," she said with a big toothless grin. "We look the same." We laughed, showing our pink gums.

There were no presents for my birthday. It was name days that were celebrated, but I wasn't sure what day that fell on, or even what month. I did hope that Mikulás would leave me something nice in the boots we left out the night before—maybe some nuts or raisins; maybe even a chocolate Mikulás wrapped in shiny paper.

But the night of my birthday, I went to sleep worried that instead of Mikulás, it would be the Krampus who'd show up at my grandmother's house, with his pointed horns and fiery tongue, carrying a long switch with which to beat me. He'd spank me, then stick me in his big bag and take me far away to some place even colder, far from my grandmother, and even farther from my mother and father. Zoli Bácsi said so.

"Be good," he'd say to me before I got into the red wagon for my grandmother to take me to the kindergarten. "Or the Krampus will take you away." Sometimes he said it with a smile, but I could tell he meant it. Maybe it was he who had the Krampus take Ildikó away to school. I tried to be nice to him so he would see that I was good.

"Goodnight, Zoli Bácsi," I said to him that night. "I hope you sleep well."

"Hrmph," he grunted, and slammed the bathroom door.

I tossed and turned on my grandmother's mattress. I looked up to the window over my head. The birch was shaking from the bitter cold, its bare white arms rapping on the window. "Let me in," it seemed to say. "It's cold out here." It was the perfect night for the Krampus to go rambling from house to house looking for bad children. I was sure he'd come for me, that Zoli Bácsi had sent for him. He would not forget how I glared at him on the train from Mohács, how I shouted at my aunt and told her the food she made was poison. I was a bad child; that's why my parents weren't coming home. That's why they went to Vienna and then to that other city. Maybe they would keep going and never come home.

I thought back to last Christmas. Our apartment in Mohács was cozy. A huge tile heater that took up an entire wall kept it that way. The kitchen smelled of Juliska Néni's stuffed cabbage and poppy seed strudel. Radio Free Europe played Silent Night, and though my mother said we had to keep it low so the neighbors wouldn't hear, we were listening to it on Christmas Eve because my mother said it was the most beautiful song ever. We had a huge tree; its top branch nearly reached the ceiling.

"You want to put the angel on the top?" my father asked. He was happy that day too, happy for the yummy smells coming from the kitchen; maybe like me and Tibor, he was looking forward to the presents we'd be opening later that night. I held out my arms and he lifted me high above his head. I held the white angel in her shiny white dress and reached for the tiny, wiggly branch at the top. But just as I did, my foot slipped into the pocket of his brand-new pajamas, ripping the seam. From a height of more than six feet, he plunged me to the floor so fast I thought I'd fall through the floor of our apartment to the neighbors below. I was terrified. When I looked up, his face was red hot, like the Krampus, and he was yelling loud, yelling at my mother, yelling so loud we could no longer hear Silent Night. I ran to my bed and hid under the covers. There were no presents that night.

Finally my grandmother got into bed next to me.

"You're still not sleeping?"

"No."

"Is something wrong?"

"The Krampus. Maybe he will take me away. He'll take me away because I've been bad."

"Oh Juditka, that's not going to happen," she said, patting my sweaty head. "You are safe here with me. And you are not a bad child. You are a good girl, a very good girl." She hugged me and held me until we both finally fell asleep.

¤ ¤ ¤

I woke up at dawn, even before my grandmother had a chance to heat the rooms, excited that I was still there, that maybe the Krampus went to someone bad, like Gábor, who is the one who I thought really needed a lesson. I peered through the frosted glass and opened the door to the small porch. It was so cold I could blow smoke rings through the air. Sure enough, my boots were there and filled with candy and not one but two chocolate Santas! "Look Mamika," I shouted. "Look at all the candy."

"I think it means you were a good little girl."

I hugged her, then unwrapped and ate both my chocolates for breakfast.

¤ ¤ ¤

With Christmas coming, my aunt and grandmother were even more busy than usual. My grandmother went back and forth to the store and to Kati's house and to some other neighbors. From Kati's family, she bought a ham and eggs, and from the store she brought home potatoes and milk in plastic bags and juice for the soda maker and bread and butter and the best part, *szalon czukor*, chocolates with a yummy filling wrapped in shiny paper, that we would string on the Christmas tree. She bought them in big boxes.

"Now don't touch these, Juditka," she'd say. "They are for Christmas."

It took every bit of willpower I had to not eat them.

Katus Néni cleaned the whole house, washed all the extra sheets, and set up the guest beds for my cousins' homecoming. She found a small tree and set it up in the heated bedroom. To the branches she clamped metal holders for the sparklers that we would light on Christmas Eve. She found decorations from years past, like gold-and-silver globes, and hung them on the tree.

In kindergarten, we cut circles out of colorful paper and weaved them together to bring home for our Christmas trees. We sang songs about big snowflakes and Father Winter. I was excited for my cousins and the presents!

Christmas Eve finally arrived. Ildikó and her sister Piroska came home earlier in the day and had already finished decorating the tree. The boys, Árpád and Zoli, helped my grandmother haul water and coal inside. Katus Néni cooked and served supper. For the first time since I'd arrived at the house, we ate together as a family around a big table in the parlor. After supper, we gathered around the tree. My cousins sang Silent Night. There was no fighting, no one yelled at my grandmother or sent her out to the cold snowy yard for more coal or water. Even Ildikó, home from her school, smiled a little. Katus Néni looked around at her four children, and she seemed happy. Zoli Bácsi took out his camera.

"Hold it up! Show us what you got for Christmas, Juci!" he said, looking through his camera, and calling me that name I hated. I sat on a small stool in front of the Christmas tree and held up a set of toy dishes. I refused to smile for him, but I was happy for my present. Tomorrow, I'd cook Zsuzsi Baba a feast!

¤ ¤ ¤

My grandmother saved the best present for Christmas day: a letter from my mother.

"She wrote this just to you," she said, handing me a blue envelope. The envelope was thin. I held it up to the light, and could see the letter and even the shape of the words inside. The return address said Rome.

My grandmother showed me how to open it carefully with scissors so the envelope and the letter inside it would not rip. Then she took out the letter. My mother's handwriting was small and precise. She wrote to me in block text rather than cursive. It didn't matter because I couldn't read. So my grandmother read it for me. *Drága Juditka*, she read. We hope you like your new kindergarten. Mamika says you are making new friends. We wish you a happy Christmas. We hope we will see you very soon."

She stopped reading.

"Read more!" I demanded.

"That's all she wrote."

"No. Read more," I yelled again.

"That's all she wrote. There's no more," she repeated.

How could that be? This was so short.

"Turn it over. To the other side."

"That's all there is."

I didn't understand. How could she be gone for so long, go to all those places—to the palace with 1,000 rooms and that old city with the broken building and even visit the pope—and only write a few words? "This is the worst Christmas ever," I

71

yelled at my grandmother. I spent the day in the heated bedroom. I didn't make Zsuzsi Baba a feast.

¤ ¤ ¤

It was not much later that my grandmother decided it was time we had a talk.

"Come in the parlor," she said. "I have something important to tell you."

In the parlor? What could it be? The parlor was the fancy room in the house, a few steps up from the hallway with the blue linoleum. It was separated with big sliding doors made of frosty glass. Someone had hung tiny black plastic cutouts of Fred Flintstone, Barney, Wilma, and Betty on the doors. It was one of the few fun things we had in the whole house. My cousins told me that in some other countries, you could watch Fred and his friends on television and they came to life, walking and talking to each other. Fred with his club made me laugh and I loved how Wilma had the same name as the street on which we lived: Vilma Utca. The parlor was where guests stayed in the summer. It was also where my uncle hosted visitors from time to time, sitting in a big comfy chair, inhaling the tobacco in his smoking stick. It was the biggest room in the house, with wide windows on every wall. In the summer, when my grandmother rolled up the heavy wooden blinds, the view from that room was pink oleander and white hibiscus, and wildflowers all the way to the willow tree and the railroad tracks. But the windows were black now and covered with frost, and the room was freezing cold. We only heated it on special occasions like Christmas, and sometimes not even then.

"Sit," my grandmother said, pointing to a chair next to a large wooden table in the center of the room. "Let me warm up the room a little." She walked over to the heater, threw some black coal inside, and lit it with a match. She sat next to me, and took another blue envelope from her pocket. I was excited,

72

thinking surely my mother had more to tell me about the palace or the cake or maybe my brother. Did he get a chance to go fishing after all? Was he still practicing piano somewhere? Did they see the broken building? Did she visit the king in the palace? Was my father happy visiting all those new places? Did he like the cake with the chocolate frosting?

Maybe she had good news. Maybe they'd be coming home. Maybe they finished seeing all 1,000 rooms in the palace of that first city, and were finally done seeing every broken building in that other one. Tibike would have to start school in the middle of the year, but that's okay because he learned so much. He could even be the teacher.

"You know that your mother and father and brother are in Rome," my grandmother said slowly.

"I know, Mamika. You told me last time . . . visiting that man, the one who lives in the castle. The king."

"The pope. Yes, he lives in Rome. That's where they are."

"Open the letter, Mamika! What does it say? Are they finally coming home?"

"It's like this, Juditka . . ."

"I can go home then. And Tibike will go back to school and Anyuka will go back to the babies and Apuka to the hospital. And we can come back here and visit you in the summer like always, when it's nice and warm, and we can swim in the lake and eat ice cream and . . ."

"It's like this, Juditka," she repeated, interrupting me. "Your family—they are not really on a vacation, Juditka. They couldn't tell us before because they weren't sure whether they could really go. But they were able to get as far as Rome, and now in this letter, they finally were able tell us that it looks like they will be going to America. Moving to America."

"America?"

"That's right. America."

"Where's that?"

"Well, it's kind of far."

"Farther than Rome?"

"Yes. It's on the other side of the ocean."

"Is that big?"

"Yes. Very big."

"Bigger than the lake?"

"Much bigger ... And because it's far, it means they can't come back to *Magyar Ország*."

"Why not?"

"Well, to get there, they will have to fly in a plane."

"Can't they fly back?"

"It's not that easy."

"Why not?"

"Because once you leave *Magyar Ország* to go so far away, to go to America, you can't really come back."

Can't come back? Can't come back! The words made no sense. If they could go there in a plane, why couldn't they come back in a plane? If you go in a car to Mohács, you can come back in a car. I was confused. Then my stomach started to hurt like I'd eaten a huge loaf of bread, and my pinky finger felt like it might break and fall off.

"They want to live there . . . in America."

I was cold. I started to shiver. I tried to think of what to say, but couldn't think of the right question or even words. And before I could speak, my grandmother's face brightened. Her eyes grew big and she smiled like it was Christmas again.

"The best part," she said, "is that you will be going to America to be with them. Can you believe it, Juditka? You are going to America!"

"Me?"

"Yes. To America. They have everything there," she continued as I sat in the freezing cold room shivering, listening to her. "It is like paradise there. There are big buildings and many stores for shopping and beautiful things to buy, pretty sweaters and shoes and dolls . . . And . . . you don't have to heat the rooms with coal like here. The heat comes out of the wall, like magic, and water comes pouring from pipes. And the buildings . . . the buildings are so tall, they touch the sky."

She kept talking and talking and as she did, my stomach settled and my finger went back to feeling regular, and in front of my eyes, I could see tall buildings piercing the blue sky, and beautiful clothes and shiny shoes, and stars and rainbows and a palace and cake and green grass and flowers and dolls and toys.

"Really?"

"Really."

"How tall are the buildings?"

"If you go to the top, you can look down and see the whole world."

"And I will live there?"

"Yes. One day. You will all be there together as a family."

I didn't ask my grandmother why my parents would want to go to America. Who wouldn't? I also forgot to ask her when this would happen. Time was not something I understood well. A day came and went when the sun set; a week ended with each Sunday when my aunt went to church, and started with each Monday when my grandmother pulled me in the wagon to kindergarten. Summer came and went and now it was winter. But what was a month? Was it three Sundays, or four or eight? What was a year—how many Sundays? And what did it matter? It seemed like such a small thing compared to America.

¤ ¤ ¤

"Guess what Mamika told me today?" I whispered in Zsuzsi Baba's ear as we sat on my grandmother's musty mattress that night. "We are going to America! We are going to a beautiful place with all kinds of pretty things, with houses so tall they touch the sky, with yummy cake and chocolate and candy and pretty shoes and sweaters to wear. We're going to be with Anyuka and Apuka and Tibike."

I told Kati the next day. I told her about the heat that comes from the walls and the water that pours from pipes. "I'm going there," I told her. "I'm going to America."

I told Laura and Péter and even Gábor.

"Guess where I'm going?" I told them. "I'm going to America! I'm going in an airplane over the ocean. It's so big. It's bigger than the Balaton."

We ran around the schoolyard, stuck our arms out and pretended we were all flying to America. "Follow me," said Péter, and we did, making the sound of a loud airplane engine. "Hello down there," Laura yelled to the pretend people watching us from below. "We're flying to America!"

Eight

Blind Crow

Winter just wouldn't leave. The days remained short and freezing cold and now my grandmother was going to and from the shed many times a day fetching coal for the heaters. She'd pull her raggedy old coat snug, tighten her black kerchief around her white hair, then slip into her old sneakers with the heels worn down at the back and shuffle over to the little hut, filling her metal bucket with black squares. Hunched like a shepherd's crook, she lugged the bucket back inside. Each time she fed the hungry heaters, Zoli Bácsi yelled.

"Would it hurt to stick on a coat?"

"Some of us have warmer coats," my grandmother snapped, sizing up my uncle's wool military jacket. The moths that shared the pantry with her all those years ago had eaten holes in hers.

"We can't keep this up; it's only February."

"What do you want me to tell you? We have children in the house."

"That's the problem. One more mouth to feed; one more body to keep warm."

"They left enough."

"Chump change. He was a rich man. With the car and vineyard and all that fancy furniture. But no. It wasn't enough for him. He takes off for America and leaves his kid here and expects us to feed and clothe the brat. *Büdös Zsidó*. Stinking Jew." He made a face like the toilet bowl was full of poop.

I was in the parlor looking for Zsuzsi Baba. The glass doors opened to the narrow hallway, where the two of them were arguing—again.

"Do you have to talk so loud?" my grandmother said.

"Don't I have enough problems? We barely have fuel to heat one room in this goddamned house?"

"Piroska sent some money last month and she promised to send more once they are settled in America and have jobs."

"Yes. She sent a little money. From two rich doctors in America, I would have expected more."

"They also left money they saved."

"Like that's going to last forever . . . Just stop sending every damn cent up the chimney." He turned around and marched back into his den.

"Never mind," she called after him. "I'll pay for the coal myself."

"*Boszorkány!* Ugly witch!" he shouted from his room.

I stayed in the cold room. I didn't feel like listening to my uncle calling my grandmother names. It was not the first time I heard them bicker. They fought about the heat and food and money all the time now. But now there was a new word: Jew, a stinking Jew. What was it? A thief, a monster with sharp fangs and claws, a devil with horns and red tongue like the Krampus? What?

I tried to remember my father, to see his face, his dark wavy hair . . . see us catching the beach ball in my grandmother's garden: "*Fogjad meg, Juditka.*" Catch the ball. He would throw it straight at me, then way high, then way low, making me work for it. I'd see us walking to the beach, his tanned muscles gliding down the street toward the beach, the red inflatable raft balanced on his head. How we giggled and laughed in the water. The south side of the Balaton was shallow far out into the lake. We could walk far from the shore, and the water still only reached his belly button. I'd splash my arms and wiggle my legs the way he taught me to stay afloat. And when I started to sink, I'd reach for his back to hold me up, or scramble onto the red raft. He would dive under the water and stay down a long time. I waited nervously for him to surface, scanning the lake, trying to see his shadow under the murky water. And then, just when I thought he'd drowned, he'd come shooting up from under me, lifting me in his arms, carrying me higher and higher, over his shoulder. And then suddenly, without any warning, from way up there, he'd let me drop into the lake. I went plunging beneath the surface, holding my breath, then just as I came bouncing to the surface, he splashed a fistful of water in my face. I was terrified but laughing ear to ear. "Do it again, Apuka! Do it again!"

My mother had to drag both of us from the water.

I saw him back in Mohács. It was my birthday, or maybe my name day in December and it was snowing hard. Enormous wet flakes fell from the sky, covering the sidewalks, the roads, the rooftops, the green dome of the church, the square, piling high, turning our city into a frosty white paradise. It was impossible to walk or drive or ride a bicycle. My father put on boots, a long wool overcoat, a felt hat and leather gloves. Juliska Néni dressed me in a white fur coat. I don't know where the coat came from. Maybe Austria or Italy—another trip my parents took somewhere far away. He found a wooden sled and off we went. He strutted ahead in his long black overcoat, his strong back carrying him forward in swift long strides, moving fast through the silent, snow-covered streets. The sled moved fast behind him, almost flying. I clung tight to the sides, my small hands in mittens, gripping the wooden slats, thrilled but scared to death. He didn't look behind to check if I was still there. He just kept moving forward. I was determined to not fall off, to show him I was his brave girl.

Bells rang as he opened the doors to the tiny toy shop. My father didn't ask me what I wanted for my birthday. He just looked around the shop and pointed to a huge brown bear slouching against a wall.

"We'll take that one," he said to the clerk, pointing to the bear.

"Yes sir, Dr. Boros," she said. "I'll wrap it for you."

"No need. We'll take it as is."

I hugged the bear tight as my father pulled both of us on the sled back toward our apartment. As we passed the clinic where my mother worked, he hollered up to the window. "*Piri, gyere ki*," and she appeared miraculously in the window, the snow falling on her dark hair, his felt hat, his wool coat, my white fur, the huge brown bear.

"Look at this, Anyuka," I called up to her. "Look at my new present!"

"*Nunus*," she called from the window, astonished. "It's as big as you!"

The bear was gone now, and so was my father. He used to be the most important doctor in the hospital in Mohács. He had his own office with a telephone on his desk and a pretty lady who worked in that office and answered the phone when people called him. People in Mohács called him Dr. Sir. Patients brought him gifts because he knew what to do to make them better. We'd get plump chickens and ham and sausage delivered to the house, and Juliska Néni would make us a feast.

But then he started traveling to other cities. We weren't told why; if he'd lost his job or if he got a better one. I knew that he didn't want to be just another doctor in a small city. He wanted to be the top doctor in a big city. My mother told me how when they were in medical school together, he wasn't satisfied unless he got the best grades in their entire class. If he earned anything less than an excellent, he would go up to the professor, and ask to retake the exam.

"Not good enough for you, eh?" the professors asked, annoyed.

He didn't want to stop going to medical school when it was over. He wanted to keep going, to specialize in radiology. My mother held up my hand to a light to show me how an X-ray might let you see the bones beneath your skin. But my father never got to learn more about X-rays. The people in charge, the people who decide such things, sent him back to Mohács, where he grew up. He wasn't happy about that, my mother explained. My father loved new things, new places, new adventures. Mohács was old. He knew every square inch, old and new. He knew the people who lived there before . . . and he knew them now. He wanted to work in Budapest, or even Pécs, where the university was, where his half brother lived. But this is the job he got. My mother was happy though. Mohács was her first choice. She grew up in an even smaller town, a farm, really, and to her Mohács was a big city. It had a brand-new hospital. When she opened the envelope with her assignment, she was thrilled.

¤ ¤ ¤

Now that he was no longer working in Mohács, my father only came home once during the week, on Saturdays. He was often in a dark mood. He would yell at Juliska Néni and my mother. The soup was cold, the furniture dusty, the shoes out of place, we kids messy. On those days it seemed like nothing could make him happy, especially us. My brother and I would hide and listen, scared, as he railed about everyone and everything; his new job and new boss, how he had to live in a small room, about not being able to come home and about having to come home, about Juliska's cold soup, and our bad manners, and my mother's hair; about Kádár and Kállai and

Khrushchev, and a whole bunch of other people whose names I didn't know.

Maybe my uncle was right. Maybe my father wasn't really what I thought he was. Maybe he was . . . what was that word . . . a Jew? Maybe that's why he had to go away and take my mother and my brother.

¤ ¤ ¤

Kati came over to play sometimes. But I was especially excited when she invited me to visit her. Kati's house was a whole other world. The house itself was short and squat, with small rooms and a straw roof. Inside, the walls were covered with tapestry that her grandmother made by hand. It trapped the heat but also made it so stuffy, I could hardly breathe, especially when Kati's mother was cooking. Sometimes it was sweet pastry; more often, it was something spicy and pungent, smells that sent us scurrying outside, holding our noses. On this day, her kitchen was warm and cozy, so we made a small space to play near the stove. We put a blanket on the floor and set out my play dishes and pretended to feed our dolls. Just as we were getting ready to feed them pretend cake, Kati's mother came in from outside, the door slamming behind her. In her bare hands, she clutched a shrieking, live chicken. She had it by the neck and was nearly choking it as the bird struggled, feathers flying everywhere. "Out, out," her mother shouted at us, trying to hold on to the frantic bird. "I need the kitchen."

"We want to watch. Can we please stay?" Kati said. I wasn't sure I wanted to watch. I was scared to death for the bird and even more scared that it would escape from her mother's clutches and attack us with its claws and sharp beak.

"Why would you want Juditka to see such a thing?" her mother said. But she let us stay anyway.

"Watch this," Kati whispered.

Then with a smart twist of her knuckles, Kati's mother snapped the chicken's neck. After all the clucking, it was suddenly so quiet I could hear Kati breathe. Taking a large knife, she cut off the bird's head and threw it in the trash, eyes and beak and all. Blood gushed from the chicken's body, but Kati's mom deftly directed it into a pan on the stove sizzling with onions and spices. "It's good for you," her mother said as I stared at her cooking the chicken's blood.

I ran out to keep from vomiting.

"I guess you've never seen a chicken get its head cut off," Kati said, coming after me.

"Or cooked blood for dinner. I never want to see that again."

"It's just a chicken. It's worse when they kill the pigs."

"You've seen them do that?"

"Every Christmas. We just killed one last month."

"Poor pig."

I wanted to go home, but Kati pulled me toward the shed in her yard. "Come, I want to show you something."

There, in a dark corner on top of a pile of straw lay a big fat black dog licking her pink nipples.

"Touch her belly."

"Eww."

"It's okay. Don't worry."

I put my fingers on her swollen tummy. It was soft and silky, her skin tight. Kati's dog was beautiful—pitch black like a moonless night. But she seemed very tired and barely moved. "Is she okay?"

"She's pregnant," Kati whispered. "Her puppies will be born soon. My mother said you can have one if you want."

"Really?"

"Yeah. She'll have like eight."

"That would be so fun. I'll ask my grandmother."

I imagined having a puppy of my very own, a warm furry friend to keep me warm at night. I imagined my puppy following me everywhere, and welcoming me home with slobbery kisses. I imagined taking him to the Balaton to swim, chasing him through the wildflowers behind the house. I imagined a friend who'd never leave.

I asked my grandmother the minute she arrived.

"Please, Mamika. Please!" I begged, showing her Kate's pregnant dog.

"A dog is a lot of work, Juditka. You have to feed it and train it."

"I can do that," I promised. "I'll give him my supper."

"Well, I don't think you have to do that. Table scraps will be fine. But you will have to make sure you feed it."

"I will Mamika, I promise." I sensed her giving in and I jumped up and down, hugging her tight around her waist. "Thank you, Mamika. Thank you."

"Maybe it will be good for you," she said.

I was so happy, happier than I had been since I arrived at my grandmother's house. Then my thoughts wandered to Zoli Bácsi. To him, a dog would be just one more mouth to feed, like me. I was sure he would say no.

"Do we have to tell him, Mamika?"

"No. This will be our decision alone."

I loved my grandmother. I loved her more than a big ice cream cone on a hot day, more than the lake in July, more than anything in the world.

¤ ¤ ¤

We picked up the puppy from Kati's house in late winter. I named him *Vak Varjú*, Blind Crow, because he was black like a crow, so black I thought maybe he was blind. He was tiny enough to fit in the palm of my hand. I held him in my mittens and kissed his little pink nose.

I was allowed to keep Blind Crow inside the house for the first few weeks of his life. The puppy joined my grandmother and me on the mattress on the floor, snuggling between us. He kept us warm all through the end of winter and early spring and licked my face before I fell asleep at night. He wagged his little tail and jumped all over me when I got home from school.

¤ ¤ ¤

Blind Crow grew quickly, and I did not know how to train him. Neither did my grandmother or aunt or my cousin Ildikó, and certainly not my uncle, who took no interest in him, except to yell at him regularly. By late spring, he was out of control. He bounced around our yard like a big baby who doesn't know his own size or strength, nearly knocking my grandmother down. He jumped on my aunt, shoving the food from her hands, and stealing off with whatever he could grab with his jaws. He stood on his hind legs and stole bits of bacon or ham from the kitchen table. None of us knew what to do.

"Whose idea was it to bring this devil into the house," my aunt cried.

He barked at the mail carrier on his bicycle, chasing him down the street, once even grabbing his pants with his teeth until he fell off.

"I'll get you!" he cried, picking up a stick and running after *Vak Varjú* like he was going to beat him.

"Leave him alone," I yelled at the man. "He's just a puppy."

"Then teach him how to behave!"

From the front yard, Katus Néni saw me yell at the man. "Get inside, Juditka," she yelled. "You can't speak to grownups like that . . . I'm sorry," she said, turning to the man. "It's a new dog."

"You better get him under control before something happens to him," he said, getting back on his bicycle.

When *Vak Varjú* barked at night, Zoli Bácsi got mad.

"Get that dog to shut up, or I will," he said.

"Hush," I told *Vak Varjú*. You must be good or else they will send you away. I pet his black fur and he licked my face.

But I could not get him under control. He continued to bark and jump on everyone. So Zoli Bácsi tied *Vak Varjú* to the tree in the front yard. And because the yard was so muddy, he was no longer allowed inside. He was to sleep in the shed. I stayed outside with him, stroking his black fur until the sun went down behind the train tracks and twilight turned to night.

"I'll never leave you," I promised him as we sat shivering in the shed. "I'll stay right here all night long no matter what."

But the sky turned blacker than *Vak Varjú*, and the wind howled through the cracks in the shed, and before long, I gave up my vigil and went inside, leaving my dog alone in a pile of straw, where he slept thereafter every night.

"It's all right," my grandmother explained. "Dogs are supposed to sleep outside. They protect the house."

When fall came, I went back to school and ran home every day to see *Vak Varjú*. He was there day after day, jumping on me, licking my face until one day, he wasn't. I walked around the yard amid the wildflowers, the willow tree, and the tall grass calling his name. "*Vak Varjú! Hova mentél, kis kutya?* Where are you?" I searched every inch of the house, out back under the tree house, in the woodshed, behind the outhouse; I even lifted the cover of the well, thinking maybe he had drowned. There was no sign of *Vak Varjú* anywhere.

I cried myself to sleep that night. I worried he would get lost and get hit by the train, or even by a car. There weren't many that came through the village, but there were a few here and there on the main road and if he wandered off, he wouldn't know how to not run in front of a car. I worried he would have nothing to eat and he'd starve. I worried the mailman would find him and beat him with his stick.

I didn't want to go to school the next day.

"Maybe he will come home, Mamika. I have to be here when he does."

But my grandmother said no. School was important. I couldn't skip it on account of a dog.

It was my grandmother who eventually found him and told me what she suspected happened. Someone, maybe the mail carrier, maybe someone else, decided they'd had enough of my dog's barking and fed him sausage laced with sharp pins. He ate it heartily, and lumbered off toward the railroad tracks, where my grandmother said she found him dead. A piece of sausage laced with the deadly pins lay by his side, she told me.

"Good riddance," Zoli Bácsi said. "That dog was a goddamned nuisance."

¤ ¤ ¤

That night, I dreamed about dying. I dreamed that morning came, and I didn't wake up. Like my dog, I too had disappeared. No one remembered that I had lived. No one knew my name or my face, my black curly hair, my blind, black dog, my doll Zsuzsi Baba. I had lived and now I was dead, with nothing of me left. I woke up sweaty and scared in the dark room, my grandmother snoring by my feet. What happens to you when you die? I looked at my grandmother's wrinkled skin, her hunched back, her white hair. What will happen to her when she can no longer work or pull water from the well, or even walk, or eat or take a sip of water? I thought of *Vak Varjú*, dead by the railroad tracks. Does a part of you float up to heaven? Go to hell? Do we just melt into the soggy ground like the apple cores or cherry pits we toss into the garden, like the rotted plums that fall from the tree only to be eaten by flies and maggots? The priest at church talked about being good so our souls will have what he called everlasting life. But what did everlasting life feel like? Look like? Was it a green meadow with wildflowers? Was it endless servings of ice cream? And what did it matter anyway, if after we died, no one remembered that we even lived at all?

And then, lying there in the dark, the solution came to me. Before I die, I decided, I must carve a statue of myself. It might be made of white marble like the statues of important men or heroes in a city square back home in Mohács. It might be small, made of bronze, like some people might have in a garden. It might be made of shiny green Zsolnay porcelain, like the one of a little girl corralling her ducks, which sat on a shelf in our home in Mohács. My statue would be a little girl holding her black dog, my dog. Boros Judit, it would say. Born: 1963. Even if I did nothing else, even if my parents had gone to America and forgot me here, even if I died and melted into the brown earth like apples and plums, like *Vak Varjú*, people would at least know that I lived.

With that, I went back to sleep.

Nine

The Orphanage

"Stand back," Gábor shouted. "I'll show you how it's done."

He strutted over to the tree at the center of the kindergarten yard, and reached for the limb. The girls stood back, letting him butt into our game, the game I started, in which we were all competing for a spot in the next Olympics. The tree had gone from a dungeon with prisoners deep in its rooted cells to a stage for the Olympic trials. The goal was to wrap your hands around the limb and twirl around it flawlessly: twice to qualify; three times to win.

It was an unfair game. I had so much practice on my gymnastic rings, there was no way Laura would beat me, or Ilona. The only other girl who had a shot was Kati. I could hold on to the rings and twist around, stick my legs through and swing high, hook my legs in with my hands to make the bridge, and point my toes in the air for the candle. I was going for gold.

Then Gábor sauntered over. All the girls backed up and stupidly allowed him into our game. They knew Gábor messed up everything, tore up their drawings and blasted through the doll house. Instead of kicking him out, they stood back and acted all silly, giggling and laughing. He reached for the limb, threw his legs up and made it over twice. Not bad, I thought. But I wasn't going to let him beat me.

"That's nothing. I can do that," I shouted.

"Oh yeah? Prove it!"

He got down and moved over to the pack of girls, who made a path for me to mount this Olympic stage. Now I was nervous. He may have been a bully, but I had to admit he was pretty good. I walked over to the tree, and reached for the limb. It was a little higher than I thought and I had to stand on my toes and stretch my arms further than I expected. I touched it with the tip of my fingers. One more inch and I was able to wrap my hand around the branch. It felt coarse, not at all like my polished wooden rings. Still, I grabbed it firmly and lifted my feet off the dirt. One more pull and I was able to push myself high enough to get the limb to my stomach. I was ready to do the somersault. I knew I had to push off hard to make it over. I lurched forward with all my might and found myself spinning around the limb with a mighty force, once, twice, about to make it over three times! My mind was abuzz with victory.

But before the third spin, I lost my grip. In an instant, I fell to the ground and landed with a thud. I lay on the ground in a puddle of defeat. Teachers and kids came rushing. I was bleeding from my nose and couldn't move my right arm. From the corner of my eyes, I saw Gábor strut off.

"Does someone have a handkerchief?" the teacher called. Two girls, twins, stood directly in front of me. They were not my friends. They had each other, so they didn't play with anyone else. They were dressed exactly alike in a white shirt and red skirt. Their red hair was covered with red handkerchiefs. They looked like dancers in an old-fashioned Hungarian folk dance.

"You!" the teacher called to one of the twins. "Hand me your handkerchief!" Blood gushed from my nose and my arm felt like a horse trampled it. Trying to help, the teacher nudged it just a bit. "Ouch." I yelled.

But the twins just stood there, staring blankly, not moving.

"The one on your head," the teacher pointed, losing patience. "Come on. Hurry up. Hand it over."

Then as if in slow motion, she shook her head no. The teacher turned to the other twin. "You?" She, too, shook her head.

"She's going to America," I thought I heard the girl say. "She doesn't need our handkerchief."

The teacher stared at them, stunned. Laura finally ran over and offered us her white hanky, and the teacher quickly wiped the blood from my nose. An hour later, I was at the doctor's office, and before the week was out, my arm was placed inside a heavy, stiff cast. And there it stayed for the remainder of that school year and well into the summer. I couldn't swim. I couldn't play on the gymnastics rings. And I was forever humiliated by that stupid Gábor. It would be my first summer on the lake without my parents and brother, without Juliska Néni, with nothing to do. There'd be no going to the beach every day, no raft, no jumping from Apuka's shoulders.

¤ ¤ ¤

The first guests of summer arrived with the end of school. They settled into freshly-made beds with downy covers in the same room I shared with Juliska Néni last summer. Katus Néni smiled at them. "Look at those rosy cheeks," she said, patting one little blonde girl on the head. "I bet you will have fun at the lake. We'll have supper waiting for you when you return. What do you like better? *Palacsinta* with chocolate, or jam?"

Zoli Bácsi surfaced from his den to greet the summer tourists. "I'll be at the lake tomorrow with my camera if you want some photos," he told them. "You'll want to have something to remember your vacation." He may have been a scary old man, but he was a skilled photographer. It was he who took those first-ever color pictures of my whole family and my cousins swimming happily in the lake last summer. He was now taking pictures of all the tourists arriving from East Germany and Poland and Czechoslovakia. He'd sling a 35mm camera over his shoulder, mount a noisy old motor scooter, and take a ride to the beach. He'd find vacationers who didn't bring cameras. There were many. Only the fat East Germans had them, he told us. The skinny Poles and the Soviets were too poor. He'd snap shots of happy children swimming and playing. Then he'd take the film back to his room, which he turned into a darkroom with a clothesline strung over the bathtub bed. From a basin filled with cool water came white sailboats, ice cream cones, and happy smiles. He placed the black-and-white photos on the outside table for the tourists to choose.

"Come with me, Juditka," my grandmother said. "Let's pick some strawberries from the garden. We'll make some jam." The blonde family with the cute children finished their breakfast, packed their toys, and went off to the beach, followed by Zoli Bácsi on his scooter. I followed my grandmother's black dress to the strawberry patch in the back yard. "Take the stems off, and put the strawberries in here," she said, handing me a bowl. I crouched down to pick the strawberries and watched my grandmother walk off to lug another heavy load of sheets and towels to wash in the tin tub. It took her all day to wash everything, then hang it all up to dry, pinning each piece carefully to the clothesline.

I found a ball and spent the rest of the day bouncing it against the yellow stucco wall of the house with my good arm. 1, 2, 3 . . . 43, 47, 44. Each time I missed the wall, I started over. Once I got all the way to 52. How many numbers were there? How many days 'till summer ends? How many days 'till I can see my family?

¤ ¤ ¤

It was almost the end of summer when the cast finally came off. The doctor cut it off with a saw as if he were cutting a limb from a tree. After it fell off in two pieces, he asked if I wanted to keep it, but I made a face and shook my head. Why would I want to keep that ugly smelly thing that ruined my summer? I was happy to be rid of it.

At least I had my arm back for the start of elementary school. What I didn't have were clothes that fit. I was still wearing what Juliska Néni packed for me the day we left Mohács: my favorite red flannel beach dress, a green-and-red plaid skirt, and my knitted pink sweater, which my mother had brought back from Germany when we lived in Mohács, the not-so-distant past that now seemed like a lifetime ago. I loved that sweater. I wore it almost every day, picking and pulling at the threads. The sleeves barely covered my arms now and the thread was slowly unraveling. Still, I clung to the sweater. It came from my mother.

It was cool and cloudy as we left the house on Vilma Utca and headed for the train station to get the new clothes. I wondered why we couldn't just go to the one shop at the end of the street, across from the ABC market. It was a tiny shop and dark inside. There weren't many choices. Skirts came in blue or black; pleated or plain. Shirts were either white or light blue. The clothes were stacked on a shelf behind the counter, and you had to point and tell the lady what you wanted. She'd pull down a shirt or a dress covered in dust and if you smiled nicely, she might let you try it on. My grandmother said they wouldn't have what we needed in that store. Besides, she added, it was a chance for me to see another city.

Our little town faded in the distance as the train pulled out and headed north, past small houses with straw roofs, past the church, past Jesus on his cross with flowers at his feet. The houses turned into wide-open fields tended by men with donkeys and mules. Poor things, I thought. They had a harder life than my grandmother. They were working outside in the cold and rain all day. It was raining hard by the time the train pulled into Keszthely and we got off. The city reminded me of Mohács because there were paved roads and stop signs and lights that lit up the roads and buses and even traffic lights. There were cars on the roads. It was fun to watch the lights change from red to green in the drizzle; fun to watch the cars with their headlamps, the bus stops with people getting on and off, busily going places. The city was so alive. Without an umbrella, we walked the wet sidewalks, my grandmother carefully avoiding the puddles so her feet wouldn't get wet in her old canvas sneakers with holes in them, while I purposely looked for the best ones to jump across, or land splat in the middle. "Juditka," she scolded. "You're going to get us both drenched." But I knew she wasn't really mad. Besides, we were both already wet. So I kept on stepping in and around the puddles until a shop window caught my eye. There, smack in the center and all lit up by the shop lights, was the very thing I wanted for the start of first grade: a shiny light blue school jacket just like the one Laura's mother bought her for the start of school. It was so beautiful. Its lightweight fabric sparkled like the sun on the lake in summertime.

"Please, Mamika, can we stop and buy that jacket for school? Look how pretty it is …" I tugged on her dress, trying to pull her into the shop.

"Those are much too expensive, Juditka," she said.

"But Laura is getting one. Why can't I get one?"

"You already have a school jacket from Ildikó. It will be fine."

"But it's so old fashioned, Mamika. It's so dark and stiff."

Ildikó got her jacket from Piroska. It was navy blue and made of heavy canvas.

"We need the money for other things, Juditka, like heating the house. Ildikó's old jacket will be fine."

"But Mamika, please. Just look how pretty it is."

She wouldn't hear of it. "School is not about how you look," she said. "It's about learning."

We left the storefront. My joy over the city, its twinkling lights, and the possibility of starting a new school year in a sparkling jacket were snuffed. I'd be stuck with Ildikó's ugly old hand-me-down. I pouted unhappily as we walked in the drizzle until my grandmother came to a stop in front of what looked like a large school surrounded by an iron fence twice as tall as each of us. Its yard was noisy with the sound of children playing outside despite the rain.

"Mamika, look at this school. They have a swing!" It was the first thing to catch my eye. Inside the heavy iron gates, there were dozens of children, all with short hair, all dressed in shades of gray and black. They were running around the yard chasing one another. This must be like Ildikó's school, I thought. I was happy to see children laughing.

"It's not a school, Juditka. It is an orphanage."

I remembered the sound of that word and I didn't like it. What did it mean? Who was it who first said those words? Was it Kate? Or Laura?

"I don't like this place, Mamika. Let's just keep going."

"This *is* where we're going."

"I don't want to go in there. Let's just go, please." I pulled on her arm to get her away from the iron fence when a girl wandered over.

"Is she coming to stay?" she asked my grandmother hopefully, sticking her nose through the fence. She had short hair like all the kids, boys and girls. And she wore a coat like that of every other child playing outside.

I looked at my grandmother and remembered the meaning of the word.

"Don't leave me here, Mamika. I don't want to live here," I said, tugging on her arm.

She looked at me, suddenly realizing what I was thinking. "No, Juditka. I'm not going to leave you here."

"But you said it's an orphanage. For children with no parents. Like me."

"Yes, but you're not staying here. Why would you even think such a thing?"

"Because Zoli Bácsi doesn't want me."

"Oh, that man."

"I heard him say it. I heard him say I'm not his problem."

"Oh . . . sometimes I just want to . . . never mind."

"Then why are we at the orphanage?"

"We're here because you need new clothes. And we can get some here—for free."

"You'd like it here," said the girl, turning to me. We have those swings and even some toys inside, and the food is not bad."

"No, she's not coming to stay," my grandmother answered quickly, grabbing ahold of my hand and pulling me toward the entrance. She could be a good friend, I thought. Maybe it wouldn't be so bad. Maybe the teachers were nice. Maybe they read you bedtime stories. I'd have friends . . . friends who I could play with from morning 'till night. I wouldn't have to wander around the house bored and alone, feeling like I was always annoying someone. We would eat breakfast and dinner together at a big table. We'd sleep in beds next to each other, and whisper secrets through the night.

"*Szia*," I said to the girl as we headed toward the front door.

"*Szia*," she waved. "Maybe I'll see you sometime."

Inside, my grandmother looked through some bins of clothing, talked to the adults, signed some papers, and we were on our way, leaving the children behind the iron fence. I looked back and saw the girl who had come over to say hi. She was standing alone by the fence. I wished I could have run back to her, at least to say goodbye, and tell her I was sorry I couldn't stay and be her friend.

Outside, my grandmother took a small cardigan from the bag, told me to take off my pink one and put this one on instead.

I took a sniff. "I don't like it," I said, holding my nose.

"We'll wash it when we get home. Look how nicely it fits you!"

I didn't like the new sweater. It had never touched my mother's hands; it did not come from Germany. But at least the sleeves reached my hands and the thread wasn't unraveling. My grandmother let me keep my pink one; I clutched it close to my chest as we made our way back to the train station.

¤ ¤ ¤

Back at my grandmother's house, everything was topsy-turvy. While we were gone, a truck had arrived from Mohács filled with furniture and boxes from my family's home. Everything was scattered in the front yard—boxes of clothes and shoes, dishes, and art. I ran my fingers across the green velvet chairs, bounced up and down on the sofa. I tore through boxes filled with my mother's clothes. I inhaled the smell of her sweaters, her winter coat.

"Why is this all here?" I finally asked my grandmother, amused at the sight of my family's old belongings in the yard.

"Mamika," my aunt called from one of the guest rooms. "Come and help me. I've been working since you left. Everything arrived on the truck just as soon as you left. They didn't even give us notice that today would be the day."

"It sure took long enough," my grandmother said.

"Mamika, Mamika . . ." I tugged on her dress, begging for attention. "Why is this here?"

"Your family doesn't need all this anymore. They have nicer things now," she said.

Zoli Bácsi inspected the furniture, and sat on the sofa. "Payment for services rendered," he mused, talking to himself. "What good is all this anyway?"

"It will make the guest rooms nicer," Katus Néni chimed in. "Maybe then we can charge a little more."

"Who's got money to pay more?"

"It's something," my grandmother said.

"Yes, it's something. More work to move it all inside. Why did that Jew need all this anyway? What's the use?"

"He wanted nice things for his family."

"I doubt it was for his family. Anyway, it doesn't solve anything. It's not like I can sell it to pay for heat and food. Maybe we can chop it up for firewood."

¤ ¤ ¤

Over the next few days, my aunt and grandmother managed to move everything inside. Zoli Bácsi didn't help them. He went back to his room to smoke. They moved my brother's bed into the room where we all slept. My grandmother didn't need to sleep on the floor any more.

They moved the green velvet sofa and chairs into one of the paying guest rooms. They tucked the fancy china in the pantry next to the flour and the salt and sugar. We never ate dinner together. There was no need for fancy china.

Katus Néni unpacked my mother's things. Her sweaters were small, almost small enough to fit me. They had pretty buttons, red, pink, and green. They were soft like kittens.

I took one from the box and held it up to my cheeks, feeling the soft knit against my face. It was much nicer than the sweater from the orphanage.

"Can I have this one, Katus Néni," I asked my aunt. "Look how pretty it is." I held it up against me to show that it fit.

"No, you're too little for it."

"I'll take care of it."

"No, Juditka! With your climbing on trees and running around in the mud? What do you think will happen to it?

"Please?"

She didn't let me have it. She put all the sweaters in a cabinet in a cold guest room and locked it with a key.

¤ ¤ ¤

I followed my grandmother into the room where they put the furniture. I sat on the green velvet sofa and watched her dust and polish the cherry wood edges. I tried to remember what the furniture looked like in our home in Mohács. My mother told me that my father drove all the way to Budapest to buy the furniture. He had spent several days looking for the perfect living room set. It was a few years after the apartment on Szabadság Utca was assigned to them. Assigned because it was the party that decided who got to live where. Before that apartment, they lived in a small room in the hospital where both my mother and father worked after they were married. Tibor was born there and he lived there with them, sleeping in a small crib. My mother held up the tiny black-and-white photos that showed the three of them in that tiny room. My father had thick black hair. Tibor was a chunky baby, not like he was when they left, all skinny with black, slicked-back hair. They were a family then, and they were a family now, somewhere.

My mother told me how happy they were to get the place across from the onion-domed church and the big square. It was just a small apartment at first, because they were a small family. But my father knew the people who made those decisions. Just a little bit of money and they could arrange to get you more space, and so by the time I came along, we had three apartments put together. The furniture he had brought home for the living room was heavy, made by one of Budapest's finest craftsmen. Once it was set up, though, my brother and I were

99

banned from the room. If I sat on the sofa and my shoe just as much touched the fabric, he'd yell loudly and I'd run from the fancy living room to my brother's room and hide my face in Juliska Néni's lap. Even my mother wasn't allowed to sit on the furniture without a towel under her. What kind of furniture did they have now? Maybe my mother would send a picture soon.

Ten

Ugly Shoes

The mail carrier was bringing more tissue-thin blue envelopes now—all marked AIR MAIL. My grandmother showed me the return address in the far-left corner and a stamp with an airplane and the words United States of America. She told me the letters were coming across the ocean in an airplane from New York, the city with the tall buildings.

"The ones that touch the sky?"

"Yes," she said. "Do you know what this means, Juditka?"

"What?"

"It means your family made it to America. Where they wanted to go."

"In an airplane?"

"Yes, in an airplane."

"Where I'm going?"

"Yes. Where you are going."

"Can you tell me what she wrote, Mamika?"

"She says they flew in a plane from Italy and they lived in a big hotel for a while, in New York. Now they have an apartment with a small kitchen and Tibor has his own room."

"What else?"

"Your father has a job. Tibike started school."

"What grade is he in?"

"Oh, I don't know, seven, maybe eight." The eighth graders at my new elementary school were so big. I could hardly picture my brother like them in a new school.

"And Anyuka?"

"She is learning how to speak English."

"Will I learn how to speak that?"

"Yes. You will."

"How?"

"Well, school I guess. That's how Tibike is learning."

Then she took out something from the envelope. I thought maybe my mother had sent some pictures. I wanted to see everything; their new home, the streets, the buildings that touch the sky, my brother in his new school. But there were no pictures. Instead, my grandmother pulled out what looked like paper *forint* hidden in the letter. It had the number twenty on it. From the center stared a scary man with stick-up hair.

"What is it, Mamika?"

"They call them dollars."

"What's that?"

"It's American money. Like the *forints* we use here."

"Can we buy things with it?"

"If we exchange it, yes. Maybe a new coat for winter."

"And the shiny school jacket?"

"Maybe that too."

"And shoes, Mamika. Laura just got these new shoes. They are black and so shiny you can see your face in them."

"Yes, maybe we can get those too."

¤ ¤ ¤

To buy anything with the green dollars with the stick-up hair man, my grandmother had to walk more than a half hour, farther than the kindergarten or my new school, to a small branch of the *Magyar Nemzeti Bank*, the Hungarian National Bank. After school one day, we walked over there together.

"Why can't we just take the dollar to the store?" I asked my grandmother.

"Because every country has its own money and here, the stores only take our money. But this is American money," she said, grinning. "We should be able to get a lot for it. I think I can even pay the heat with it this month."

"Then we won't have to be so cold, Mamika."

"That's right."

We stood in line at the bank for a long time. When it was our turn, she handed the dollars to the clerk behind thick glass.

"Where did this come from?" the clerk asked.

"That's our business, I believe."

"It's American money. If you want to change it, you have to fill out this form."

My grandmother didn't have a choice. She had to fill out the long form detailing exactly where she got the money, with names and addresses.

"Is this your family?" the clerk asked when my grandmother handed her the form.

"Would it make a difference if I told you?"

"It wouldn't make any difference."

"Then I'd rather not say."

"Suit yourself," said the clerk. She then handed my grandmother a stack of *forints*.

"Thank you," she said, as we left the line. On our way out, she counted the money and that's when all the happy lines in her face turned upside down.

"This is not nearly enough," she said. She cut in line in front of everyone and returned to the clerk.

"Please get back in the line," the clerk said.

"But you made a mistake," my grandmother said. "We waited in line the first time."

"There is no mistake, I assure you."

"But this is half what it should be."

"There is a tax on exchanging American dollars."

"How could it be so much?"

"I don't make the rules."

"But this isn't right."

"Be grateful you got something," said the clerk. "Most of us around here don't have money coming from America."

When we left the bank, my grandmother was still fuming. I'd never seen her so mad at anyone before except maybe Zoli Bácsi. I was too afraid to speak up until we were almost home.

"Does this mean I can't get a new sweater, or shoes, or the school jacket?" I asked her finally.

"Maybe we can get one of those things, but not all three."

I hung my head. How could I choose between a shimmery new school jacket and new black shoes?

She made the mistake of telling Zoli Bácsi what happened. "Tell your rich son-in-law to send more next time," he said. "After all, we're caring for his brat."

"Forget it," she said.

Still, that month at least, we didn't have to wear our coats in the house all the time.

¤ ¤ ¤

I didn't really know what people had to do to get dollars or *forints*. But I was learning. I could see that every summer the guests left money for staying in the rooms. I could see that every summer my aunt went to work as a maid at a hotel at the beach. It wasn't a big hotel, just two stories. But few places along the Balaton even had one. It meant that by the end of the summer, Katus Néni had enough money to send Ildikó back to her school with a new dress or two.

While our house didn't have running water and the electricity came and went depending on the state of the wires that crisscrossed the cracked walls, my cousins always dressed nicely. They too had jobs in the summertime when they came home from school. My cousin Árpád left on his bicycle every morning to work at what he said was the water treatment plant. I didn't know what that was, but I was glad someone treated the water. My cousin Piroska worked at the only restaurant in the village and collected tips. She said the nicer she looked the more money people gave her, so she spent what she made on eye liner, lipstick, and perfume. She looked beautiful.

I didn't see Zoli Bácsi work—except in the summers when he took photos of the tourists and sold them for *forints*. Other than that, he stayed in his room, read the newspaper all day, and complained about his food and the people he read about. They were the same names my father yelled about. I figured Kádár and Khrushchev were bad guys. Sometimes I was afraid of them at night, but then I'd see their pictures on the news and the man on the TV said Kádár was a good man who did nice things for people, like make sure they had jobs and enough food and fuel. I wished Kádár could get my uncle a job too. Maybe then he would complain and smoke less, and stop yelling at my grandmother for heating the house.

¤ ¤ ¤

I ran to the mail box every day looking for more new blue envelopes. "Read it, Mamika. Read it!" I'd beg when one finally came. She would show me a small part of the letter that my mother wrote just to me.

"*Drága Juditkám, Reméljünk hogy jól vagy.* We hope you are well and that you like school. We miss you very much. We hope we will see you very soon."

"Read the rest, Mamika," I begged her. But like her Christmas letter, that's all there was for me. The rest was for the grownups.

"Read that part! Please."

But she said it was not about anything for children. It was just boring grown-up things.

"Tell her next time to send fifty dollars," Zoli Bácsi said, when he saw her with the letter. "Or maybe a hundred. Tell her the kid needs more clothes and food, and money to heat the house."

So eventually my grandmother wrote on thin blue paper, asking her for just a bit more, money for new pants, a skirt, a new coat for winter. She'd choose a new black-and-white photo of me, one with an especially big smile, tuck it inside the thin paper, and walk to the post office to send it to America.

The next time we got two twenty-dollar bills, and my grandmother took me to the shoe store.

"The bank will take most of it, but I think we can finally buy those shoes you want," she said.

I was so happy. My feet had grown and my shoes pinched. Plus they were so plain. I couldn't wait to get shiny shoes like Laura's.

"I'd like those," I told the clerk behind the counter when we stopped at the store the following week. "The really shiny ones." From a small stack of boxed shoes behind the counter, she handed my grandmother the shiny shoes. "These don't even need to be polished. Just wipe them down like this," said the clerk, running a soft cloth over the toe.

"Thank you, thank you, Mamika," I said.

I loved my new shoes and wore them to school the very next day. But then Katus Néni said it would be best if we saved them for some special occasion. I wondered what special occasion was coming, but couldn't really think of one.

"The school yard is so muddy, Juditka. Don't you want to keep those shoes looking pretty for when spring comes? For church?"

"No, I want them for school so everyone can see . . ."

"I will put them in the box and save them for church," she said, and with that, she took the new shoes and locked them away in the cabinet in the cold guest room, next to my mother's sweaters.

I should have been grateful to have those shoes, even if they had to be locked away. Except for Laura, whose mom was the Russian teacher, most of the kids at our school wore the same pair of pants every day, and hand-me-down shirts and shoes. Kati was still wearing the same dirty cardigan she wore in kindergarten. Compared to her and everyone else, I had many nice things: a plaid dress, a knit sweater with Nordic designs, a corduroy dress, a pleated skirt. I had knee-high socks, and now that my hair was growing long, red ribbons tied in two ponytails. But I wasn't grateful. I hated the orphanage clothes and Ildikó's hand-me-down jacket. But what I hated more than anything was my mother's boots. I would have given anything for my aunt to let me have one of my mother's sweaters, but not her boots, with their uneven soles, one tall, one short.

Then came one snowy day. It snowed in big giant flakes from the afternoon and through the night until Vilma Utca disappeared. My grandmother couldn't pull me in the wagon and the snow was too high even for the sled. And since school was not going to shut down, I'd have to make my way there on my own two feet. Buying snow boots for my growing feet was out of the question, especially when there was a perfectly good pair left behind by my mother. My grandmother dug them out of a closet. They had sheepskin lining and thick soles to grip the icy ground.

"These will be perfect for today," my grandmother said, happy to have found a solution for getting me to school. "They will keep your feet nice and dry. Try them, Juditka."

I kicked the boots across the room. "I'm not wearing those," I shrieked. "They're ugly." I thought about walking into our first grade with those boots, limping like my mother. I thought of how she hobbled behind my father who never waited for her, how she could never keep up with him, or run and skip and jump with me. I thought about all her other ugly shoes. I thought about how she could never wear pretty shoes, red shoes, shoes with heels, shoes with open toes to show off painted nails, shoes with fancy straps, or even shiny black patent leather shoes like mine. She always had the same ones: brown, square, and plain, one tall, one short. I thought of how the whole class would break out laughing if I were to walk in wearing those boots. I thought of how they'd point and call me names. "*Sántos béna*," Gábor would mock, and the whole class would follow along, chanting, laughing, calling me a cripple.

My grandmother, who had never said an angry word to me, glared and raised her voice. "Don't you ever let me hear you talk like that!" she said. "You are being given something good, something useful. You are lucky to have warm boots to wear. Many children have nothing for a cold day like this."

I sat on the floor and stared at the blue linoleum, tears streaking my face.

"Why did she walk like that anyway? Why did she have to wear shoes like that?"

"She was born that way, with one leg longer than the other. That's why she needed one shoe to be taller. Shoemakers don't make pretty orthopedic shoes."

I looked up at her. "Couldn't someone fix it? Couldn't they make her legs the same?"

"We tried. Her father took her to a surgeon when she was little. But the surgery didn't work."

"I just don't want everyone to laugh at me. I don't want them to think I'm like that."

"And what if you were, Juditka? Would that make you any less of a person?"

"I don't know. . ."

"She's still your mother."

"But you said no one would marry her because she was like that. That's why she didn't go to the dance. That's why she got books instead of pretty dresses."

It was my grandmother who looked at the linoleum now. "People make mistakes," she said.

"What people?"

"Me. I made a mistake."

"What kind of mistake?"

"In thinking the way I did. In thinking that going to dances was more important than books and school. Your grandfather knew better. He gave your mother books. Told her to study. That's why she is a doctor, a doctor who heals children. You know how much everyone in Mohács loved your mother? Many children today are alive because of her."

¤ ¤ ¤

I thought about my mother and how she always had her head in a book. At night, with my little bed tucked up against hers and my father's, I'd watch her sit on the white goose down comforter and read her book long into the night. They were big books with lots of pages. Sometimes, I'd wake up hours after falling asleep, and she was still awake, reading. During car rides, she and my father recited impossibly long poems from memory. At times, when she got to the end of a long poem, she'd cry.

"Why are your crying, Anyuka?" I asked.

"Because it's so beautiful," she'd say.

I didn't understand how something beautiful could make you cry. I didn't understand how she could memorize all those lines of poetry. Practice, she'd say. She told me she started learning poetry in the fourth grade and never stopped. There were many poets lurking on the bookshelves of our apartment in Mohács: Petöfi Sándor, Arany János, Ady Endre, József Attila. She knew them all.

I thought back to the lines that formed outside the children's clinic. How she was often away on her bicycle to get to families who could not get to her. And I remembered a story my brother once told. He was walking home with a friend when a group of boys, much bigger than they, stopped them on a dirt path. They were carrying sticks.

"You're in the wrong part of town, little boy," one of them said.

"We're just trying to get home."

"I hope you make it," said the biggest one, blocking the path and raising a stick.

"Just let us go," my brother said. "We mean no harm."

"*You* mean no harm," one boy laughed, looking up and down at my skinny brother dressed in a clean shirt.

"Hey, you look familiar," one of the boys then said. "Aren't you related to that doctor? What's your name?"

"Tibor. Boros Tibor."

"That's the one. She cured my sister when she had fever. She came out to the house. She's a nice lady, your mom."

The boys stepped aside and let Tibor and his friends go.

¤ ¤ ¤

I stared at the linoleum again. Then I got up and put the boots on. They fit perfectly. The next morning, I trudged across the snow-covered streets in my mother's boots. I expected everyone to point and laugh. My ears burned when I stepped inside the classroom. I was so ashamed, but I just took my seat in the second row behind András. To my shock, he said nothing. Neither did Laura, or Gábor, or Péter, or Magda. We stood up to greet the teacher when she walked into class like we did every morning, saying hello with one voice. No one said anything to me about the boots, even when we went outside to play in the wet snow. And my feet were toasty and dry.

Eleven

Secrets

The elementary school was at the border between our town and the next. It was just a few kilometers, but to me, going that far was like going to the end of the world. My grandmother still brought the wagon along, but I was too proud to sit in it now, lest some eighth grader see me. On either side of the main road stood pastel-colored stucco houses, each with a window box filled with red geraniums, each with a straw roof. Upon each straw roof was a chimney, and upon each chimney a large stork's nest. I was especially interested in the stork nests because it was the storks that brought cuddly new babies to each house. Every day to and from school, I'd watch for the huge white birds and see if I could spot one with a baby in its beak. I believed in this firmly, like I believed in Santa Claus and the Krampusz and the feather ball. It was true, undeniably true. I believed this until my new school friend Ilona informed me that I was a dunce.

"Babies come from inside their mother's stomachs, stupid," she whispered in my ear at school one day.

"You mean like where the food goes?"

"It's true."

"How can it be true? How would they get out?"

"You are really stupid. They cut them out, of course."

"Cut them out with what? Scissors?"

What if they killed the mothers, or cut the babies? But all the kids said Ilona was smart about these things. She was part Gypsy, and everyone said Gypsies knew such things.

School was a long stucco building with embroidered curtains in the windows and our country's red, white, and green flag flying alongside the Soviet hammer and sickle. Lenin's stern portrait hung over the teacher's desk in every classroom. It was enough to frighten all of us into obeying the teacher and doing as she said.

"Good morning, Mrs. Novák." We would stand in unison to greet the teacher when she walked in. We saluted both flags, then took our seats in neat rows. On holidays, like May Day, the entire school—teachers included—lined up in the schoolyard to march around the building carrying the Soviet and Hungarian flags and Lenin's picture, singing songs to the man who broke our chains and freed us from the capitalist slave drivers. I didn't know what capitalist slave drivers were, but I was glad that Lenin broke our chains. I didn't like chains. It reminded me of the time my uncle tied my black dog to the tree in front of our house. He always cried. On these special days, we got to wear white shirts and pleated skirts and the blue scarf of the Little Drummers. The older kids—the Young Pioneers with red scarves—got to carry the flags. I couldn't wait to be like them, to lead the rest of the school in the march and the songs. The songs always made me happy; they gave me goose bumps.

There were twenty of us in the first grade, and we'd stay together until graduation from the eighth grade—except for me because I was going to America. I already knew some of the children from my kindergarten. Laura, who had green eyes, freckles, and light brown hair, was here. Her mother, the Russian teacher, was what my aunt and grandmother called divorced; I didn't know what that meant, but I knew Laura lived just with her mom. She was the only lady like that in town. But she was a teacher and very smart, so it was okay. Gábor, the cause of my broken arm, was here, and Péter, who had the cutest cowlick and a nice smile. I planned to marry him and bring him to America with me. There was Ilona, the all-knowing half Gypsy with dark skin. She had a small scar on her left cheek but she never told how she got it. She was our inside source not just on babies, but how to kiss a boy by puckering up your lips and sticking out your tongue. There was Klári who had the longest hair in the class, and Vera, who thought she was special because she always got the best grades and had thick blonde curls. And then there was me, with my long legs, giant front teeth, and unruly black hair, which on good days my grandmother managed to tame into thick ponytails. Usually, it was a knotty mess.

Even before I set foot in elementary school, everyone seemed to know me. They knew that my parents were gone, that I lived with my grandmother at the other end of the village, and that one day, I'd be going to America. The adults—the teachers, the cook, the priest, the clerks at the store—all shook their heads when they saw me and patted me on the head. "*Szegény Juditka.*" "Poor little Judit . . . Such a pity."

But not the kids. I wasn't "Poor Little Juditka" to them. I was "Going to America Judit!" They knew America was special. It was the Wild West. It was cowboys and Indians. It was big open land; it was snow-covered mountains and roaring rivers; it was deserts with canyons and cacti and lizards. It was blue oceans with hot sandy beaches. It was skyscrapers and bright lights; it was big cars, blue jeans, and rock and roll. America even had a jungle with screeching monkeys! It was everything we weren't, everything we didn't have.

How did we know all this? Television!

We had two black-and-white channels, one of which though fuzzy, worked somewhat well, and was the official station of Hungary. There wasn't much that was interesting on this channel. In fact, the screen had nothing but black-and-white static most of the day until some stiff people came on the nightly news to read from their notes to tell us how great our country was, how our good friend Russia would soon be flying people to space, and stood ready to protect us from the greedy capitalists bent on destroying us. My aunt watched it every night, mostly for the weather report that came at the end.

It was the other channel we looked forward to, the one from Austria. My uncle said it was illegal but much better than our own channel, which he called "horse shit." It was hard to get a good picture on the Austrian channel, but if my uncle twisted the rabbit ears on the top of the television set just right, we could get a fuzzy picture and a good enough sound. On this channel, we could even get American films! Of course I wasn't allowed to watch any of it. I was supposed to close my eyes after the story hour, which came on before the news. But Katus Néni kept the TV on after the news almost all the time, and switched it to the other channel. I pretended to be asleep, pulled the covers over my head, and turned my body so my face was where my feet were supposed to go, and I could watch from under the covers without her even noticing. And that's how I got to see a fuzzy John Wayne ride through the black-and-white canyons of the Wild West, and Tarzan swing from one giant vine to the next, and James Bond leap into his fancy sports car.

I wasn't the only one watching either, because in school, everyone knew the stories or heard about them from others. I'm sure not everyone had a television. But the stories went around anyway. They were in the air, somehow, and in the schoolyard, we made them real. We pretended to have cars with names like Ford and Citroen and Mercedes Benz. At recess, I'd jump behind the wheel of my Citroen, and making engine sounds, chase Laura, who was driving a Ford, and Magda, who had the Mercedes. I picked the Citroen because I liked the way that word tasted on my tongue. I always imagined my Citroen as bright yellow, like a *citrom*, though lemons, like oranges, were a rare sight in our village. Mine was always the fastest car in the schoolyard.

The boys pretended to be cowboys and Indians. Péter stole his mother's kerchief, tied it around his mouth like a cowboy, and pointed the fingers on both of his hands like pistols to shoot András, who whooped like an Indian holding his hand to his mouth. András fell to the ground. "I'm dead! I'm dead!" he'd yell. Péter would stand over him, turn him over on his back with his pretend cowboy boots like John Wayne on the illegal channel, and blow on each finger in triumph. This is why Péter was coming with me to America!

At the edge of the schoolyard stood a cement ramp. None of us knew why it was there, but to us, that ramp could be anything. One day it was Mount Everest.

"I'll beat you to the top," I yelled to Laura. "Wanna ski?"

"On your butt?" she laughed, and we'd go flying down on pieces of tossed cardboard. Other days, it was an Egyptian pyramid. We'd hike to the top, wipe our brows, and pretend the sun beamed down on the desert sands and us. Some days it was the Eiffel Tower; we climbed its steel beams, then slid to the bottom, pretending we were falling and needed to be rescued by the ambulance. Péter drove it, steering the wheel, and wailing like a siren at the top of his lungs.

I told my classmates about New York and the buildings that touch the sky, and we pretended to climb the 100 stories to the top of the biggest building there ever was.

"I wish I could come with you for real," Laura said.

¤ ¤ ¤

I was a good student. I did my homework, raised my hand, and never spoke out of turn like some of the boys. Laura was the same. She had to be. She couldn't make her mom look bad. Maybe that's why the teachers were more than a little surprised the day she and I and three of our friends took up a dare from the boys. I should have known better, learned my lesson from breaking my arm in kindergarten. But on a bright fall day in the first grade, when red and orange leaves swirled around us like magic, when the sun shone down and warmed our happy faces, I forgot all about that lesson. All I could think of was how much fun it would be to take the boys up on their challenge to run around the school yard with our pants pulled down.

The dare had its origins in our toilet situation at school. Being in a small village, we didn't have a flushing toilet. We didn't even have a ceramic toilet bowl, like we had at home. All we had was a stinky outhouse with a wooden seat that gave you splinters. On most days, we also didn't have toilet paper. What we did have were leaves. The school yard was littered with them. The best leaves were the fresh ones that fell in the fall. Once they sat on the ground for more than a day or two, they were either too soggy or too dry and brittle. The important thing was to remember to collect the leaves before you went into the outhouse. If you forgot, you had to send a friend to find them. If there was no one around, you had to sneak outside with your pants pulled down in search of a leaf. The boys decided to turn this into a game, and dared us to run the length of the schoolyard with our pants around our ankles.

"What will you give us if we do?" I asked.

Laura's jaw dropped. "We can't do that. We're going to get in so much trouble."

"Don't worry," I told Laura. "It will be fun."

"Toilet paper," one of the boys shouted back. "We'll give you toilet paper."

Ilona looked at me. I looked at her. "Could we trust them?" Toilet paper was expensive. The ABC sold it, but only in the summertime to rich tourists. Maybe one of the boys would bring it from home, I figured, and we could hide it and keep it just for us. A whole roll would last us girls a long time.

"Probably not," Ilona shrugged. "Do you know anyone who has toilet paper? But what the heck. It will be fun!" She was smart and sassy and always up for an adventure.

We got in a line, and on the count of five, we hiked up our school jackets and pulled our pants down to our ankles. We held on to each others' waists, and formed a train. Somehow, we managed to stumble around the outhouse like this, circling the small building. I was in the lead, Laura right behind me, Magda and Klári in the middle, Ilona in the back.

"I can't believe we're doing this," Laura said. We laughed so hard we fell in a heap into the crisp fall leaves.

The other children froze in their tracks; the boys cracked up.

Our adventure lasted less than a minute because the big fat day-care teacher noticed the commotion and came out, brandishing a wooden ruler.

"Shame on you," she barked, her face the color of paprika. "Laura . . . you of all people, and Juditka. Wait 'till I tell your grandmother. Hold out your hands."

The ruler came down swift and hard. Five smacks on each hand. She took her time, counting slowly, allowing each blow to make its full impact. "That'll teach you." She then grabbed us by our ears, two girls at a time, and dragged us inside, where we were ordered to stay for the rest of the day.

"I told you we shouldn't have done it," Laura whispered, clutching her red ear lobes.

"It was worth it," I whispered back, clutching mine.

¤ ¤ ¤

Mrs. Novák, our regular teacher, was a small lady with chestnut hair, and pretty eyes. She was short, like my mother, and when she spoke, her soft voice reminded me of hers. She treated me like the smartest person in the class, and called on me often. I knew she liked me because every time we lined up, she patted my head and told me how pretty I was and what nice hair I had. No one ever said anything nice about my disobedient black hair. She even asked me about my grandmother and how things were at home. She knew that my family was in America. She knew because everyone knew, but also because she was married to a town official who knew everything that happened in the village. She was a patient teacher with reading and writing, and encouraged me to practice my writing with letters to my family in America. She'd even hold my hand as I put the pen to the white-lined paper, and help me format the proper shape of letters.

One day, Mrs. Novák offered to walk me home from school. That's weird, I thought. What would we talk about? Subtraction? I was nervous as we left the building together, me holding my hand-me-down satchel and she, her pocketbook. We walked side by side, past the houses with bright geraniums and stork nests. When we reached the ABC, she pulled me inside.

The ABC was the biggest store in the village and had just gone through a makeover. They still kept the fresh bread and meat behind a counter, where men and women in white jackets waited on a long line of customers, but everything else was laid out on bright shelves, where we could reach up and choose things for ourselves. Best of all were the giant ABC letters on the front of the store, lit up in colorful neon lights, one red, one blue, one yellow. It made our village a little more cheerful in the gray winter months. In the summer, the plaza in front of the ABC buzzed with tourists. While inside, they shopped for colorful rafts and floats, sandwiches for the beach, and now, even soda. Next door to the ABC was a restaurant where my cousins waitressed during the summer. On top of the restaurant stood the tallest structure in our town besides the church, a recently built triangle-shaped dance hall that thumped with music and smelled of tobacco on hot summer nights. It was all closed now, but the ABC, with its shiny bright letters, beckoned.

Mrs. Novák walked to the toy shelf. There wasn't much there: a dusty chess set, a few stuffed animals, and a few dolls. "Do you like any of those?" she pointed.

I was nervous. I looked up at Mrs. Novák's face. I hesitated. "I like that one," I said, pointing warily to a doll with black curly hair and blinking eyes. She took it off the shelf, took it the checkout counter, and paid for it. "It's a present," she said, handing it to me.

"But it's not even a holiday."

"You don't always need a reason for a present, but if you must have one," she said, "consider it a present for an outstanding report card." Then Mrs. Novák bent down and whispered in my ear. "Don't tell anyone. This is our secret."

I felt a little guilty, knowing she probably wasn't going to buy a doll for every child with a good report card. But I felt special too.

"I'll walk you home," she said.

"I can do it alone . . . It's not much further from here."

"I know you can. But I want to talk to your grandmother. See how she is."

We walked up Vilma Utca side by side as I clutched the doll nervously. I worried that my grandmother would make me give it back.

My grandmother came out to greet us on the street. "Good evening, Mamika," my teacher called. Everyone called my grandmother by the same name we called her. Maybe everyone wanted to have a Mamika like mine. "I took the liberty of walking Juditka home. I hope you don't mind."

"What a nice surprise *Tanito Né*," she said, brushing ashes from her dress and wiping her brow. "How is your husband these days?"

"He is managing. And you? I hope not working too hard."

"We are lucky there is work to be done."

"I guess that's the right way to look at it."

"Mamika, look . . . look what Mrs. Novák bought me!" I tried hard to be polite and let the two of them talk, but I couldn't wait. I unwrapped the new doll from its packaging and held her up for my grandmother to see.

She took the doll from my hands and looked it over. "*Novák Né*, we cannot accept this. You shouldn't have."

"No, no. Juditka deserves it. She is making excellent progress in school."

"Well, thank you," Mamika said to Mrs. Novák, then turned to me. "Juditka, I hope you said thank you."

"*Nagyon Köszönöm, Novák Né.*" I was happy and relieved that she didn't make me give it back. Zsuzsi Baba would finally have a friend.

"Now, go play with your new toy," she said, shooing me away. I walked to the shade of the birch and sat down to play with the new doll.

"I wanted to tell you something, Mamika. It's not easy for me to do this and I probably shouldn't even say anything, but I was concerned."

"What? I hope Juditka is not being naughty again."

"No, no . . . It's about Zoli Bácsi," she lowered her voice to a whisper. "My husband told me something I think you should know."

"To be honest, when it comes to that man, I'd rather know less, but what is it? What should I know?"

"It would appear that he has filled out paperwork petitioning the government to declare Juditka abandoned by her family."

"Abandoned? Why her parents are sending us money regularly! Lászlo saved up his salary for a whole year and left the money with us for her support."

"That's why I was suspicious. It didn't seem right."

"Abandoned?" my grandmother repeated, stunned. "That's crazy!"

I heard my teacher and saw the expression on my grandmother's face. But I didn't understand their words. Like all the hushed grownup conversations, it left me confused and a little scared. "Don't worry," I told the new doll. "Mamika will make sure it all turns out okay."

"He filed the papers a few weeks ago. He is her official guardian, so he is within his rights. But I don't think it's good for Juditka."

"Why? What do you mean?"

"I am not sure of all the details. But my husband says it might make getting permission for her to go to America harder. She is in effect a ward of the state."

"A what?"

"A ward, a dependent of the state. She belongs to the state. Zoli gets paid to take care of her. Instead of living in the orphanage, the state pays him to take care of her."

"So that's why he did it. The devil."

"I don't know if it's too late to do anything. But I wanted you to know. I must go now. I will come by again; maybe my husband has some advice. Just please . . . don't tell anyone I said anything. I'm not supposed to pass on information from him, and well, you know."

My grandmother nodded. "I understand. Thank you."

My teacher said goodbye and left. It was getting dark. We went inside the house. My grandmother put extra sugar and coco on my cream of wheat that night. I washed up in the tin basin, slipped under the covers with my new doll, said good night to Katus Néni, and after she turned on the TV, peered from under the covers to watch Tarzan swing from tree to tree. "We'll be there soon," I told my new doll. "You and me and Zsuzsi Baba."

Twelve

Cold Christmas

Another Christmas was around the corner, the second at my grandmother's house, and my cousins were all coming home. There was much work to be done, the house to be cleaned, a tree to be found, food to be bought and prepared. My aunt hummed Christmas songs to herself as she went about dusting and cleaning the big empty house. She went to the ABC and back, thinking about what decorations to buy for the tree, what presents to get, what food to prepare for Christmas dinner. She seemed almost happy.

My grandmother liked shopping the way she always did—bartering with the neighbors. One day before school, we stopped at the house of a neighbor. Like Kati's family, these neighbors raised chickens, and pigs, and other animals. They had a small house with a door around the back. Inside the fence were white geese, a loud dog, and a pair of magnificent peacocks. I stared at the beautiful birds strutting around like princes in royal robes.

"Come inside, Juditka," my grandmother called. "You can play with the children."

It was bitter cold outside, so I peeked my head in the door of the little house with the straw roof. There was a dirt floor and what looked like an open fire. It was a Gypsy family. I shook my head. "I'll just stay here," I said. While she went inside, I entertained myself by chasing the peacocks and when they ran off, the geese. When they too ran off, I found a patch of ice and pretended I had skates. I skated like the skaters I remembered from the Olympics, trying to lift up one leg while sliding gracefully with the other, imagining myself in a pretty leotard, when suddenly the ice cracked and I fell knee-deep in freezing water.

"Mama! Mamika!"

My grandmother came running from the house.

"Juditka, what happened?"

She pulled me from the puddle, and helped me over to the sled she brought to carry the food home. She pulled off my shoes and sighed. My socks and pants were soaking wet.

The dark-skinned woman came out of her house with a wool blanket and covered me up. "Take it," she said to my grandmother. "You can bring it back tomorrow."

"Thank you," my grandmother said.

"You should have come inside when I told you to," my grandmother said, turning to me. "It's too far a walk to go home now. I'll have to bring you to school."

I didn't dare look at her. I just let her pull me to school in the sled, her small, stooped figure bent against the bitter wind. She had no gloves, and only her raggedy coat. She had no boots, only the shoes with holes. Her feet were probably colder and wetter than mine, her hands freezing against the frayed rope. But she didn't say anything. She just kept walking in silence. I didn't say anything either. I pulled my legs underneath the wool blanket and stared ahead as the wind drew tears from my eyes. She went home in her soaking wet shoes; I stayed at school, where the teachers gave me dry clothes and let me sit before the ceramic heater. I made it through the morning's lessons, shivering. But by noon, when the cook filled my plate with the one thing I hated most—pureed green beans—my throat hurt and I gagged.

"Eat," the day-care teacher commanded. "It's good for you."

I forced it down, but within seconds felt the beans come right back up. I threw up all over the dry clothes.

"Look what a mess you made!" the teacher bellowed. She pulled me from the table, and stuck me back on the stool in front of the heater. My face was on fire. All I wanted was to lie down and hide. But she made me sit on that stool for what seemed like hours with everyone staring at me. And just when things could not get worse, I soaked my underwear with diarrhea.

"Jesus Christ, what next?" the teacher cried, exasperated as all the kids pulled away, holding their noses.

Someone sent for my grandmother and she came, trudging through the ice to take me home on the sled. I didn't protest. She didn't say a word the entire way home, which made the whole thing that much worse. All I could do was sit there and feel shame over what I'd done, holding my nose, and not going into our neighbor's house. Who made me better than those people anyway? I wanted to tell my grandmother I was sorry, but I didn't know how to put it all into words. So I just sat there silently, shivering.

By the time we got home, we were both soaked to the bone. By bedtime, my mouth was dry, my throat ached, and I was so hot, I kicked off all the covers. By morning, my fever was so high, my grandmother called for the doctor. He came to the house with his black bag and stethoscope

"No wonder you feel sick," he said. He held up a mirror so I could see myself. One whole side of my face was swollen like a giant peach. "Looks like you have the mumps."

"The mumps?" said my grandmother. "That's bad."

"She will be okay," he said. "Just make sure she takes these." He handed my grandmother a bottle filled with enormous black pills. "It will be hard to swallow, but make sure she does."

My cheeks burned. My head throbbed. When I tried to swallow the pill, I gagged and almost threw up. It looked and tasted like the lumps of coal my grandmother used to heat the house. All I wanted was my mother to stroke my hair and tell me everything would be okay. But she was far away. My aunt gave me her own bed to sleep in, and packed two of the heaviest goose down blankets she could find on top of me, determined to sweat the fever from my body.

"Eat this, Juditka," she said, spoon-feeding me hot soup. "It's good for you." She then brought hot tea with honey and took my temperature hourly, putting her hand against my hot skin. "We want you better for Christmas."

She was so nice, I thought maybe I should get sick more often.

Home from her school, Ildikó found a book of stories by Hans Christian Andersen and sat at the edge of the bed.

"Want me to read to you, Juditka?"

She was taller, and getting prettier each day. She smiled and opened the page to "The Little Match Girl." I listened as she read, but my thoughts were fuzzy. I dozed off and as I did, my mind drifted to the city street where the little match girl stood alone in her raggedy hand-me-downs. She had lost the boots that had belonged to her mother, and now her feet were bare against the cold snow. She was looking through the brightly lit windows of a big brick house, watching a family gathering for Christmas dinner. A giant roasted goose sat in the middle of a table set with fancy china and glittering silver; a Christmas tree stood majestic in a corner, shimmering ornaments dangling from green branches. She was cold, so she lit one match, SCRATCH, and she warmed her bare little hands, her face, her naked feet. But it went out quickly, so she lit another, SCRATCH, and now there before her was a Christmas dinner even more beautiful than the one in the window; a thousand candles burned on the tree. But this match burned out too, just like the others, so she lit another and another and another until the matches burned hot like fever, like shooting stars. And now, before her appeared a vision of her mother, waiting in a place so bright, so beautiful. "I'm so happy you are finally here," she said, embracing the little girl with arms open wide.

I woke up covered in sweat. The book of Hans Christian Andersen lay at the foot of the bed, a little duckling on its cover. Ildikó was gone. I didn't know if it was morning or night. I'd been in bed for what seemed like weeks. Katus Néni came in the room humming a song and carrying more tea. "Drink up, Juditka," she said. "We want you all better for Christmas Day."

¤ ¤ ¤

Piroska arrived the next day in the middle of a snowstorm. Katus Néni let her in, hugging her.

"It's so good to see you," she said.

Piroska was so beautiful, even more beautiful than last year. She was taller somehow, and had a stylish short haircut, pencil-thin eyebrows, and thick black eye lashes. Under her winter coat she wore a short blue dress and black boots.

Ildikó eyed the fabric jealously. "What is this?"

"It's called jersey. It's a new fabric. See? It stretches."

"Where did you get it?"

"At a store near the university."

"Go say hello to your father," Katus Néni said.

Piroska let out a long sigh. "It's late. Isn't he asleep?"

"I'm sure he wants to see you."

She reluctantly knocked on his door.

"Apa, it's me. I'm home from school."

"Come in," he called.

"How have you been?" she said, standing in the doorway of his room, but going no farther.

He sat up in his chair, snuffed the cigarette in an ash tray, and put on his eyeglasses. "Is that a new dress?"

"Yes, do you like it?" she said, smiling.

"It looks expensive."

"It wasn't . . . "

"You're wasting your money. Didn't I tell you to be careful?"

"*De Apa*, I'm working. I paid . . ."

"You think I'm made of money?" His gaze shifted to the boots. "And those . . . I suppose your internship paid for that too. Next month, pay your own rent!"

"Zoli. It's Christmas . . ." Katus Néni interrupted.

"It's all right, Anyuka," Piroska said. She shook her head and left the room.

¤ ¤ ¤

The boys came home the next morning. They didn't get the same interrogation. They talked about school and living in a dormitory and becoming engineers. None of it made sense to me. But they seemed happy to be home and together. The day before Christmas, they left the house wearing black pea coats and furry hats, and carrying a small axe. They came home with a bright green Christmas tree. It wasn't tall like the tree in "The Little Match Girl." In fact, it was so small it had to be propped up on a table. Still, it was beautiful and smelled like the forest. Then the cousins set to work decorating the tree with garlands and chocolate candy wrapped in shiny foil and sparklers.

I lay in bed on Christmas Eve as the family gathered in a circle, just like last year, to sing "Silent Night," to eat dinner, and exchange gifts. My throat ached, I was in pajamas, and sweaty from the fever that came and went. My cousins were all dressed up, cheerful and happy. I didn't want to spoil their fun.

"Juditka, it's Christmas Eve." My grandmother came looking for me. "You can stay in pajamas, but come, join us."

"I'm too tired."

"Don't you want to see what you got for Christmas?"

I really didn't. I didn't want a new doll, or a new set of play dishes or a teddy bear. My eyes were so tired. I just wanted to sleep.

"Come . . . I'll help you," she said. "Everyone wants to see you." She helped me out of bed and into a clean shirt. She let me keep my pajama pants on. We went to the parlor, where we found everyone sitting around the ceramic heater, exchanging presents and eating the candy wrapped in shiny foil. "Juditka, come have a piece," Piroska called. I didn't even want chocolate.

Zoli Bácsi took a family photo before the Christmas tree. With my shirt stuffed into pajamas and my cheeks all puffed up, I must have looked like one of Kate's Christmas pigs, the kind they stuff all through the fall to be ready to eat on Christmas Eve.

After the photo, my grandmother handed me a blue envelope. "It's from your mother," she said. "From America. I was saving it for tonight."

It cheered me up like few things could have that night. I opened the thin blue envelope carefully, unfolding the blue tissue inside, hoping she had written more than last time, hoping she'd written stories about New York and what it's like to live among the skyscrapers, about the shops and fast cars, about Tibor and his new school, about my father and what he was doing every day, about her job—whether she was still taking care of babies like she used to.

There was a long section in cursive addressed to my grandmother, and a small part in print for me. "*Drága Juditkám*," I put my fingers on the letters and read slowly, pronouncing the letters one by one just like our teacher at school had taught us. "We want to wish you a Merry Christmas and Happy New Year. We miss you very much. We hope we'll be together by this time next year."

That's all there was—again. Just like last year. Nothing about New York, or her job, or Tibor's new school or my father or what it was like to walk the streets of a big city, drive a big car, shop in a big store. I read it again, more slowly this time. Maybe I missed something.

Then I read those words at the bottom: next year.

Next year?

Next year?

When I was just five and first came to live with my grandmother, I didn't know how much a year was, or a month or a week. But I turned seven earlier that month. I knew better now. I knew that a year had twelve months and that a month had thirty days. I couldn't multiply yet, but I could add. And when I added up thirty days twelve times, I knew that was a lot of days. More than 300 days!

I wanted to ask someone what the letter meant, why my mother said next year, and why she said "hope." Why she hadn't written more. I wanted to know if maybe she had written something in the long cursive part that might explain. But my cousins were talking and sharing stories of their schools, Katus Néni and my grandmother were already washing dishes in the kitchen. Zoli Bácsi had gone to sleep. Even if I asked, I wasn't sure any of them had answers. No one ever had answers.

I threw the letter on the floor. I didn't want to see it ever again. I left the parlor and went back to bed. I stared into the darkness around me, at the ceiling, at the windows with the trees scratching the black glass, and thought back to my last Christmas with my family, how I ripped my father's pajamas, and then about the day I broke his sunglasses.

It happened in the vineyard on one of those early spring days when the air is still chilly, but the flowers are eager to peek their heads out from under all that winter snow. My father wore a heavy cable sweater the color of mustard and a bright red striped scarf. He spent the day planting fresh baby vines with Tibor, who was eager to work alongside him, to show him he could. My mother was weeding the rows to get the ground ready; so was my grandmother, bending down alongside my mother, pulling chunky green shoots from the rows they prepared the previous fall.

On the hill overlooking the Danube, my father had a swing set built, a real honest-to-goodness swing set. Not many children had such a thing. Not even the schools had one. But we did, at the top of a hill, no less. It was here that I spent the afternoons playing while everyone else was hard at work. My father walked over to take a break. The sun was high in the sky and he put on his sunglasses, his brand-new sunglasses.

"How high?" he said, giving me a little push.

"The highest," I said. "To the tippity top!"

He pushed again, harder this time.

"Higher, Apuka. Push higher," I screamed, so happy to have this little time with him. He pushed me again, then higher again until I could see over the top of the grape vines and the trees; I could see down to the valley and to the ships making their way up the Danube. I could see all the way to the little island where Gyuszi Bácsi took my brother fishing. I was a robin, flying over the river, flying high above the world, free and happy. But then his new sunglasses slipped off his nose and fell to the ground. I picked that very moment to jump off the swing, landing squarely on the sunglasses, twisting the frame and crunching the glass.

When the swing stopped, I hung my head.

"I'm sorry, Apuka," I said. I said it nicely, the way my mother taught me to do when I did something to make my father mad. But he was really mad this time. He liked those sunglasses a lot.

"Na . . . look what you did!" he yelled. "Do you know what this cost?"

He didn't push me in the swing after that for a long time.

Tibor would never break my father's things, I thought. Tibor was smart. He got good grades in school. He knew the names of countries; he could find Vienna, Rome, and New York easily on a map. He could name every sea, every bird, every fish that swam the Danube. He knew the names of trees and flowers. He could play the piano, and even though he hated it, he sat and practiced every day, his back stick straight, his fingers properly placed on the keys. He would never disappoint our father.

Me? I banged on the piano keys. I shredded pajamas and broke precious sunglasses. I threw tantrums, I sucked my thumb and I cried.

That's why they took my brother to America, I thought, and left me here in the village. That's why my mother said next year, a year that may never come.

¤ ¤ ¤

Piroska woke me Christmas morning. Our room was warm and snug. The white light of the winter sun shone through the bedroom windows. She sat at the edge of the bed.

"Good morning, sleepy head. You look a little better today."

I did feel better. My body felt cooler. I touched my cheeks. They weren't puffed up like a squirrel's cheeks anymore. The day was just starting, but she was already dressed up pretty, wearing her high boots and a miniskirt with a turtleneck sweater. I wondered where she found such beautiful clothes, what shops she went to. I rubbed my eyes awake and sat up in the bed. She handed me a small package. "I got you a little present," she said. "I know that Mamika had to take you to the orphanage for clothes. I know that getting hand-me-downs doesn't always feel good. So I got you something . . . something new."

The present was wrapped in Christmas paper and tied with red yarn. I held the package and shook it. "What is it?"

"Open it!"

I untied the ribbon. In the box was a white sweater, as soft as my mother's. I held it to my face. It felt like a baby rabbit.

"Thank you," I said, hugging her.

"I have something else, something I've been listening to. I want you to hear." She walked over to the table, where earlier in the week she had set up a large reel-to-reel player. I watched her carefully thread the metallic film from one wheel to the second, then turn the power button on. The tape moved to the opposing reel and from this movement flowed music. It was like magic. I studied the contraption, unable to understand how the movement of film created sound. It made no sense. My grandmother didn't understand it either. But that didn't matter now. Piroska and I cuddled up next to each other on my aunt's bed, our feet under a warm wool blanket, the fire going in the heater. "Listen," she said. "The words are in English."

"Michelle ma belle," the tape player crooned. "I love you. I love you. I looooove you."

"Try to say it. It's English. You'll need to speak it in America."

"I love you, I love you I love you," I sang, trying on the strange soft sounds. They curled around my tongue like melting vanilla ice cream, drippy and syrupy.

"I'm not sure I like it. It feels weird."

Piroska laughed and squeezed me closer. "Well, you're gonna have to get used to it where you're going."

"Maybe. I don't know." I looked at my feet.

"Of course, you know. You'll be speaking English in no time."

"Maybe not," I said, thinking back to my mother's letter. "Maybe I won't ever go."

"Of course, you're going."

"Not for a long time. Maybe a whole year."

"A year can go by fast."

"No. It takes forever. Besides, she said the same thing last year. Maybe I'll never see them again."

"They'll find a way."

"Piroska," I said, looking up at my beautiful older cousin. "Why do you think they left? I mean to America?"

Of everyone in my aunt's family, she seemed the smartest. She was at a university now. I remembered when she graduated gymnasium because she went to the one in Mohács. Her graduation ceremony was held on the square across from our home. She was carrying a bouquet of flowers. Afterwards, we went to the Turkish coffee shop where she drank coffee from a tiny little cup. She let me taste it. It was so bitter, I spit it out. She let me dunk sugar cubes in the coffee. That was much better. My mother and I ate tiny square-shaped cakes; I chose the one with pink frosting. I figured if anyone knew why my family left, and would tell me about it, it would be her.

She shifted a bit, and paused before saying anything. "That's a hard question, Juditka. In many ways our country is not an easy place to live. Hungary used to be big and rich, but not anymore. We're a small, poor country compared to places like Germany and America. And your father, well, remember how he always wanted nice things? Well, those things are not possible to get here."

"You find nice things," I said, hugging the plush sweater.

"Yes, but your father wanted more than sweaters."

I looked down at my feet, sticking out of the blanket covering us. I thought back to our apartment in Mohács, at the piano, the TV, the pretty paintings on the walls and porcelain on the shelves and I wondered what my father wanted that he could not have.

Piroska sighed and shifted closer to me. "It's complicated, Juditka. Your father's decision has to do with so many things in our country, our history, politics, the people in power. One day, you will understand."

"And Anyuka. Did she go because she wanted more things too?"

"I think for her it was different. She adores your father. It was hard for her to think about being without him."

"But why couldn't I go with them? Why couldn't we all go together?"

Another long sigh. The tape player kept playing. "I need you I need you I need you . . ."

"It's hard to explain, Juditka. You are too little. One day you will understand. What we must do now is help you so you can be with your family soon . . . Now, it's Christmas. I know Mamika has some fresh rolls for you. I think she even has oranges! Come. Up we go."

But I didn't want to get up.

"I don't feel so good," I said. "I think I need to sleep more." I buried my head under the covers, and stuck my thumb in my mouth.

¤ ¤ ¤

It was late afternoon by the time I woke up again. The house smelled like ham and potatoes. It made me think of Kati's little pig. My grandmother came into the room to add more coal to the heater. Next to me was a small package.

"It's about time you opened your eyes," she said, closing the door to the heater. "You've practically slept the day away. It's all right though. It's good for you to sleep. It will make you better."

"What's this?" I said, noticing the package next to me. "Is it my Christmas present?"

"It's been waiting for you all day."

It was from America. I ripped open the package. Inside were two small delicate dolls, each with shiny black hair like coal, and cheeks like ripe tomatoes. They could have been Snow White, but their eyes looked different—and their clothes. Instead of a dress, they wore silky blue pajamas and tiny red slippers.

"I think they are Japanese," my grandmother said.

"Japanese?"

"I think it's near China."

"Did she go there to get these?"

"No," she chuckled. "But they have everything in America. Even Japanese dolls."

I introduced the Japanese dolls to my other dolls and sat them around a pretend Christmas tree. I found my play dishes and made them all a feast. Before putting them to bed, I brushed their silky black hair with a tiny brush.

"Don't be jealous," I told Zsuzsi Baba, whose black curly hair had grown frizzy and knotted with neglect. Her face was dirty, her eyelids were creaky and her mouth was almost gone. She stared at me as I cuddled the new dolls, holding them gingerly.

But she was jealous.

"I like their pajamas," Zsuzsi Baba whispered in my ear.

"They are very special," I told her. "They are from Japan."

"Can I try them on?"

Her own clothes were worn, faded, and full of stains. It would only be fair, I thought.

"Okay, but first we need to wash you." I spit on a handkerchief and started scrubbing her face. A small patch of the rubber brightened up and I could see the pink peeping through the layers of dirt. When she looked a little better, I started to undress one of the Japanese dolls, carefully unlooping the button on the front of the tiny little silk jacket and removing one arm at a time. When the jacket was off, I pulled her pants down. The Japanese doll, made of cloth, looked frail and flimsy without her shiny silky outfit. I started to pull the pants on Zsuzsi Baba. It was a bit of a struggle, for she was bigger and fatter and made of rubber. That's when my aunt walked in.

"Juditka," she scolded. "What are you doing to your brand-new present?"

"Nothing." I hid the undressed Japanese doll behind me.

"Show me," she said, holding out her hand.

I did.

"You just got this today and already you are taking it apart. Those dolls are special. They are for show, not undressing like this. You nearly ruined them."

"I know but . . ."

"Give them to me," she demanded.

"But Anyuka sent it to me."

"Give it to me now, or else."

She rarely spoke like that to me and I wasn't sure what she would do if I refused. I doubted she would spank me. But maybe she would tell Zoli Bácsi and he would.

I handed her one doll.

"The other one too," she said.

I pulled the pants off Zsuzsi Baba and handed my aunt the other doll along with the silk pajamas. She took them, and walked into the freezing cold adjacent room, the room with the large armoire where she kept my mother's clothes, and the cherry furniture that used to be in our home. I heard her open the door to the armoire, then close and lock it. "When you are older, you will appreciate that I saved them for you," she said.

"I'm sorry," I told Zsuzsi Baba, who was now naked and freezing. I picked up the tiny brush and tried to fix her coarse black hair. But it was too tangled and all I managed to do was pull most of the hair from her head. I flung the brush filled with rough wooly hair across the room and shoved Zsuzsi Baba off the bed. It was too late for her. She was dirty and ugly. She'd never be beautiful again.

¤ ¤ ¤

My cousins got all dressed up for Christmas dinner around the big oak table in the parlor. The tree was set up in front of a window, now all fogged over from steam. My aunt spent all day cooking baking, and boiling potatoes. For dessert, she made chestnut puree, grinding the boiled nuts with a hand-cranked meat grinder clamped to the kitchen counter, letting the pureed meat of the nut fall into a bowl. The women scurried to and from the parlor carrying dishes, glasses, and trays of food.

Katus Néni's face was ruddy and sweaty by the time she sat down at the table across from my uncle. Her hair was pinned in a bun and she wore a short-sleeved sweater. It looked familiar. My grandmother barely sat. The boys each wore neat collar shirts and polished shoes. Ildikó was dressed in a cardigan and short skirt. Piroska came in wearing her new blue dress. Her black hair shone like that of the Japanese dolls. Even her eyes looked a little like that of the dolls—with thick mascara and eyeliner.

Zoli Bácsi put down his soup spoon when she came in the room, looked at her eyes, then looked at the dress.

"What did I say about that dress? It's wasteful. You should return it."

"I bought it with my own money."

"You should spend your money on more practical things like food and rent," Zoli Bácsi said, "not foolishness."

"It's my money," Piroska said.

"Not when I pay your rent and food."

"My rent costs you nothing and I get all my food from the commissary."

"In that case, you can make a contribution to . . ."

"Zoli, not today. Please don't start," my aunt interrupted. "It's Christmas."

"I'm not starting anything. I'm just saying as the oldest child, she can help the family."

"Not today, Zoli, please . . ." my aunt begged.

"I'm not doing anything. I'm just pointing out that things are getting more expensive, food, and heat. And who knows how long we will have Judit . . ."

"Stop it," my grandmother interrupted sharply, dropping a piece of the ham in front of my cousin Árpád with a thunk. "You complain about money. But I know you have the money.

So don't you say another word! You . . . you thought I didn't know. But I know."

Everyone was silent.

"Mamika? What are you talking about?" Árpád finally asked.

"Ask your father," my grandmother said.

Everyone turned to my uncle.

"She's going insane in her old age."

"What is she talking about?" Piroska said.

"Nothing. I've had enough of all of you." Zoli Bácsi got up, shoved the table, and left the room. My grandmother left too.

Thirteen

The Haircut

The summer Ildikó turned fourteen, her father brought her back home to live. I didn't ask her what it was like to live away in school all those years, or why she was sent there in the first place. Neither did she want to talk about it. She was old enough to work, Zoli Bácsi said, so she'd be earning money for the family now. Ildikó put on the short skirts that were in style then and applied for a job serving food and drinks at the dance hall on top of the ABC market.

Now that she was home, there was just one thing Ildikó said she wanted--a room of her own. There was a small room carved out of the back of the house where the old Spanish verandah used to be. But it was supposed to be for summer guests. Giving the room to Ildikó meant losing the income for the room, so my uncle didn't like the idea. But Ildikó insisted and Zoli Bácsi finally allowed it, provided Ildikó paid for the room with some of her earnings and tips. And there was one more condition: she'd have to share the room with me.

I didn't know why I had to move. I was perfectly happy sleeping in the same room as my grandmother. And this new room was all the way on the other side of the house, far from my grandmother.

"I don't want to move," I told my grandmother. "I want to be near you."

"But you are getting big now too," she said, "like Ildikó. It will be good for the two of you."

"But it faces the meadow," I told her.

"That's nice, you like the meadow."

"But it's where *Vak Varjú* died."

"That's no reason not to have your own room. It will be nice. We'll move the beds. We'll get you a pretty blanket. You'll see."

"But it's next to Zoli Bácsi's room," I whined. There was a door that opened to his bathroom. I didn't want to have to listen to him coughing all night.

But my grandmother said that was no reason either, so we packed up our few possessions and Ildikó and I both moved into the guest room on the far side of the house. She was thrilled, even if she did have to share the room with me. She got to have her very own dresser and even a small table where she kept makeup, mascara, and nail polish in pretty shades. As for me, I hoped that sharing a room would help us become friends, or at least that she would spend a little time with me. But the more I wanted to be with her, the less she wanted to be with me.

Like the ugly duckling in my storybook, Ildikó had transformed in the past year into a graceful swan. Gone was her short stringy hair, arms that drooped to her knees, her boxy figure. She now had curves, soft curls around her face, pencil-thin eyebrows, and long brown legs. The change pleased her. She spent what seemed to me hours before a mirror every day patiently plucking her eyebrows, painting her eyes and lips, brushing her long locks, and finding the exact pair of socks, shirt, and miniskirt to emphasize her new body. No longer was a quick wash in the basin enough. The upkeep of her new face and body needed cotton balls, tweezers, brushes of all shapes and sizes, and powder in all shades from pink to lavender to highlight what she knew to be her good features, like her big brown eyes, and to diminish bad ones, like her father's nose. To have me in her face day and night to watch her preparations and pampering must have been torture for her. But it was fascinating to me. I wondered what shade she would choose each day to emphasize her eyes, or what color nail polish she would paint her toenails. I couldn't wait to be fourteen!

"How do you do that?" I asked, staring as she put the finishing touches on her eyes with a tiny brush.

"You'll learn when you get older," she said, staring in the mirror.

"Doesn't that hurt?" I asked, sneaking up behind her as she plucked an eyebrow.

"Oh my God. Can you stop following me around?"

"Can you brush my hair to look like that?" My hair had grown almost to my waist. Sometimes, when my aunt or grandmother had the time, they'd brush it out and pull it back in pigtails. Just as often, it was left unbrushed and tangled. I borrowed Ildikó's brush and imitated the way she pulled the brush through her long brown curls, but I only made a mess.

"That hair would take an hour to brush out," she said. "What you need is a nice short haircut."

No way, I told her. I would never want my hair short. But she kept at it, telling me my hair was an embarrassing mess.

"If you don't start brushing that rat's nest," she said, "I'm going to take the scissors and chop it off myself."

Terrified, I imagined Ildikó sneaking up on me in the middle of the night with a pair of giant scissors and chopping my hair to bits while I slept. I couldn't sleep. I'd lie awake until I knew for sure she was sound asleep and would not wake up to take away my hair.

She didn't, but she did convince my grandmother to take me to the hairdresser, who cut my hair so short, I could feel the peach fuzz on my neck. "It looks stylish," Ildikó said when I walked in the door. "Short hair is so in style now."

I didn't believe her. I didn't believe her because she had long hair and looked beautiful while I looked like a boy. I didn't believe her because I missed the hair that everyone said reminded them of my father. I missed the hair that Mrs. Novák liked to stroke in the hallway at school when I passed by, calling it "so pretty." I hated my spiky boy hair.

¤ ¤ ¤

It was around this time that more packages started arriving from America. There weren't many, because my grandmother explained to my mother that boxes from America cost too much in tax, even more tax than the dollar bills she sent. When the mailman brought a slip of paper for a package from America, she grumbled. "I wonder what they'll charge for this one?" How can she complain about presents? I thought. Excited, I'd grab the slip from her hand and tug on her dress to go to the post office. I lived for those presents from America! My mother sent things no one in the village had, like purple socks and colorful hair ties.

But then Ildikó saw the hair ties and said, "I don't think you need those anymore." She was right of course. What good were colorful hair ties when you had spiky boy hair? They looked lovely in her long hair, though.

When a blue cardigan arrived in another box, she told me it was too big on me. She promised to set it aside and keep it safe until it fit better. I didn't realize that setting aside something meant wearing it to the movies on Saturday night.

One time my mother sent the most special gift of all: a silver necklace with a heart-shaped pendant. The note from my mother said the heart was a symbol for love and that she loved me very much. I folded the letter, kissed it, and put it under my pillow. It made me so happy. It made up for last

Christmas and the Christmas before. I showed the letter to my friend Laura and I showed it to Mrs. Novák in school.

I showed Ildikó the necklace.

"It's beautiful," she said.

"Can you help me put it on?" I asked. I wanted to wear that heart around my neck all the time. It would remind me every day that my mother was thinking about me and that she still loved me. I told myself I'd never take it off.

"I can," she said. "But I'm worried it might break. You're kind of little for something like this. What if it breaks?"

"I would never let that happen," I said. "I will take very good care of it."

"What if someone snags it at school?"

"I won't let anyone do that."

"But it could happen. Some of those boys play rough. So do you."

She was right. Péter and András still liked to play cowboys and Indians and we chased each other around the schoolyard all the time. I chased them as much as they chased me.

"You'd feel really bad if it broke," she said.

"I guess . . ."

"How about you let me take care of it for you? I'll make sure it stays safe." She then showed me a small box on the top of her dresser. "Here," she said, "we'll keep it here. And if you want to wear it someplace special, I'll put it on you."

It sounded like a good plan. But later that week, getting ready to go somewhere in the evening, I watched her put the heart around her beautiful long neck framed by her soft brown curls, look in the mirror, and smile. She did the same the next weekend and the one after that until the necklace just stayed around her neck all the time and somehow it just became so much a part of her that the thought of me asking for it back, or wearing it, seemed very strange.

I told myself it was okay. I thought that sharing the gifts from America meant we were friends, that it would make her want to spend more time with me, or take me places she was always going to now, like the little movie theater in our town where once a month someone set up a film projector and set out enough stiff-backed chairs for fifty or so people to come and watch.

In the summertime, her girlfriends would meet at our house wearing pretty bikinis in blue, yellow, or pink. They'd flip flop to the beach carrying towels in brightly-colored beach bags. I wanted her to take me, since no one else would. I begged her, running after her in my red flannel dress with the fish pockets, which was now so small, it barely covered my behind. But she always said no. "Stop following me everywhere," she would hiss. "I'm sick of babysitting you all the time."

My grandmother saw me walk back to the house, and she'd pour me chocolate milk to cheer me up. But chocolate milk was not the Balaton. So she would ask some of the houseguests to take me to the lake. "She won't be any trouble," she told them. "She's a very good girl." Then she'd reach into the pocket of her black dress and pull out two *forints* to hand the guests to buy me an ice cream cone.

But I didn't want to go to the Balaton with strangers. I didn't want them looking at me like I was some orphan.

¤ ¤ ¤

Then on a hot day in July, the best present of all arrived, something that would make me look as grown-up as Ildikó's friends, something that might make Ildikó happy to take me to the beach with her. I went to the post office with my grandmother to get the box. I couldn't wait to open it and promised myself that whatever was inside, this time I would not let Ildikó near it. When we got home, I tore open the box. Inside was the most wonderful summer dress and a two-piece bikini, almost like the ones Ildikó and her friend wore to the beach that summer. How did she know that this is what I wanted more than anything in the world? Surely Ildikó would take me with her to the lake now. I'll be like one of the teenagers.

I ran my fingers across the feather-light fabric and admired the beautiful pastel peach color. I ran inside to shed my old clothes and slip inside my new present. The bikini felt light against my skin, like the wings of a dragonfly. My skin was way too white but I figured I could now go to the beach and lie in the sun and get tan like Ildikó and her friends.

I ran outside to the backyard where my grandmother and Katus Néni were washing the linen.

"Very nice," my grandmother said, looking up from her work, a clothespin in her mouth.

"Do you think maybe you can finish your work later and we can go to the beach?" I asked her. I don't know why I thought she would take me. She was always too busy. And truthfully, deep down, the last thing I wanted was to go with my grandmother, dressed as she always was in her drab black frock.

"Juditkám, we just got home from the post office," she said as if I should know better. "That took up half my day."

I turned to Katus Néni, hoping maybe just this once she would take me. "I can't, Juditka," she said, her hands wringing the sheets in the tub, smelling like bleach. "There is this load and two more waiting. Ask Ildikó."

Ildikó was inside our summer room packing up towels. Two friends were on their way to meet her. "Please, Ildikó. Can I come with you? Just this once? Look, I have a new bikini from America."

I regretted those words the moment I spoke them. That's it, I thought. End of my new bikini. She'd be wearing it to the beach this afternoon.

Ildikó stopped fussing with the towels and scrutinized me.

"That's your new bikini?"

"Yes. Mamika took me to the post office this morning. Anyuka sent it. It's brand new. Isn't it beautiful?" I couldn't help it. I twirled in front of her, showing off the pretty fabric and colors.

"Hmm. The fabric seems kinda light."

"It's the latest style . . . from America."

She looked at me again and shrugged. "If you say so."

"Can I come with you? Please?"

"No. You're too little."

"Please, Ildikó?" I begged and begged until finally she turned her head and yelled, "I said no! Now go away. If you keep this up, I'll tell my father." She turned and walked out, heading to the gate to meet her friends. She didn't even turn around as she and the other two strutted out the gate and down the street in their flip-flops.

I couldn't bear sitting at home on another hot summer day. I decided to follow her to the beach. I snuck back into the house, grabbed my towel and without saying a word to my grandmother or aunt, left the house, trailing Ildikó and her friends, hiding behind trees and shrubs, staying just far enough behind so they wouldn't see me. At the beach, I spread my towel in the shade of a tree, keeping Ildikó and her friends just barely in sight. I was almost surprised she had not spotted me. When I saw them lie on their stomachs to sunbathe, I left my towel and went into the water, eager to show off my new American bikini.

The lake was blue-green and dotted with white sailboats. Badacsony, the mountain on the north shore, loomed clear and bright, its vineyards and red tiled roofs visible. The sky was cotton candy. Children were everywhere but I played it cool, way above them. I was a teenager, alone at the beach, here to sunbathe and maybe take a little dip in the water when I got hot. I walked slowly toward the water's edge, swaying my hips just a little, the way I'd seen Ildikó do. I got to the steps that led down to the water, dipped my toes in an inch and stood there, holding on to the rails, leaning back just a bit, letting my bikini show off what I imagined were long tanned legs. I lingered, the way teenagers and ladies like to do, slowly, leisurely, anticipating the cool of the water, but not giving in to temptation.

I could only stand this grownup behavior for so long. I followed my heart into the water I loved, sinking down to the bottom, squeezing the mud between my toes, then shoving off for a swim along the water's edge. I turned right and headed into deeper waters, proud of my nice long strokes. I stuck my head under and turned a few somersaults under water, then cupped the water with my hands the way my father taught me and squirted water as far as it would go. I stayed until I was good and tired. I hoped to sneak back to my towel, quickly dry off, then follow Ildikó home—all without her spotting me.

But the minute I stepped out of the water, I realized my mistake. My American bikini turned translucent in the water and now that I was out of the water, clung to me like jellyfish. This was no bikini!

I ran from the water, desperate to get to my towel before anyone would see me. But it was too late. Vera, the tall blonde girl from school, who thought she was so much better than everyone else, the girl with perfect hair and perfect grades, spotted me.

"What are you wearing?" she laughed.

"It's my American bikini," I said. "It's what everyone wears there."

"Looks to me like underwear!"

My face turned red. "That just shows what you know about the latest styles," I managed to stammer as I pulled a towel around me. "I'd stay but my grandmother is waiting for me at home."

"Did you come alone?"

"I did. I'm allowed to do that now."

There. I sealed it. The ultimate victory over Vera, who still needed her older sister to babysit her. But before I could free myself, I saw Ildikó coming over the grass. "Did you follow me here?" She was yelling in front of everyone. "Didn't I tell you to stay home? Wait till I tell that you snuck out."

She shook her head. "You should not have gone in the water alone. You could have drowned."

Vera laughed. "I'll see you another time," she said. "Maybe we can play."

I walked home with Ildikó even as she continued to berate me. It was the worst day of my life. How could I be so stupid? How could my mother do this to me? How could she embarrass me like this?

At home, I changed into my old flannel beach dress, found my cardboard box and a book, and climbed inside. I found the box in the woodshed that summer. I don't know what was so big that it was sent to the house in such a big box, but it was big enough that I could crawl inside it, and close the flaps. It was cozy, and mine alone. I went there whenever my uncle yelled at me, when my aunt ignored me, when Ildikó took my things. At first, I just took Zsuzsi Baba with me and we entertained each other, but then on Ildikó's shelf, I found an old copy of *Grimm's Fairy Tales*. I was a good reader by then and I could read that book from beginning to end, no problem. I would drag the cardboard box under the oak tree in the back yard, climb in with my book, and follow Hansel and Gretel into the deep dark forest; I'd climb the stairs into Rapunzel's lonely room and accompany Little Red Riding Hood on her journey to her grandmother. I'd read and read and read for hours on end in my box while my aunt and grandmother cooked and dusted and washed sheets in the tin washtub, while Zoli Bácsi smoked and read his newspaper and hollered for his dinner, while Ildikó went to the beach without me. I'd read until my skin was sweaty and my eyes tired and I'd fall asleep like Sleeping Beauty for a week, a month, a year . . . until someone, maybe my mother, maybe my father, maybe my brother, would cut through the weeds and brambles that grew like magic around my grandmother's house and take me home.

I grabbed my book now and hid from everyone. I didn't want to face my grandmother or listen to more of Ildikó's scolding. I just wanted to escape into those stories where the evil witch is vanquished, where the mean stepsister gets what she deserves, where the youngest daughter always wins her father's heart. It felt like hours before my grandmother finally found me.

"Juditkám. . . I've been looking everywhere for you."

"I'm not coming out . . . I'm never coming out."

"Na . . . mi történt? What happened? Tell grandma."

"Nothing. Go away!"

"You're going to get sick from the heat in there."

"I'm reading."

"Juditka, please. Tell grandma what happened."

"My mother doesn't know anything."

"Juditka, don't say such things."

"She sent me underwear."

"You mean what you wore to the beach?"

"Yes. It's not even a bikini."

"Is that why you are upset?"

I didn't say anything. I stared at the walls of my box.

"Well, I thought it was a bikini too. The top matches the bottom. Anyone could have made that mistake."

"No. Vera knew it was not a bikini. So did Ildikó!"

"Juditkám . . . Come out of there. It's boiling in there."

"No!"

"Your mother loves you. She always sends such nice things."

"She doesn't love me."

She opened the flaps, leaned over the top of the box and reached her hand inside to stroke the top of my head. I started to cry. "She doesn't love me," I repeated. "She left me because she doesn't love me."

She didn't say anything else. She just stroked my hair while I cried and cried.

¤ ¤ ¤

I did not go back to the beach soon. My aunt and grandmother were always too busy and Ildikó kept a watchful eye on me to make sure I would not sneak off or follow her again. From the house, I could hear kids shrieking and laughing and playing in the lake, the hum of the motorboats, and the call of the ice cream vendor. I stayed home and tossed my ball against the side of the yellow house, or retreated to my box. I wanted to be just like Ildikó, but I also hated her. I swore I would never forgive her for leaving me out, making my grandmother cut my hair, and taking my silver heart-shaped necklace.

Then I found the blood.

I went to the outhouse one day that summer, latching the hook on the wooden door behind me. I turned to sit on the seat and found the bowl clogged with wads of blood-soaked cotton. I saw Ildikó walk out of the outhouse before me, so I knew she was the last one to use it. The blood was hers for sure. She has some horrible disease, I thought. Ildikó's dying. I was too afraid to ask her about it or my grandmother. But I watched for signs of the disease that I thought would kill her. I studied her face in search of a pale complexion or a fever. I listened for a cough. I sniffed for hospital smells and searched her things for big black pills that look and taste like chunks of coal. I resolved to be nicer to her. I smiled at her when she woke up. I brought her fresh crescent rolls in bed. I would have kissed her goodnight if I thought she'd let me.

But Ildikó did not die. She just seemed to get sadder as time passed, fighting more with her mother and especially her father. One night, she never made it back to our room. I couldn't sleep. Ildikó drowned in the lake, I thought, or bled to death on a dark street. Katus Néni wrung her hands, but eventually went to bed. Zoli Bácsi puffed his cigarettes and grumbled late into the night.

When I woke up the next morning, Ildikó was sprawled on the bed, still in her daytime clothes. She had one shoe on and one off. Her long brown hair clung to her face, knotted and sweaty. Black mascara streaked down her face. She looked bad, but she was home and she was alive.

Zoli Bácsi banged on the door, startling both of us.

"Ildikó, get up!" he shouted. "I want to see you."

Reluctantly, she got up and went to his room. She wiped the mascara from her eyes only to smear it more. I followed her into Zoli Bácsi's smoky den. He sat at his table across from his makeshift bed on the clawfoot tub.

"Where were you last night?" He lit a cigarette, put out the match, and looked her up and down. "You look like crap."

I went around them into the kitchen and sat down to eat breakfast.

"Why do you suddenly care about where I go and what I do?" Ildikó shouted.

"Why do I care? I'm your father."

"My father? The father who left me at that home for five years? You don't care about me. You never have. You sit around here all day, smoking your stupid cigarettes, telling everyone else what to do. What's it to you if I don't come home?"

"You little shit. Who do you think you are?"

I was shocked at what Ildikó said. Just stop it, I thought. Don't say anything. Don't make him mad.

But Ildikó egged him on. "You want to know where I went last night? I went to my boyfriend's house and we fell asleep. There. Now you feel better?"

That did it. Zoli Bácsi, whose breakfast was still sitting in front of him, lifted his bowl of hot cereal and hurled it at Ildikó. She and I both ducked just in time, and the mush landed on the wall behind us. Shards of porcelain and hot cereal splattered everywhere. "*Te kurva*; Slut! How dare you?"

Ildikó ran from the room. I stared at my uncle, who then turned his anger on me. "What are you looking at?" he yelled. "Get out and don't come back."

I ran after Ildikó. I thought maybe now, we could finally be friends. I thought she would see what I had seen; that we did after all have some things in common, starting with how we both felt about Zoli Bácsi, with his pointy nose, his coarse mustache, his tobacco smells, his coughing and his spitting. I wished him dead; dead and gone and buried in the cold ground.

I went close to her bed, where she was now lying, face down. Black mascara and tears stained her face and the white pillowcase. "What do you want?" she yelled. I meant to comfort her, the way my grandmother comforted me, to stroke her hair, to tell her everything would be all right. But before I could say a word, she shouted at me. "Get out. Get out and leave me alone."

Fourteen

What is a Jew?

I passed Jesus on the way to school every day. There he was, on his wooden cross, so sad, so real, his eyes half-closed, blood dripping down his broken body. I watched the village ladies come in their black frocks and kerchiefs, kneel before him, and leave tulips and red geraniums by his naked feet. I saw Jesus in our town, and at the intersection of every other town. I saw his image painted on the church walls; I saw him as a baby in his mother's arms, I saw him carry his heavy cross, I saw him ascending through pink fluffy clouds to heaven.

Who was this man? What made him so important that people kneeled before him? How did this man become a god? That's what I wanted to know on the few occasions I went to church with my aunt. I stared into Jesus's sad eyes and wondered how he got off his cross to fly to heaven, because if he could fly to heaven after people nailed him to a cross, maybe I could fly to America.

At the church, I kneeled before taking my seat, just like Katus Néni; I crossed myself like Katus Néni, stood up to sing, and kneeled to pray, just like Katus Néni. Maybe if I did what she did, I could discover what she knew. I could learn the secret that made prayers come true. There were so many people in that church, they had to know something!

But the answers were not coming from Katus Néni. At church, she just did what the priest told her to do: stand up, sit down, sing, pray, kneel; stand up, sit down, sing, pray, kneel. Did she even know the meaning of the words she sang? Did anyone? When on the way home from church I asked her why they nailed poor Jesus to the cross, she said he died for our sins. What sins? I wanted to ask. It made no sense at all.

That's why I was so excited to start religious school in the second grade. It would be my chance to learn the secret, the secret that everyone seemed to know but me.

Zoli Bácsi said church was superstitious hocus pocus. He said praying was a waste of time, that the only people who could change anything were the powerful people in the world, but they were crooked politicians who didn't care about anyone but themselves. But if it meant that someone would feed me and take care of me for a few hours after school, then so be it. I could go.

My grandmother wasn't sure.

"They may not approve of her going to those classes," she said to my aunt one day. My aunt was washing dishes; my grandmother was drying.

"The priest knows us, Mamika. He will see to it."

"I don't know . . . maybe I should ask *Novák Né*. She can ask her husband."

"It's not like she is the only one going. I've heard that almost all the children in her grade are enrolled."

"All the Catholic ones."

"Well, that's just about everyone here, isn't it?"

I wasn't sure what they were talking about, but that night, I told my grandmother how much I wanted to go. "I heard they'll have a big party at the end of the school year, Mamika," I told her while putting on pajamas. "We'd have to get a new dress, a white one, and I can wear my patent leather shoes."

154

"You'd also have to sit through church every Sunday with Katus Néni," she reminded me.

"I guess. But everyone from my class will be there. Maybe we can play afterwards."

"Well, maybe it will be all right," she said. "What harm could it do?"

¤ ¤ ¤

The church was just across the street from school, but it was the priest who came to school to teach us instead of us going to him. When he entered our classroom and stood under the portraits of Lenin and Kádár and the other stiff, scary men on the wall, we all stood up to greet him. He was a chubby man with thick jowls hanging over his white collar. He looked like he had just swallowed an apple. The only part of him that was visible under his black cloak was his head and pudgy hands. He had thin white hair and a red splotchy face. He winked as he entered our classroom.

"I am Father Pál," he said, peering above reading glasses to size us up. "Now, who do we have here?" He looked at Magda in the first row. "Little Magda. How is your father? Is he recovering from the accident?"

What accident, we wondered? Father Pál seemed to know things the rest of us didn't.

"Juditka, I saw your aunt at church on Sunday. Did she find a new job?"

"I . . . I don't know." How did he know that she was looking for a new job? I didn't even know. Maybe this man really had the answers.

He placed a stack of freshly printed books on the teacher's desk under Lenin's nose. "These are your textbooks. Treat them kindly." He walked down the aisle and handed each of us a book. I held it to my nose. It smelled of fresh-cut trees and was filled with colorful illustrations. Our schoolbooks, by comparison, looked like ancient papyrus.

He started us off with the Ten Commandments. He said it was important for us to memorize so we would know right from wrong. "I am the Lord your God," he read. "You shall not take the name of the Lord in vain . . . Keep the Lord's day holy."

I was clueless. What did he mean by taking the Lord's name in vain? But we didn't dare ask and the father pushed on. The goal was to memorize, and we mouthed the words after him, eager to please our new tutor. "You are going to know these words backwards and forwards," he said, "by next week."

Afterward came lessons about all kinds of things that had nothing to do with Jesus. We opened our books and read about how to wash our hands, how to dress, how to speak politely to adults, how to avoid getting sick and make sure we got eight hours of sleep. We learned to make sure we ate enough fresh fruits and vegetables and how to wash them before we did. There were even illustrations of red apples in a colander under running water. I wondered how that water came so easily from a pipe, and how lucky that person was to have a colander. I'd never seen such a thing. Maybe, I thought, we could get one of those for my grandmother, and one of my cousins could learn how to put a pipe in the house so she would not have to haul water inside from the cold in a heavy bucket.

It was months before we finally got to Jesus. Father Pál said his birthday would be coming soon, so it was time we learned.

"Jesus was born poor," he said. "There is no shame in being poor." He told us Jesus's real father was not Joseph, but God himself and that his birth was a miracle. I didn't care much about any of it. All I wanted to know was how Jesus wound up bleeding on a cross, how he got off, and how he managed to fly to heaven. One day, I finally raised my hand and asked.

"If Jesus is the son of God, how come they nailed him to that cross?"

"That's a long story," Father Pál said. "And we will learn it all, but for now, I can tell you that there were many people who were threatened by his goodness. People like the Romans who ruled over the land where Jesus lived and the Jews, who didn't believe he was the son of God.

The Jews? The Jews that Zoli Bácsi talked about? They helped kill Jesus?

I didn't ask any more questions. I was too scared by what the father said because if what he said was true, if what my uncle said was true, then a Jew was really something to be feared. A Jew might leave you to go to a land far away and take your mother and brother; a Jew might be too cheap to feed his child, like my uncle said. A Jew might kill Jesus.

I looked for a picture of a Jew in our textbook. I flipped backwards and forwards, hoping for a glimpse of the Jews who helped the Romans hang Jesus. I couldn't find a thing. Sometimes Katus Néni brought home little pamphlets from church filled with prayers. But all I could find in those were pictures of Jesus with his beautiful yellow halo and pictures of Mary with big sad eyes. I would have looked for more books if we had any, but the only book I had was *Grimm's Fairy Tales*. I looked there too. There were fairies and dwarves and wicked witches with mean ugly faces; there were cruel stepmothers and vain stepsisters; there were vultures and wolves who ate grandmothers. There were the trolls and deadly snakes with red tongues and fangs. But no Jews.

¤ ¤ ¤

I thought of my father's face, his thick black hair, his laugh, his strong shoulders. And I wanted to cry. How could what the priest said be true? How could what Zoli Bácsi said be true? My father could be mad, irritable, and impatient. Sometimes he scared me. But he was no killer. And there was this: if my father was a Jew, was I? I knew I had my father's curly hair. I knew that my father had his mother's curly hair. Who told me this? Who was my father's mother? Who was his father? Did he have a family somewhere? Were they Jews too? Were we all Jews?

As I walked home from religion class one evening, past houses with windows lit up with families sitting down to supper—mothers, fathers, grandmothers and grandfathers—it occurred to me that unlike Laura and Péter and Kati, I had just one grandparent. Just one. The others had four, or at least two or three. Even if they weren't alive, they knew them. They knew their names or where they lived or when they lived. Some knew grandparents who were buried in the cemetery behind the church in a grave with a mound and a gravestone, where their names were carved in pretty letters, where their children and grandchildren could visit on Sundays after church and leave flowers. Besides my grandmother, I didn't know anything about any of them.

Thinking about these grandparents I never knew made me realize that my being alive was not a given. I did not have to exist or exist in the shape I did. I could have been born a sheep or a fish, an ant on the ground or a bird in the air. I could have been nothing. Maybe I was a Jew, but I was also a living, breathing human being with big front teeth and curly brown hair. I didn't have freckles like half the kids in my class, or blonde hair like Vera, or a cowlick in my hair like Péter, but what I did have had something to do with these people. And I didn't even know their names.

"Mamika, who was your husband?" I asked my grandmother as we walked home from school together on a snowy cold day. "What was he like?"

"My husband?" The very word seemed strange on her tongue, a taste long forgotten.

"Well, didn't you have one once? You need a husband to have children. And you have children."

"Yes, you are right," she nodded, looking ahead. "You need a husband to have children."

"What happened to him?"

She sighed. She smiled for a moment and then the smile faded. "He died," she said. "A long time ago."

"Do you still think about him?"

"Sometimes."

"What was he like? Was he like Zoli Bácsi?"

"Ha! No. Not at all."

"Was he nice?"

"Very nice. He was a good man. He loved his family. He loved your mother especially."

"Really?"

She nodded. "He used to take her to school in a horse and buggy. He taught her how to read. It's because of him she went to the university to be a doctor."

"What else did he do?"

"He took care of the land for a rich man. He grew grain and fruit and vegetables. He oversaw all the workers."

"On a farm?"

"A big farm."

"Is he still my grandfather?"

She sighed again. "So many questions, Juditka. What's going on?"

"Well, is he?"

"Yes, he is still your grandfather."

We walked further toward home. The trees were bare. It was twilight, my favorite time of day because the sky was so beautiful, a deep blue green like the color of the lake. Soon it would be pitch black in our tiny village. But the stars were beginning to emerge and the handful of streetlights that lit up Vilma Utca came on. Electric lights lit up a few windows from the inside.

"How did he die?"

"One day his heart just stopped. He was young, just fifty-one." That didn't seem young to me. It seemed old, but then I remembered my grandmother telling me once she was seventy.

That meant she had been without him for almost twenty years, which seemed like an eternity too.

"Do you miss him?"

"I used to. But it's been so long."

Until that moment, I never thought of my grandmother as part of any other family. She was always our Mamika. The thought of her belonging to anyone else was unthinkable. But here was this man who was smart and kind and maybe even loved her.

"What was his name?"

"Lajos," she said. "His name was Lajos."

After supper that night, she showed me a photograph. My grandfather Lajos was short, fat, and bald. In the photograph he wore knickers and a double-breasted coat; the hat on his head had a feather tucked in its brim.

"He was a caretaker on the count's estate," my grandmother explained, holding up a fading, brown photo with fringed edges.

"The what?"

"The count. Before the war, before the Russians came, rich people like the count owned huge pieces of land. Your grandfather oversaw it all, the crops, the animals, the workers. He loved his job. We had a nice life . . . until . . ."

"Until what?"

"Until they took the count's land and he lost the job."

I didn't understand what she meant, why anyone would take anyone else's land? I didn't know what she meant by "they." The grownups were always talking about some mysterious "they," who had the power to give and take away, the power to grant permission to do things, or not. But I did not want to talk about "them." I wanted to talk about my grandparents.

"Do you have pictures of my other grandparents," I asked her. "My father's parents?"

She stopped and looked at me, puzzled. "Your father's parents?"

"Yes, he must have had them—parents I mean?"

"Oh . . . well . . . yes . . . of course, but no, I don't have pictures," she said. "I never knew them." She got up from the table and began washing the dishes.

"Time to clean up and get to bed," she said.

I thought about these other grandparents, my father's parents. They must have names, like my grandfather Lajos. Even if they were Jews, they were alive once, or maybe still were. Did they have a house or an apartment somewhere? What were they like? Was my grandfather a doctor like my father or did he take care of a count's land like my grandfather Lajos? Was my grandmother a good cook like Katus Néni? Was she nice like my grandmother, with magic pockets that held chocolates? Or were they like what Zoli Bácsi said? Was being a Jew something inherited, like my black curly hair? Was it something you chose, like being a doctor? Or was it the result of some terrible accident, a birth defect like my mother's limp?

¤ ¤ ¤

Since there were no books to turn to, I asked my grandmother.

"Mamika," I asked her as she was loading coal into the small hallway heater one day. "What is a Jew?"

"A Jew?" She put the shovel down, turned around and looked at me sharply. "Who called you that? If it was that Gábor again, I will tell your teacher tomorrow. She'll teach him!"

"No one, Mamika. No one called me that. I heard it from Zoli Bácsi. He keeps calling Apuka that word. I heard him say it. Is it bad?"

"Oh, Juditkám," she said, turning back to the stove. "Your father is a good man, a hard worker. Don't listen to what your uncle says. He is a good man and he loves you. That's all that matters. Now, go to your room and get ready for bed." She went back to shoveling. Soot was flying in her face, her eyes, turning her hands black. She coughed, turned to pick up a broom, and said nothing more.

I went back to our winter room confused. The only thing I knew for sure is that no one wanted to talk about this, or anything else that seemed important.

I continued to go to religion class like I was supposed to. I soon learned to say the entire Lord's Prayer by heart. I cupped my hands and kneeled before the statue of Jesus on his cross. I looked him in the eye and I promised him I'd be good. I promised I would not talk back, I promised I would do as I was told. I promised to always help and never think bad thoughts about other people. It seemed like that's what Father Pál wanted; wasn't it what Katus Néni and my grandmother wanted too?

I watched my aunt walk up to the altar every Sunday to receive communion. I watched her stick out her tongue and receive the white cookie that the priest called the body of Christ. I saw her walk back to the bench with hands clasped in prayer. And I wondered if she was happy now. I thought of her sitting at the side of her bed every evening, watching the news for the next day's weather. I thought of her daily life, waiting on a man who she didn't seem to love and who didn't seem to love her back. I thought of her scrubbing the hotel toilets and washing clothes every day until her hands were raw. I thought of how she'd grown so old. And I wondered about this Jesus she prayed to every night. Did he think of her just once? Did he love her back? Would he love me?

¤ ¤ ¤

My first-grade teacher, Mrs. Novák, visited us again that spring. She came by herself, knocking on our door early on a

Sunday morning. The new dog greeted her, barking and pulling on the rope that tied him to the silver birch in the front yard. His name was Csutak and he was a good dog, with bright orange bristly fur. Zoli Bácsi got him from a neighbor to guard the house and this he did well. He didn't cuddle up with me, though, nor did he jump up and down and lick my face when I got home from school like Vak Varjú. He was the family dog, not my dog.

Mrs. Novák smiled when she saw me doing homework at the little desk my grandmother set up in the hallway outside the kitchen. "Now I know why you are the smartest girl in the class," she said.

"*Novák Né,*" my grandmother called to her. "It's so nice to see you. Are you checking up on Juditka, making sure she does her work?"

"No, I know she is doing a good job. She is a good student. I'm here to talk about something else."

"Is everything all right?" my grandmother asked.

"Well, I just wanted to see if there is anything more I can do, or my husband. It's been a long time now with Juditka's family gone and . . ."

"Almost three years," my grandmother said as she moved toward the front door, away from me, and lowered her voice. "It's very upsetting. Piroska wrote that she has gone to the Hungarian embassy there in New York. They told her she chose to leave and she can forget about getting help from them. There is nothing they can do. They said she is lucky Juditka is with us, and not in an orphanage. They said she can forget about ever seeing her child. Can you imagine, saying such a thing to a mother?"

"She must be devastated."

"She's heartbroken."

"Mamika, you remember what I told you last time I was here, what Zoli Bácsi did?"

"I remember, but what can I do about it? I can't talk with this man and he wouldn't listen even if I tried."

"Well, we have to try something. Nothing will happen unless someone really takes an interest in this and goes after this, advocates on her behalf, goes to Budapest, appeals to the right people, writes letters. Zoli is doing none of these things."

"But what can I do? No one listens to an old woman."

"Well, we have to find someone. Maybe you have a relative who can try? But this is not all I'm here to tell you. I've been talking with my husband and he wanted me to let you know that he seriously recommends that you take Juditka out of those religious classes. I know Katus Néni is very devout and it's important to her. But the government doesn't look kindly upon this."

"Who's saying this?"

"My husband, he is a party member, you know. He hears things. I think you should follow his advice."

"Hmmm. I'm not a big believer. But I find it interesting that the government that would keep a child from her mother is so suddenly interested in what should be a private matter."

"I understand. Still . . ."

"Yes. We will do it. Thank you, *Novák Né*. Thank you for taking the time to come out."

"It's the least I can do. In the meantime, let's both think about who can help make Juditka's case to the authorities."

She left, waving goodbye.

That night my grandmother explained that I would not be going to religious school that Tuesday, nor the one after that.

I was confused, scared about missing out on something that everyone until now seemed to think was important. I didn't tell her my bigger fear: that I was being expelled for being a Jew.

"But I like going," I told her. "Everyone goes."

"It's important that you don't."

"Is that why Mrs. Novák was here?"

"It is. Her husband is an important man. He knows people. It was his suggestion."

"I don't understand."

"It's like this," she explained. "The people who run the country don't believe in religion. They don't believe in God. They don't believe in Jesus. So if we want anything from them, we need to do like they say."

"But I like the father. He's really nice and he gave us all new books."

"I know. But this is important. You want to go to America, right?"

I nodded my head. But I was confused. What did going to America have to do with me learning about Jesus or learning to say the Lord's Prayer? I almost had it totally memorized.

¤ ¤ ¤

The following week I walked home with Laura, the only girl in our class who didn't go to religious school.

"My mother thinks religion is silly," she said as we made our way home past the houses with the straw roofs and storks' nests and geraniums. "She says there is no God. That people just make it up so they don't feel sad or lonely. She says it's superstitious, like believing in fairies."

I wasn't sure what to believe. I knew now that storks didn't bring babies and that the presents on Christmas came from my grandmother, not Santa Claus, but not believe in God? Who'd answer my prayers?

¤ ¤ ¤

While I never went back to class, my grandmother was able to make a deal with the priest. Come May, I would be allowed to take my first communion with the rest of the second grade. My teacher told her the authorities would probably overlook this small offense.

Two days before that big day, I sat under the dangling light bulb at my makeshift desk in the hallway of my grandmother's house. My assignment: to make a list of all my sins, so that I would not forget anything when I made my first confession to the priest. I thought for a long time, chewing on my pencil as I made one list after another. This was my final list:

I've been selfish. I let my grandmother do all the daily chores without ever asking if she needs help.

I hated my uncle; I've even wished him dead.

I've been mean to Ilona. Our friends and I have left her out of our games on purpose because she is half-Gypsy. When she cries, we ignore her.

I am a girl. If I was born a boy, surely my parents would have taken me to America.

I may be a Jew.

I wrote the last line, then erased it, afraid of the words, afraid of what the priest would say if I said them out loud. I folded my list and took it to confession the following Saturday morning.

"Go ahead," my grandmother said when we arrived at the the church, reassuring me. "Don't be afraid."

It was early, but already the line was around the corner. So many people! I wondered what bad things they might have done. When it was my turn, my grandmother gave me a small nudge into the confessional and I closed the door behind me. I kneeled, as I'd been instructed to do, and tried to make out the face behind the wooden slats. It was Father Pál. I had hoped for his assistant. This was bad news. Now he would know my deepest secrets. Slowly, I unfolded the piece of paper I had brought from home and read him my list, worried about what he'd say. He listened silently. Then he told me to go kneel before the altar, say three prayers to the Virgin Mary, and go home.

"That's it?"

"That's it."

"But I was mean and selfish."

"Jesus will forgive you."

But I may be a Jew, I thought, but didn't say it out loud.

"Three Hail Marys," he repeated. "Go." He made the sign of the cross and pointed to the altar.

I didn't know whether to cry or shout for joy. I wanted explanations, answers—at least reassurance. I wanted a more substantial punishment. I didn't understand how a simple prayer could result in God's forgiveness.

But I did what he said. I walked over to the altar, knelt down on the cold marble facing Jesus and said the prayers the priest wanted me to say. When I was done, I looked up at the face of Jesus on his cross. "It's all right," he seemed to say. "It's not your fault."

I walked out into the brisk, bright sunshine of that lovely Saturday morning in May, and it was strange. The thing I expected least was to go home feeling happy. And yet, I was. Not just happy—but blissful, ecstatic, jumping from a high swing ecstatic, wind in your face on a fast bicycle ecstatic, leaping into a cold lake on a hot day ecstatic. Was it the sunshine, the smell of fresh grass and tulips blossoming on a magnificent May day? Or was it the simple act of forgiveness? I didn't know; it didn't matter. I skipped all the way home.

¤ ¤ ¤

For my first communion, my mother sent a dress from America. It was white, lacy, and delicate. It felt like she was making up for the cursed bikini because when I took it out, smelled it, and touched the fabric my mother touched, I felt her love. When I put it on, I felt like a princess in a fairy tale. It also barely covered my behind, for I had grown about three inches in the past year. But she didn't know that. And I didn't mind. Short skirts were all the fashion. The dress was perfect.

Sunday, the sun was high in the sky. Everything, even the drab steely-gray church, sparkled. My aunt came to the church, as did my grandmother. She wore a clean black dress for the occasion, and even found a pair of real shoes to squeeze on her calloused feet. Zoli Bácsi came, lugging a long electric wire behind him to light up the church so he could capture the day in photographs. Villagers glared at him because of the racket he caused, and he was not one to apologize. But I didn't care, because for once, his lens was on me, and I was smiling. I alone in the village had photographs of the ceremony.

I stood with my classmates, Kati, Vera, Magda, and Péter. We cupped our hands and prayed for Jesus to love us and forgive us and take us in to his holy Catholic family so that one day all of us could ascend to everlasting life in heaven. I opened my lips and allowed Father Pál to deposit the body of Christ on my tongue. I let the wafer melt inside my mouth, surprised by the bland taste, unsure whether I could touch it with my tongue and wiggle it free from the roof of my mouth, where it was stuck. Was this a lesson I missed after I was expelled?

After the ceremony, we were treated to lunch on picnic tables outside Father's Pál's house. Among the guests were Mr. and Mrs. Novák. She was wearing a small gold cross around her neck. Had I missed this too?

The following day, in the small bathroom where he slept and ate, my uncle developed the pictures he snapped. He closed the shutters, and under purple lights, coaxed the black-and-white images to life, then hung them on a clothesline to dry. The next day he put them in a translucent blue airmail envelope and sent them to my mother across the sea.

Fifteen

Serious Consequences

I was outside playing on the gymnastic rings when I heard the car rumble to a stop in front of the house. I jumped off to investigate. Few cars came through our village, and none of them ever stopped in front of our house. So it was no ordinary occurrence. I saw two tall people get out: a man and a woman. They looked familiar somehow, but I couldn't quite place them. They were definitely not from the village. The man had a square jaw, square-shaped glasses, and thinning hair. He looked smart, like someone who was curious and might like asking questions and finding answers. The woman wore blue jeans! She had shiny, shoulder-length hair, like the people on the covers of glossy magazines left behind by tourists from East Germany. She had on a striped V-neck shirt and carried a beaded purse. I saw my grandmother open the gate to greet them; I followed in her footsteps. The woman reached down and hugged my grandmother tight.

"Mamika, it's been so long. How good it is to see you." Then she turned to me, and her eyes lit up. Her voice was like honeysuckle. I buttoned my orphanage sweater and straightened my pilled sweatpants. It occurred to me that my grandmother should not have holes in her shoes.

"*Te jó Isten* . . . My Goodness, Juditka," the woman said. Her big smile put me at ease. "Such a big girl. I hardly recognize you. You have grown so much. I can't believe my eyes. The last time I saw you, you were this little." She pointed to her waist.

I knew that voice, but how? Where had I heard it? As she spoke and reached down to hug me, bits of memory came rushing back, and I could see us back in Mohács on the square in front of our apartment. I am holding her hand with one hand, my mother's hand in the other. We are walking, playing, running, on the huge open square in front of our apartment in Mohács.

"I am your godmother, don't you remember?"

I do, I remember. Of course I remember. I named my doll after her! Or maybe she gave me the doll? Zsuzsa was beautiful, as beautiful as my cousin Piroska but in a different way. She was older and more like a mother, but a young mother, cool and smart, but also sweet and kind.

"Do you still have your doll? Zsuzsi Baba?"

"I do. She's inside." So that's how I came to have her.

"You won't remember this, Juditka, but when you were born, we got you a little gold necklace, the one with the hexagon shape."

I'd never worn the necklace, but I'd seen it—in a drawer in the armoire, with my mother's nice things. My grandmother showed it to me once. She said it was precious, too precious to wear, but important to keep. Inscribed in the gold was my name and birthdate.

"We had that made for you when you were born," she went on, "when I became your godmother."

"I don't suppose you remember me?" said the man who looked maybe like a scientist.

"Juditka, this is Szilárd, your godfather," my grandmother said. "Say hello."

"*Kezit csókolom,*" I said, using the formal greeting.

"Ah, you don't have to be so formal, Juditka," he said with a wink. "We are old friends." He bent down to hug me. "I hear you are one lucky little girl."

"Lucky? Why?"

"You are the only one I know who is going to America and I know a lot of people."

"I am so glad you came," my grandmother said, ushering them into the house. "Piroska wrote that she would ask you to help. I can't tell you how grateful we are."

"Of course, Mamika. We came as soon as we got your letter. And Piroska's letter. We will do everything we can," Szilárd said.

"This business is just too hard for me. You are both educated. Maybe you can do more."

She walked them into the parlor. I clung to my godmother. When she sat down, I sat in her lap as she stroked my hair. I could not stop staring at her beautiful smiling eyes and touching her shiny, brown hair. "Do you want to see my doll, Zsuzsi Baba?"

"Go play outside!" my uncle said, lighting his long cigarette holder. "We have grownup business to discuss."

"But I want to stay here," I whined.

"Go, Juditka," Zsuzsa said. "You can show me Zsuzsi Baba when we are done talking. I promise."

I got off her lap reluctantly and followed my grandmother out of the parlor and into the kitchen where she prepared tea and crackers. She slid the glass doors shut behind her. Inside, my uncle and my godparents sat down to talk. My grandmother returned to the parlor, carrying a tray with delicate pink teacups. "Juditka, go play," she said as she went inside the room, leaving the door behind her ajar. I didn't leave, though. I stayed by the door. I was too curious about these two nice-looking people from the past.

"We came to talk about Juditka's situation," my godfather started. "We received a letter from her mother. Did you know they are thinking about coming back? They aren't getting anywhere with the consulate there. They turned them away, said they would never let Juditka go. I'm concerned, Zoli Bácsi. I don't think it would be a good decision for them to come back, but. . ."

"I did not know that they want to come home," my uncle said. "But I have had contact with the district judge here, and frankly he is not optimistic. His feeling is that the parents were traitors."

"Did he suggest anything that can be done?"

Zoli Bácsi took a long puff on the cigarette hanging from a wooden smoking stick, blew, and spoke slowly. "He did suggest that I have her declared abandoned—legally speaking that is."

"Abandoned?"

"Legally. Yes."

"What does that mean?"

"It means the state is her legal guardian and they pay me a small stipend to keep her here instead of the orphanage. You must admit that's better for her. As for us, it means a little more income. Not much. But it helps."

"Do her parents know this?"

"I had assumed they would have been notified."

"You mean to tell me you had their daughter declared officially abandoned and you did not tell her parents?"

"I didn't think it was my job to do that."

"I don't even know what to say," said Szilárd, stunned.

"You know Szilárd, it's not easy taking care of another kid. We need to feed her, clothe her. It adds up. This way, the government gives us a little something every month."

Szilárd's jaw dropped. "Have you actually done this? Legally that is?"

"Did I do it? Did I do it? Of course I did. We need the money."

"Do you understand that this could have some serious consequences?"

"I didn't see you dropping everything to take the kid . . . You . . . with your university appointment and your modern apartment and one kid to feed. Please don't tell me what I should and shouldn't do to look out for my family."

"But, but László and Piroska left plenty of money. An entire year's salary from what I remember."

"Yes, and that lasted for a year. Look around you. Do we look like we live in luxury? This is an old house, expensive to heat. Do you want to see what it costs me to buy coal in the winter?"

"I think we have found the root of the problem. This must be why the process is stalled and everything is taking so long. With all due respect, Zoli Bácsi, do you understand what you might have done? That money they pay you, that extra little bit to pay the heating bills, means the state has legal custody of Juditka. They can make this process as hard as they want, and it seems like they are."

"Now you see, that's where you are wrong. That is not the problem," I heard my my uncle say. "The problem is that Jew who left the country and abandoned his kid. Good riddance, too, I say. They should all leave. Let them all go to America, or Israel, whatever's left of 'em. Let them go wherever they please. Piroska should come back. She made a mistake marrying that man in the first place. Now she can finally undo it. Let him stay there. Let her come back and take back her kid."

I stopped listening. There was that word again. Like a bad dream, it kept coming back. And now, a new word: abandoned. Had my parents really left me here for good? I went into the bedroom, I found my big cardboard box, climbed inside, closed the flaps, and opened *Grimm's Fairy Tales*. I turned to the story of Cinderella. I imagined my mother was like Cinderella's mother. She is in heaven, in paradise. She wants to come back, but she can't. She is calling to me, telling me it will be okay.

Wait patiently. Just one more Christmas. She's looking to find a way. But she's trapped. The gates are closed. She can't get out; I can't get in. I am Cinderella stuck with the mean stepmother who doesn't care and the vain stepsisters who just care about being pretty. They take the things my mother sends and go to parties, leaving me home. But wait: there's a fairy godmother. Perhaps she's come.

The sun set early, the room grew dark and I fell asleep with the book glued to my face. It was nighttime by the time I heard my grandmother come in the bedroom and peer into my box. Zsuzsa and Szilárd had gone home, she said. They realized I was sleeping and didn't want to wake me. My mother was gone, and now my fairy godmother was gone too.

¤ ¤ ¤

Szilárd, however, came back many times. Each time his noisy white car pulled up before my grandmother's house, I ran out to greet him. He would pat my hair, and head into the parlor to speak with my uncle. I saw him carry a briefcase full of documents in and out of the room. I tried to stick by his side, sit in his lap. But I was always sent out. "This is for the adults only . . . Out you go."

Whatever was happening in that room, it seemed like it had less and less to do with me. No one ever explained what was going on, not Szilárd, not my grandmother. Three years had passed since my parents left; the hope that I'd ever get to America was slipping away. So were my memories of my family. What did Tibor look like? Did he really play the piano? Or go fishing in the Danube in a rowboat? Or was that someone else? Zoli Bácsi was the family photographer. I knew he took lots of pictures of our family. But maybe that too was someone else. Because if he did, wouldn't there be some photographs of my family? I didn't even have one picture of my mother or my father.

Pictures did eventually come from America, but they were rare. They needed a thicker envelope and more postage. When I did get a photograph, I would stare at it, examine every detail. I'd hold it to my nose to see if I could catch the scent of something American: the smell of my mother's hands, her new lotion, maybe. I'd study the background, the furniture, the pictures on the wall. In one picture, my mother wore a sleeveless dress with big red-and-brown flowers. She was standing in front of a large television set, a color television set. My father was in the picture too, his hand on the TV, showing it off like a proud parent. My mother's hair was red. Was it always red?

One time, and just one time, my father sent a letter with a photograph inside. He still had his thick brown hair. Next to him stood a man in a blue shirt, blue jeans, and bushy hair. Who was that man? Why was there a strange man next to my father? What was he doing there? Then I turned over the photo and I saw the words, Bronx Zoo. I didn't know what a Bronx Zoo was, but I repeated the words over and over, testing the vibrations the sound made in my mouth. "*Remélem emlékszer Apukádra*," my father had written on the back of the photo. I hope you still remember your father. It was signed, Apu and Tibor. Was that man my brother?

I traced the letters on the back of the card with my fingers, following the soft Es and As and hard R. I sounded the letters, repeating the words. I held it to my ear as if the photo could speak.

They had changed so much, Tibor especially. Will I ever get used to them again?

Sixteen

Dangerous Games

Seven days before school got out, the teacher wrote the word *VACÁCIO* on the blackboard. Each day she erased one letter, until there were no more letters on the board and school was finally out. We ran from the stuffy classroom, barely able to contain our excitement. But by the second week of summer, boredom set in. I thought this summer would be as bad as the last, with no one to play with and no one to take me to the beach. Then I met Attila.

His family was from Romania, and they planned to stay the whole summer. Suddenly, I had friends. Attila was the oldest, about 14, with smooth olive skin, shiny black hair, and a dimple on his chin. His cousin Gábor was 12, maybe 13. I wasn't sure. And there were the sisters, two girls, both a little younger than me, both with dark hair. We played together all day. My aunt and grandmother were relieved to have me out of their hair.

"Wake up, Judit," Gábor shook me awake early one morning in the summer room I shared again with Ildikó. "Get dressed. We're going down to the tracks."

"What? No. We're not allowed to go there. It's dangerous."

"*Te ostoba*. That's what makes it fun, stupid."

I got dressed and met them in the front yard. We stole a handful of breakfast rolls that my grandmother had put out for the guests on the table under the trellis and off we went. We didn't tell my grandmother where we were bound. The plan was just to leave, but she caught me as we traipsed through the backyard.

"Where are you going?" she called after us.

"Oh just to play," I told her. "Don't worry, Mamika. Attila is old enough to look after us."

"Just be careful."

I followed Attila and Gábor with the girls, from the back of the house to the willow tree, trampling across the wildflowers, heading toward the tracks. We climbed a small hill to the railroad bed and followed the rails, walking, running, skipping, more than a kilometer from home. Once we were far enough away from my grandmother's house, Attila got on the tracks and held up a chocolate candy bar.

"This," he said, grinning, "goes to the one who dares to stay on the tracks the longest after we spot the train. Who takes the dare?"

It was absurd, ridiculous, hardly worth risking your life for a bit of chocolate. I raised my hand anyway. The sisters had no choice. We were all in.

We waited and waited. The sun beat down on our shoulders. We put our ears to the tracks listening, feeling for vibrations. It was a slow day for the trains. We kept walking slowly, patiently, another kilometer and another under the sweltering sun. Then just as Attila was about to call off the game, there it was: smoke! We each claimed a spot on the metal tracks, determined to stay until the very last second. The train neared, roaring in our ears. The vibrations shook our knees and rattled our lungs. My heart thundered inside my chest, its rhythm matching the roar of the train. My grandmother never laid a finger on me, but if she saw this, she would have spanked me with a wooden spoon for sure. But I stood my ground. We all did. None of us was going to be chicken. Forty feet, thirty feet, twenty feet. The first of the sisters jumped off. "Chicken!" Attila yelled. "Cluck, cluck," the girl shouted back. Nineteen, eighteen . . . the other sister jumped. I gritted my teeth and held my ground. Seventeen, sixteen, and Gábor dove. There, I held out longer than an older boy. It was between Attila and me now. The train bellowed, its eyes flashing red. I could taste the smoke in my mouth; the engine loomed huge in front of me . . . fifteen, fourteen. That's it. I was done. I flung myself off to the side, falling by the tracks, heart thumping, squealing like a piglet about to go under the butcher's knife. Finally, Attila. He didn't even jump. He just stepped off. He held up the chocolate bar as the train whistled past, and took a triumphant bite. This was our fearless leader.

Past the train tracks we scurried up a small mountain, hunted for foxholes and owls, then slid down the hill on our butts. I ripped my pants, and scraped my thighs. Blood trickled from my knees, but I spit on it and washed it away. Coming down the muddy slope I laughed so hard, I wet my pants. By the time we got close to my grandmother's house, the sun was down in the sky. I gathered a few wildflowers before walking in the house.

"I got these for you," I said, holding them up to my grandmother's nose, hoping it would distract her from the ripped pants, the bloody knee, the smoke-stained face. "Aren't they pretty?"

"Where have you been all day?" she scolded. "Don't think I don't see those pants just because you brought flowers . . . Now go wash up while I make some food. Tomorrow, Katus Néni will have to teach you how to sew." She went on griping about the boys. But I knew she was secretly happy that I had friends.

Attila was back knocking on my door the next morning. "We're going to the camp. Wanna come?"

"What camp?"

"The camp on the lake. I have a plan."

Did I want to go? Of course I wanted to go.

I got up, got dressed and off we went down the street toward the lake before anyone noticed. As we passed the hotel at the end of the street, Attila dared us to climb the iron fence to fetch the ripe golden apricots growing on the trees on the grounds inside. Hungry after rushing off without eating breakfast, we all clambered up the fence, jumping down on the other side. It was a long way down, but I swallowed hard and jumped. I fell to the ground and scraped my knee. But at least I didn't rip my pants this time. Once in, we stuffed our faces, then our pockets with the juicy fruit, which left a sticky residue on our faces and hands. I was careful not to snag my pants on the climb back out to the street and we strutted off toward the Young Pioneers summer camp on the lakeshore, following Attila.

The camp gate was next to the entrance to the public beach. Walking to the beach with Juliska Néni or others, I would often glimpse over the fence at the lush green grass inside those gates, at the rainbow-colored playground equipment, the building that looked like a castle with spires and turrets. I thought a princess lived there until I learned to read the sign on the gate. Inside the fence, I'd see smiling children in clean clothes and pioneer scarves playing organized games, singing happy songs. How many times I wanted my grandmother to get me inside that camp so I could be a Pioneer!

It took Attila to figure out how. Just climb the fence, which we did, following our fearless leader, the same way we climbed over the fence of the hotel. We came down the other side, jumping on the freshly cut green lawn. The children were inside, we guessed, eating a delicious hot breakfast. While no one looked, we took over their playground. Gábor was first to jump on the glider swing set with two wooden benches that faced each other, kicking off with his feet. We all jumped aboard and held on to the metal poles for dear life as Gábor shifted his weight back and forth, carrying us so high, I thought we'd flip over the top bar. The sisters and I screeched in delight. "Higher! Higher!" We yelped. Then it was time for the see-saw. The boys got on one end, the three of us girls on the other. Outweighing us, they flung us high, then made us come down hard on the ground. We never had so much fun.

After we gorged on the apricots in our pockets, we snuck down to the lake. The pioneer camp had a dock that led out into deep water. The public beach had no such thing! We stripped to our bathing suits, and did somersaults off the dock. Attila did a three-sixty, falling into the water below like a graceful diver. I stood at the back of the dock, hoping to get a running start and then scrunch up into a ball. I landed on the flat of my belly with a thud.

"Haha," Gábor and Attila laughed. "Good try for a girl."

The water left a bright red spot on my belly. But I didn't mind. When the other girls tried, I laughed at them. And when Gábor also landed on his belly, I shrieked.

We would have stayed 'till nighttime, had a teacher not finally spotted us.

"Don't think I don't see you," she yelled, one hand up in the air, the other resting on her enormous hip. "You get out of here, you hoodlums, or I'll spank all your behinds. I don't care how big you are!"

Grabbing our clothes from the dock, we waded into the water and scurried off in between the reeds and rowboats, coming out triumphantly at the public beach. We stayed there playing until dusk, then finally headed back home.

"Don't worry, Mamika," I told my grandmother when we were safely home. "Attila is old enough to look out for us in the water. Plus, I'm a good swimmer now. You don't have to worry."

☐ ☐ ☐

One lazy afternoon, when the air weighed down heavily and all I wanted to do was stay home and read my book of fairy tales, Attila and Gábor came into the room I shared with Ildikó. The room was next to the parlor, which was rented to summer guests—not Attila's family, but another one. Between our room and the parlor were glass doors, covered by floor-to-ceiling wooden blinds. The boys wanted to cut a small hole in the blinds.

"Why would you want to do that?" I asked.

"To see what happens on the other side, stupid," Attila said, looking at me like surely I was born yesterday.

"My uncle might get mad," I said feebly.

"That old man?" he laughed. "He can barely walk."

Easy for him to say, I thought. Maybe I could outrun my uncle, but I still had to live in his house. Attila's family were paying guests, which gave them certain privileges. And no matter what, they'd go home at the end of the summer. If Zoli Bácsi saw the damage, I'd be the one in trouble. But I didn't say anything. Attila was our leader, after all.

He took out his pocketknife and carefully cut a small oval hole in the blinds—a few centimeters wide. He let me have a look. I got up on my bed and stretched to reach the hole. From that small hole, the whole room was visible. I could see the large windows facing the wildflowers and the backyard, the birch in the front yard; I could see all the beds and the large table in the center. I could see my grandmother making the beds. I stepped back and shrugged. What was the point of watching my grandmother make beds?

Later that day, when the guests using that room arrived home from the beach, we all crowded around the peephole. Attila got there first and wouldn't let the rest of us have a turn.

"What's going on?" Gábor said, pushing his way to the peephole.

"It's that blonde, remember? She checked in earlier this week with the two kids. No husband!" Then Attila whistled. It was the same sound I've heard Ildikó's guy friends make at the beach when they saw a girl in a bikini.

"C'mon," said Gábor. "Lemme look."

"Patience, patience," Attila said, not budging an inch.

"My turn," Gábor said, trying to push Attila away. But Attila was bigger and he shoved Gábor back onto my bed. "Basszd meg. You're too young."

"Am not."

"Get lost."

I left the boys to fight it out among themselves. Whatever this was about, it seemed stupid.

Attila snuck into my room all the time after that to look through the peephole. I never said anything to him, or my grandmother. I just shrugged and left the room. I assumed my grandmother knew about the peephole because she cleaned the room all the time and she never said anything. I figured the boys got away with it somehow.

Not long before summer ended and they all had to go home, Attila and Gábor snuck into my room after supper. It was late and already dark out and they carried flashlights. I was almost asleep. Ildikó was gone, working late at her restaurant job or out with her friends somewhere. Attila had a piece of rope in his hand.

"We have a new game we want to play," he whispered in the dark. "We're gonna play cowboys and Indians."

"What? No. Go away. I'm sleeping."

"It's an American game. You're going to America. You should know it."

"It's late. Go away."

"Lie down," Attila ordered. "We're the cowboys. You're the Indian and we caught you."

I figured they weren't going to leave and that Attila was too big anyway. When he made up his mind about something, there was not much anyone could do. I did what he said. Then Attila tied both my hands to the bed rails.

"I don't think this is a good idea. My uncle will hear." I struggled to pull my hands from the knot, but it was tied too tight. I tried getting up. Attila pushed me down. I fell backwards on the bed. Then he tried to pull my pajama pants down. "What are you doing? Stop. . ."

"Shh, you're not supposed to say anything," Attila said, putting a finger to his mouth. "Stay quiet."

"What are you doing?" Gábor whispered in the dark. "This wasn't supposed to be part of the game. She's just a kid. C'mon. Let's go."

Attila leaned closer, hovering just above me, his legs astride my waist. I wasn't sure what he had in mind, but this wasn't the kind of game I wanted to play. Before he could touch me, I yelled. I yelled as loud as I could for my grandmother.

Attila put his hand over my mouth. "Shut up, you idiot."

I struggled to get air through my nose. My grandmother will never hear me, I thought. The small room was too far from the bedroom where she slept. The sound would have to penetrate the parlor, the hallway, and the kitchen walls. And though the house was old and crumbling, the walls were thick plaster. Suddenly, I heard a creak and the doorknob rattle. My uncle, whose room was adjacent to ours, opened the door. He towered over the boys like a one-eyed giant.

"What the hell is going on in here?"

The boys dropped what they were doing and bolted through the back door into the darkness, just missing my grandmother.

"Bunch of hooligans," my uncle said. Then, without another word, he disappeared back into his den, leaving me tied to the bed.

"What happened here?" my grandmother said as she came in the back door. I couldn't speak. I was too ashamed.

"I should never have let those boys play with you," she said, untying my hands from the bedrail.

"I am . . . sorry . . . Mamika. I didn't know," I blurted between sobs. "They just . . . came in . . . it was a game . . . cowboys . . ." I couldn't finish.

"Don't you go near those boys again!"

She didn't have to tell me again.

¤ ¤ ¤

Attila's family stayed another week. They acted like nothing happened. No one mentioned anything to anyone. The boys and their sisters left the house like they did every morning on some new adventure. I stayed home. Earlier that summer, I found a new book on the shelf above my aunt's bed. It was a big book with a white cover. On the binding in gold letters were the words *Ezeregyszaka Meséi, One Thousand and One Nights*. I picked up the book and took it to my cardboard box and there, hidden from everyone, read through the last steaming days of August about a king who tried to kill all the young girls in his land. I closed my eyes and dreamed that I was the dark-haired Shahrazad, the brave and beautiful, who saved her own life, and many others, by telling stories.

¤ ¤ ¤

My cousins came home briefly in late August and built a huge bonfire to say goodbye to the summer. Attila, Gábor, the girls, and their whole family were there, eating and smiling. I saw Zoli Bácsi talk to their parents. They all laughed. It was a great summer, they agreed. They'd love to come back next year.

I sat by the fire and watched the flames leap like bright orange dragons into the black night sky; I watched the stars slowly come out. My cousins Zoli and Árpád dragged a big telescope out to the backyard, and set it on a tripod. They showed me how to look through the long tube with one eye. If you looked closely, they said, you could see Venus and Mars, or even Jupiter, which wasn't even a star, they told me, but a planet like the Earth. I looked through the long tube, using one hand to cover my left eye. I could see the moon bright and clear, looking like a man smiling down on the Earth.

It's not such a big world, I thought. Far away on the other side of the ocean, my mother could look up to the sky and see the very same moon smiling down on all of us.

Seventeen

My Mother's Voice

I was glad when school opened that September. Third grade meant more schoolwork, more reading, more math, and a new teacher. She was young and came from a town far away. She was pretty, but she didn't have Mrs. Novák's twinkling eyes. Nor did she know our families or us. She made us stand and recite our math facts, and if we got even one fact wrong, made us start from the top, orchestrating the recitations with a ruler in her hand. "Wrong, start over," she commanded from her pedestal at the front of our classroom. She made us read stories out loud, stories about bald fat men that our textbook called capitalist oppressors. The pictures showed them with dollar signs in their eyes and sacks of money in their pudgy hands. If we mispronounced a word, she'd have us start the paragraph over. She was strict and I didn't like her. I especially did not like the fact that she did not know or appreciate that I was going to America.

"Do you know who I am?" I wanted to tell her. "I'm going to America. I am going to live in New York. I'm going to have all the toys I want, and drive in a fancy car, and live in an apartment that touches the sky. I am special." At least I wanted to believe this. Whether it would come true was another matter, but I sure didn't want her to know that!

But she did not seem to want to know this or care. She did not walk home with me or visit my grandmother, and certainly was not going to buy me a doll—even if I had wanted a doll. In her eyes, I was just another village kid who couldn't remember the answer to seven times eight.

Still, we were considered almost big kids now. One more year, and we'd graduate from *Kis Dobos* to *Uttörö*, Little Drummer to Pioneer. We would exchange our blue kerchiefs for the official red ones.

My godfather Szilárd continued to come and go with his briefcase filled with documents.

"Don't worry, Juditka," he said. "We'll straighten this mess out." He was always cheerful to me, but he always left our house with a frown.

One Sunday morning, he came not just with my godmother, Zsuzsa, but with a little girl who sat in the back seat, refusing to get out.

"Come out, Enikő! No one will hurt you." Zsuzsa pleaded. "Juditka is waiting to play with you."

"I don't want to," said the girl, clinging to Zsuzsa's legs so that both were now stuck in the car.

Who was this baby attached to my godmother? I fixed my eyes on her mopey face, hoping a stern look in her direction would unstick her from Zsuzsa's legs. She looked about five, with wispy light brown hair, freckles, and fierce blue eyes.

But Enikő held on and refused to step out. "I'm not going in there," she wailed. "I want to go home."

I looked around our muddy yard, the outhouse, the barking dog tied to the tree, my hunchback grandmother, and my aunt in a frumpy house dress, her hair tied back in an old kerchief, her hand over her missing teeth. No wonder Enikő didn't want to get out.

"Mamika, who is she?" I whispered to my grandmother.

"She's Zsuzsa's daughter."

I sized up the situation and made a calculated decision. Enikő could be my enemy, but she could also be a playmate. She was younger. I could teach her what's what. I ran in the house and fetched the new doll my mother had sent from America. She was different from every other doll I had. She was shapely with big boobs, an impossibly tiny waist, big blonde hair, slender legs and feet shaped to fit into tiny high-heeled shoes. Her only piece of clothing was a red bathing suit. I grabbed her by her pointy toes and brought her to the car.

"They call this Barbie," I told Enikő, holding up the doll. Finally, she looked up and saw me, saw the doll.

"It's from America. You don't know about America, but it's special. You wanna play?"

"Yeah," she finally said timidly, stepping out of the car and into the mud.

"C'mon," I told her. "Let's get her pretty and make her go on a date."

That did the trick. Enikő and I wandered off to play with the doll with big boobs. We put Barbie in my aunt's tin washtub, pretending it was a swimming pool. We swished her this way and that and twirled her arms pretending she could swim. Then we stripped off her bathing suit and examined her anatomy. Enikő flipped her over and checked to see what was in between her legs. There was nothing. Whew! That was a relief. A doll with boobs was enough to handle. We then let Barbie suntan in the buff, combed out her messy hair, and put her bathing suit back on. It would have to do. None of my other dolls' clothes fit Barbie. It was time for the date. We didn't have a boy doll so we found a stick about her size.

"*Szia, Barbie*," said the stick. "Do you want to go to the restaurant or the movies?"

"Both," Barbie said. "First the restaurant, then the movie."

"Do you like Tarzan?" asked the stick.

"Oh yes yes yes, I love Tarzan," Enikő swooned. I let her play Barbie. It made her happy. We took the stick and Barbie over to the steps leading to the parlor, where my godparents were now deep in conversation with Zoli Bácsi, and set them up with play dishes for their date in the restaurant.

"What do you have this time?" I heard my uncle ask impatiently. He seemed to be growing weary and annoyed with all of my godfather's visits.

"It's like this, Zoli Bácsi," Szilárd said. "I've made some inquiries from a friend, a lawyer, who knows about these things. My hunch about Juditka's situation turns out to have been right. You have made the situation immensely more complicated by having her declared abandoned. It means that the state gets to decide all kinds of things about her now . . . not her parents and not even you. I believe this is why Piroska's visits to the embassy in Washington have been in vain. It's why we're having so much trouble here."

"I see."

"Did you know this was going to happen?"

"It was not clear."

"Well, it seems that the chance to get some money for her was clear enough," Szilárd said in frustration.

"You make it sound like I'm just after the money. What kind of person do you think I am?"

"Zoli Bácsi, we mean no disrespect," Zsuzsa said, calmly. Her sweet voice always had a way of making things better. "We just need your cooperation. Szilárd has been running back and forth to Budapest. But doors have been closed at every turn. We just want to move forward and help Juditka."

"With all due respect, Zoli Bácsi," Szilárd added. "I think your motives in this whole affair have been colored by money."

"Look around you. Does it look like I'm all about the money? It's her father that's all about money. I'm a humble man trying to make ends meet."

"Szilárd, Zoli Bácsi, please. This is not helpful," Zsuzsa interrupted again. "Zoli Bácsi, we just need your cooperation."

"Cooperation with what? I am an old man. You can see I'm not in the best of health. The doctor says the leg is bad. I can barely walk."

"There is one chance, but you need to undo what you did. You need to testify that the parents are willing to support Juditka, that they have not abandoned her."

"It's always the little man who ends up being screwed."

"Piroska wrote to us. They have someone in America who is willing to help. A politician, I think. But she must prove they can support the child. They need you to back them up. Will you help?"

"I can sign your papers, but unlike you, I am not in a position to go from office to office looking after all this."

"We can do that," Zsuzsa said.

"What about the income for the girl? Can you replace this too?" Zoli Bácsi said.

"You say it's not about money, but listen to you," Szilárd said, getting up in disgust. "It looks like you have discovered in this child the goose that lays the golden egg. No wonder you won't give it up!" He looked at Zsuzsa. "I can't deal with this anymore. Come Zsuzsa. We are not getting anywhere by dealing with this man."

¤ ¤ ¤

"Anyuka, look at this doll," Enikő said to her mother, holding up Barbie to Zsuzsa and Szilárd as they came out of the big room. "Can I have a doll like this, Anyuka? Please?" Enikő pleaded.

"I don't think I've ever seen a doll like this," Zsuzsa said, examining her more closely. "Hmmm . . . But I tell you what. If Juditka comes to Veszprém with us, maybe she can bring the doll and you can continue to play all week long!" Zsuzsa looked at me with a smile. "What do you say, Juditka? Do you want to come to Veszprém with us?"

Did I want to go? Of course I wanted to go! Enikő and I jumped up and down.

¤ ¤ ¤

Before long, the noisy white car was pulling out of my grandmother's house and I was waving goodbye to the little figure in the dark dress. My grandmother remained there waving her arm for a long time until the car went around the bend and I could not see her anymore. It was a strange feeling, driving off and leaving my grandmother. The last time I left her like this was when my parents were still home. I never thought twice about it then. Now it left a big lump in my throat. I willed myself to turn around and face forward. That's when I saw Barbie hanging upside down from Enikő's mouth, her tiny little feet wedged in her front teeth.

"What are you doing?" I grabbed the doll from her mouth. But it was too late. Enikő's front teeth were permanently imprinted in the doll's rubber feet. I was so mad I could have hit Enikő. But I didn't. I just took the doll and stuffed it in my bag.

"I'm sorry," she said.

"It's all right. It's just a doll," I lied.

As we drove from our village, Jesus faded from view; so did our school, the church, and everything I knew. It was amazing how fast the village evaporated, how in less than five minutes, everything that was my world, my universe, dimmed and vanished. Szilárd looked at my sad face from the rear-view mirror.

"Maybe this will cheer you up, Juditka," he said. "We weren't going to tell you until you saw the bridge, but instead of taking you straight to our house, we are going to take you to Budapest."

"Budapest?!"

"Yes, Budapest. And there is more. I have a friend who has a telephone, one that can make overseas phone calls. We are going to call your mother, and you can talk to her by telephone."

I forgot all about the teeth marks in my doll, about leaving my grandmother, my vanishing village. Eniko and I were practically jumping in our seats with excitement.

"You're finally going to hear your mother's voice," Zsuzsa said, turning around, smiling. "What are you going to say?"

What am I going to say? What am I going to say? The question startled me. I had no idea what I was going to say. After almost four years, what would I tell my mother? Would I tell her about my broken arm in kindergarten, about how my grandmother pulled me in the wagon to school? Would I tell her about the doll Mrs. Novák bought me, or how the bikini melted like jellyfish on my skin? Would I tell her about the teeth marks in Barbie's feet?

The closer we got to Budapest, the more I worried. I tried to imagine my mother's voice across thousands of miles of ocean. What would she sound like? I had completely forgotten the sound of her voice. I tried to imagine her calling my name from the clinic window in Mohács. But I could no longer hear the sound. What would I sound like to her? After all this time, would she remember my voice?

My godparents' friends lived in a large apartment in the Buda hills overlooking the lights of Pest and the bridges that connect the two sides. Szilárd had explained in the car ride that Buda and Pest used to be two cities. Buda was hilly; Pest was flat. There are now multiple shiny bright bridges connecting the two sides. I was in awe as Szilárd drove through the glittering city in the twilight. We passed tall brick apartment houses and wide boulevards with storefronts that were lit up all night. I caught a glimpse of the Liberty Statue on top of the Gellért hill, a strong woman holding up a single enormous palm leaf; I saw the Fisherman's Bastion and the king's castle towering over the

Buda side of the Danube, the symmetrical gothic Parliament soaring over the Pest side. I saw the Chain Bridge, the Elizabeth Bridge, the Liberty Bridge, and the Margaret Bridge, all of them twinkling like enormous chandeliers against the darkening sky. I had thought often about New York and Rome and Vienna. I had never imagined that Budapest could be so brilliant.

We parked the car on a dark, hilly street and walked into a brick apartment building. A lady in a red dress, pantyhose, high heels, and pearls greeted us at the door. There were several couples already gathered, some holding sparkling crystal glasses, others smoking cigarettes. A table in a large dining room was set with pretty dishes. Books lined one wall of a comfortable room with big chairs and sofas.

"We heard so much about your family in America," the woman said to me, inviting us into the spacious apartment, "You must miss them very much."

What should I say to her, I thought. Had I missed my family? Truth be told, I didn't miss them. Not anymore. They were no longer a part of my life. They were strangers who wrote letters about far-away places I may never get to see.

"Yes. Very much," I said. She smiled and patted my head.

Dinner was served at the table set with white linen, silver, and crystal. The adults talked and laughed. I heard familiar names like Kádár and Brezhnev and Nixon, names I've heard my uncle mention—usually not kindly. I didn't understand much about their conversation. Enikő and I ate and went into a small den to continue our play. That's where we saw the black telephone on a small table next to a couch. I sat down and picked up the receiver, just to see how it felt. It was heavy and buzzed in my ear.

"Say hello," said Enikő.

"Hello. This is Boros Judit. Are you my mother?" I laughed.

"Yes, I am your mother," Enikő said, giggling, faking an old lady sound, pretending to hold another telephone to her ear.

"America is so bright and shiny. When you get here, I will buy you a brand-new Barbie with a new dress and new shoes!"

"Okay," I said. "See you soon."

"*Szia, Juditka.*" She pretended to hang up the phone. We both laughed.

¤ ¤ ¤

Almost no one in Hungary had a telephone. To make a call, my grandmother walked two kilometers to the post office, paid a fee to a lady in a uniform behind a counter, and waited in line—sometimes for an hour. It was so hard to do this and cost so much, my grandmother only made a phone call once that I could remember, and it wasn't to America. It was nice of my godfather's friends to let us do this right from their home.

Finally, after they were finished eating, my godfather came into the den. "It's time," he said. "Come, Juditka, sit on the sofa. The cord will stretch." He picked up the receiver, said a few words to someone on the other end, then handed it to me. "It's your mother."

Slowly I grabbed the heavy black receiver and held it to my ear. A few seconds later, I heard my mother's voice.

"*Juditkám, kis angyalom* . . . my little angel." I heard my mother say.

I imagined her voice, a voice I had not heard in almost four years, bouncing across the vast Atlantic Ocean alongside the whales and dolphins, the sharks and starfish, the squid and octopus. While driving to Budapest, my godfather—who loved to tinker with cords, cables, wires, bulbs, and motors—who told me he taught mechanical engineering at the university—explained to Enikő and me how telephones carried sound across the ocean.

"About twenty years ago," he said, "copper lines were laid down on the ocean floor."

"How did they do that?" Enikő interrupted.

"With ships and tugboats and the occasional diver who had to go down and make sure it was put in the right place."

"What if the line breaks? Or a shark bites it?"

"That happens—sometimes. Then people have to bring the cable back up and fix it."

"But how does my voice get over there?" I asked.

"Well, inside the phone is a microphone. It changes your voice into electrical signals." He kept talking and explaining, but I didn't understand most of it.

"Is it like speaking into a really long tube?" I asked when he was finished.

"Kind of. But the sound is changed—into electricity. "

Enikő and I just looked at each other and shrugged. How could your voice be changed into something that lights up a bulb? My mind wandered as my godfather talked, and in the end all I could think of was this: if a long tube could carry my voice across the ocean, if people figured out how to turn your voice into electricity, then why in the world was it so hard for me to go across the ocean? If people could invent wondrous machines that can allow families to hear each other, then why do people also have to stand in between them and not allow them to see each other?

My mother's voice: it was a little distorted, cracked, but it was there by way of the copper cables on the ocean floor, by way of an invention that allowed a voice to be changed to electrical signals, by way of these people who allowed me to come to their house and use their magic machine. I struggled to recognize it. It was a sweet voice, kind, gentle.

"*Hogy vagy kis lányom?* How are you my little girl?"

"I'm fine thank you." I had thought carefully about what I would say, what I would ask. On the ride to Budapest, a million questions raced through my mind. Was it nicer in America? Was it worth leaving here? Why did you leave? Why can't I come? Why is it taking so long? What's Tibor like now that he looks like a man with a mustache? Are you coming home? In the end,

I could hardly speak. The sound of her voice sparked pictures from somewhere deep in my mind: my mother in the lake, floating and laughing on the rubber raft; my mother on the lakefront, holding my hand; my mother on a bed with white sheets reading her big book; my mother in the window of the clinic, calling my name. *"Nunus. Gyere fel.* Come upstairs my little bunny, hurry."

"Budapest is beautiful," I managed to finally blurt out.

"I'm glad you are getting a chance to see it."

"Me too."

"We will see you soon," she said. *"Nagyon Szeretlek.* I love you very much."

"Me too."

"Puszi."

"Puszi." Kiss, kiss.

It was less than a minute—and then it was over. The call was expensive, our hosts explained, and they had to be careful.

When I hung up, I was confused, upset. Why didn't I say something else? I had so much I wanted to say and ask. Where did the words go? My face burned; heat soaked my body, my shirt. All I wanted to do suddenly was run away from these people with their fancy dishes and cigarettes, patting my head as if I was some poor child. I was tired of people feeling sorry for me. They were just like all the vacationers who were asked to take me places because everyone at my grandmother's was busy. I thought of running out the apartment door, down the stairs and into the city, getting lost and never going back.

In the end, I just said thank you.

Eighteen

Running Water and Tears

The next day we drove to Veszprém, where my godparents lived. We rounded the Balaton, and headed toward the hills on the far side, hills that from my grandmother's side of the lake seemed like the end of the world to me. The city sprouted before us, fields of yellow sunflowers turning into parking lots, belching factories, and bustling roads.

"Look, Juditka!" Szilárd pointed to a crane lifting a steel beam. "They are building the tallest building in Veszprém. It's going to be twenty stories tall!"

"Can we go to the top when it's finished?" Enikő asked.

"I think so. But just think, Juditka. This is nothing compared to what they are building in New York right now. They call it the twin towers; each will be 110 stories high, the tallest in the word!"

"I want to go there," said Enikő. "Can we go there and visit Juditka?"

"First, we need to help Juditka get there. Then maybe the rest of us—some day."

We turned the corner and we were at Zsuzsa and Szilárd's apartment building, a series of four-story cement rectangles, each with a parking lot. Enikő jumped out of the car and led us up a staircase flooded with light and hanging plants. Zsuzsa unlocked the apartment door and Enikő ran ahead, down a long hallway to her very own room. It was a bright apartment with a balcony overlooking the city's red-tiled roofs. There were books here in floor-to-ceiling bookshelves, and art on the walls, and music seeping from a record player in the living room. There was a small table for eating with four chairs and pretty porcelain dishes.

"I don't know about you, but I am starving," Szilárd said.

"I'll make us something to eat." Zsuzsa went into a tidy, sun-filled kitchen. She opened the door to what looked like a white closet filled with peppers, tomatoes, cheese and milk. The closet let out a cold misty breath as if walking outside on a January morning. I stared at it, wondering what it was and why the closet was so cold inside this warm home.

"It's a refrigerator," Zsuzsa said, reading my mind. "It keeps food cold, so it won't spoil. See how fresh the peppers are?"

I touched the pepper, plump and firm and free of brown spots, blemishes, or fruit flies. She held it under a sink with a silver spout, turned on the water and washed it. My eyes opened wide. There was no need to go down three flights of steps, to dip a tin bucket in the well, to hoist the bucket full of water, and walk it up the stairs. Water came pouring from the wall through the silver spout, a river connecting to every house, every apartment. If only my grandmother could have this magic spout to wash peppers and tomatoes, to clean dishes, to make a bath. How much easier her life would be.

Zsuzsa sliced the green and yellow peppers and placed them on a white porcelain plate. She added red tomato, salami, and small triangles of soft white cheese. It looked like a painting in a museum. She carried the plate into the living room with the small table and chairs and set it all down on a cheerful tablecloth. She brought milk in a pitcher and cottage cheese and freshly sliced crusty bread. We all sat down to eat.

"Thank you, Zsuzsa," my godfather said. "Say thank you, Enikő."

¤ ¤ ¤

How different it all was. Sitting down together, talking, sharing. They were a real family, like we were back in Mohács, a long, long time ago. Or were we? I wasn't sure anymore.

After dinner, it was time to wash up. Zsuzsa showed me the bathroom—the eighth wonder of the world! Here again were things I had never seen: a bathtub with running water, a shower, a sink with a mirror, toothbrushes, soap to wash your hands, shampoo to clean your hair, and soft fluffy toilet paper! No need to hunt for leaves here. I flushed the toilet five times just to watch the water dance and swirl and disappear down the drain.

Enikő and I took a hot bath. Zsuzsa washed my back with a washcloth. A year's worth of dirt and dead skin sloughed off my back into the water and spun down the drain.

"There, that must feel better," she said, wrapping a soft white towel around me.

"Does Enikő take a bath every day?"

"A few times a week."

I was afraid to tell her how often I took a bath.

"Let's give Barbie a bath too," Enikő said. We stripped and plopped her in the tub. We pumped shampoo on her hair and scrubbed her face, her feet. I brushed her grinning mouth with a toothbrush. Enikő lent me one to use on my own teeth. "Hold it like this," she said, coaching me as we stared in the mirror. "Not sideways. Up and down." I didn't know that teeth needed cleaning too.

We got into pajamas and climbed into bed. Her room was warm. Heat came purring from a box on the wall. If only my grandmother could see this. Zsuzsa turned off the light next to

Enikő's bed. A soft nightlight came on, giving her room a warm glow. Zsuzsa lifted a book off a bookshelf filled with children's books. "Once upon a time," she read, "there was a little girl who lived in a cozy little house at the edge of the woods . . ."

Enikő closed her eyes. Stuffed animals nodded goodnight. I closed my eyes too. Zsuzsa bent down and kissed us both.

We woke up to fresh bread and salami and ate in our pajamas at the table in the sunlit room. After breakfast, we slipped into Szilárd and Zsuzsa's unmade bed, played hide and seek under the covers, then jumped up and down like monkeys.

"Enough, enough!" Szilárd finally said. "You two are going to break the bed. Let me show you a quieter game." He pulled a chess set off a shelf.

"Have you ever played chess, Juditka?"

"No. What's that?"

"Eniko, let's teach her . . . Now, pay attention," Szilárd said. "These are the pawns. They are the little guys. They have little power, you see. They can only move this way," and he moved the pawn up the chessboard by two squares to start. "They are like regular people in our socialist-democratic republic. They can't do much," he explained with a wink to my godmother, who was cleaning up the breakfast dishes. She smiled back at what seemed like a joke between the two of them. "Now, this is the knight. He can jump over the others like this. They are like the party members who can jump the line in the store to get the bread and all the other good stuff—the cookies, cakes, ice cream . . . Pawns can't do that, you see."

"I guess Mamika is a pawn. She has to wait in line at the ABC a lot," I said.

"Now you get the picture."

¤ ¤ ¤

I wanted to stay here, to be Enikő's sister forever. What a happy family we'd be. That's what I was thinking all day as we visited the university where my godparents worked as professors, as we ate pudding in the college cafeteria, as we laughed our faces off mimicking the chimpanzees at the city zoo. We went to bed smiling. Zsuzsa kissed both of us on the forehead. The stuffed animals nodded us goodnight. We were sisters. We could live happily ever after.

¤ ¤ ¤

On my third night in Veszprém, I woke in the middle of the night to sounds coming from the living room. In her bed next to me, Enikő was sleeping without a care in the world, her teddy bear tucked next to her. I went to the bathroom and sat on the toilet. At first the sounds were muffled, but not for long.

"I heard you on the phone with her and now this letter . . . what am I supposed to make of this?" I heard my godmother cry.

"You went through my mail? How dare you?"

"How dare *you?*"

"Keep your voice down."

"Really Szilárd, how could you? We are a family. And now, with Juditka, we have so much to do. Why?"

"I can't explain it, Zsuzsa. All I can say is after we get through all this for Juditka, we need to try something different. This . . . this marriage . . . it just isn't working any more."

I sat on the toilet, too stunned to move, too afraid to make a sound. I couldn't take a breath, though like a burst balloon, I had no air left inside me. I plugged my ears. I didn't want to hear any more.

I snuck back to bed and pulled the covers over me. I tried to not think about what I'd heard, but couldn't. There were no fairy tales and no fairy godparents, either.

When Zsuzsa came into the room the next morning, my eyes were red. So were hers. I swallowed hard. I knew I couldn't say anything. What would I say, anyway? My throat ached. I tried to stop the tears. But then one escaped and then another and another and suddenly, they were gushing forth and I couldn't stop. All I wanted was to be back with my grandmother in our little room, curled up next to her. I missed her so much; it was almost unbearable.

"I want to go home," I sobbed before Enikő, before my godmother. "I want to go home now."

"*De Juditkám* . . ." Zsuzsa said, trying to be cheerful. "We have so many things we still wanted to do with you, to show you."

"No. Please, can you take me home today? I don't want to see anything. I miss Mamika. I miss her so much."

"All right," she said finally. "We'll take you home . . . today."

Szilárd drove the car. I sat next to him in near silence. Enikő didn't want to come. Neither did my godmother. When we finally crossed the town line with Jesus on the cross, I could finally breathe. My grandmother's village never seemed so lovely, her hug never so sweet, her house never so much like home.

Nineteen

Dress Up and Dance

It was the end of winter; time to chase the evil spirits away.

In Mohács, Farsang was the biggest holiday of the year, even bigger than May Day. Instead of marching down the street with life-sized portraits of Lenin, people put on costumes, drank vodka, and threw a huge party. They dressed up in sheepskin coats and scary wooden masks. Some had sharp white fangs and knotted hair; others had devil eyes and horns. The masks were to scare away winter, the cold, and the dead. That's why we always held the Farsang in February. People came from all over the country to Mohács. You could hear the music from the streets long into the night and see people dancing in the street and in the square. Sometimes they danced so much, they fell down and passed out.

There was no street party to celebrate Farsang at my grandmother's village. But there was a costume contest at the school, followed by a dance. Everyone was invited, including all the old widows in their black dresses and kerchiefs. Villagers who knew how to play a fiddle or the drums came to the school to play folk songs, and the toothless old ladies would tap their feet and hum while we kids danced.

In the first grade, I dressed up as a sunflower. My cousin Piroska drew the shape on cardboard, cut it out, colored it, and sewed the flower onto an old dress. For my head, she cut out and colored orange petals and made a crown. I smiled for Zoli Bácsi's camera. Everyone clapped. I was a hit.

In the second grade, I was a Chinese girl. Our class put on a play about love and peace across the world. Mrs. Novák told me I was perfect for the part of the Chinese girl because while almost all other girls had dirty blond hair and blue eyes, I had dark brown hair and eyes. Ildikó painted my hands and face yellow and spread black eyeliner around my eyes to make them look Chinese. She made me a small paper hat and said it was like the hats Chinese farmers wore in the rice fields. András got black paint smeared on his face and hair, or maybe it was just coal dust. Our teacher said he would represent all Africans. Klári was dressed in a traditional Hungarian folk dress embroidered with red tulips and rosebuds. She would represent Europeans, or maybe Hungarians. The teacher never really explained. We had to stand on the stage and recite a poem about the color of our hands and how we all got along so well, despite the differences in our skin color. We held out our hands as our teacher instructed, turning them around for all to see. None of us had ever seen a Chinese person. I saw a black man at the university in Veszprém. He wore a suit and carried a valise like my godfather; he didn't look anything like András in black paint. It didn't seem to matter to our audience though, who loved our show and clapped loud when we finished. We all took a deep bow.

We weren't doing a school production this year, so it was up to each of us to come up with our own costumes. András was going to be a shepherd boy—he was always a shepherd boy. Péter would be a policeman. He had a toy gun and a holster. Laura was going to be a ballerina in a poofy pink dress. I didn't want to be a flower or a tree or a ladybug or anything babyish like that. I was tall now, taller than anyone else in the third grade. I was slender with arms like broomsticks dangling from my body. My hair was growing out. But the biggest change of all was my breasts! I was barely nine, but there they were, budding through my shirt, insisting on announcing themselves to the world. None of the other girls in the third grade had breasts! András, who sat in the seat in front of me at school, turned around every morning to gawk.

"I want to have babies with you," he said out loud.

Thanks to Ilona, I knew how babies got out, but had no clue how they got in. My palms got all sweaty and my face turned red.

"Just turn around," I said.

I wanted to be something grown-up this year, but couldn't think of anything. I racked my brain for weeks. Maybe I could be a waitress, I thought. I could put on a miniskirt like Ildikó, and a little white apron. Or maybe I could be a teacher like Mrs. Novák, but I wasn't sure what kind of costume I'd need for that beyond a frumpy dress. I could be a maid like Katus Néni, who worked at the hotel sometimes for extra money. But I didn't like any of those things.

It was Piroska who finally thought of an idea. She rummaged through my aunt's armoire where my mother's things were locked away and came back carrying a white doctor's coat, a black doctor's bag, a stethoscope, and a syringe. "Let's dress you up as a doctor," she said, holding up the coat.

I tried it on. Like my mother's snow boots, the coat fit like a glove. "It's perfect," she smiled.

Ildikó came into the room, and looked at me, squinting her eyes. "I have an idea."

I thought she would suggest I take off the white coat and the stethoscope. I thought she would go to her room and dig up an old ladybug costume and make me wear that. She came back with a black wig with straight hair and bangs. She put it on my head, carefully tucking in my loose strands of girlish curly hair. My two cousins stood back to assess me.

"Excellent," Piroska said. "Very grown up."

"Hmm," Ildikó said. "I think she needs one more thing." She went to our room and came back carrying black eyeliner, mascara, blush, and lipstick. She took my chin in her hand, and turning my face up to the light, carefully applied the makeup to my eyes, cheeks, and lips. When she finished, she stood back and examined me. "Perfect," she announced.

She held up a mirror so I could see myself. Before me stood my mother in her white coat, her stethoscope, and her doctor's bag. Behind me, my cousins beamed.

"Turn around, Juditka. Let us see you."

I twirled before the mirror, checking every angle. "It's perfect," I smiled.

When I walked out on the school stage on the night of the Farsang, everyone was delighted. smiled. I held up the syringe and made it squirt. The audience laughed. My grandmother laughed, showing her pink gums, and wiped a tear from her wrinkled face.

Last year, after everyone had a chance to show their costumes, my friends and I played hide and seek, rampaging through the darkened dance room and annoying the older students and grownups. This year, we danced. The band started up. Instead of old folk songs on a fiddle, the band played rock and roll.

"Wanna dance?" András asked, his brows glistening with sweat.

"Okay," I said, a little nervous.

The top of his head reached exactly to my armpits. His soft blond hair stood straight up from the electricity in the air. We shuffled forward and back to the rhythm of the new songs like we'd seen the older kids do.

Zoli Bácsi came like he did to my first communion, lugging his camera and lights to record my first dance with a boy. And all around us, old ladies with no teeth and black kerchiefs tapped their feet and laughed.

Twenty

A Town Called Auschwitz

The first thing I noticed was their shoes. The woman's were candy red and shiny with skinny heels; the color matched her lips. The man's were polished so bright he might have seen his reflection if he looked down. They tiptoed from the car, trying to avoid the thick mud surrounding my grandmother's house. The snow that was piled high just a week before had melted and turned into slush, then a deep, squishy, muddy mess. I was playing with the new dog outside. He barked when he heard the car pull up, tugging on the rope that tied him to the tree. The woman was trying to make her way to the gate, but she was obviously not good at it. She would have done better wearing my mother's warm boots this time of year. I was afraid she'd fall on her face and ruin her nice wool coat and the red scarf that matched her shoes and lips.

"So, this is the little girl I've been hearing about?" She left red kiss marks on both my cheeks.

"Don't you remember us?" said the man. He was bald and chubby with thick square glasses, smooth skin, and a big smile. He wore slacks with razor-sharp pleats, and a suit jacket. He smelled like a pine tree. I shook my head and rubbed the lipstick from my cheeks.

My grandmother let them in the front gate.

"This is János Bácsi, your uncle," she said, introducing them. "And this is Csilla Néni, your aunt. They live in Pécs."

"Very nice to see you again," the man said, taking my hand and putting it to his lips, as if I was a princess. I laughed.

"*Kezit Csókolom,*" I said, politely.

"You have grown into quite a young lady since we last saw you. How old are you now?"

"Nine . . . almost 10," I said quietly, staring at my own mud-crusted shoes.

"You were four the last time we saw you. How time flies. So, Juditka, what do you like to eat? *Dobos torta? Rigó Jancsi?*" He took a small box that he had been hiding behind his back, opened the flap, and held it under my nose. My eyes grew wide. Inside the box was a slice of seven-layer cake with a caramel-colored sugar topping.

"Don't you remember us at all?"

I shook my head and stared at the ground, eager for a lick of the shiny burnt-sugar frosting.

The man laughed.

"To what do we owe the pleasure?" my grandmother asked the well-dressed couple.

"We wanted to see the young lady . . . before she flew away for good," János said, looking down at me with a big smile.

"Well, we pray for good news every day, but . . . never mind . . . why don't you come inside."

They walked gingerly across the yard, trying to find an island of solid ground in the sea of mud. Zoli Bácsi led the visitors into the parlor, took his usual seat on one of two green velvet chairs, and lit his cigarette.

"Nice of you folks to come around," he said.

"As I said, we wanted to see Juditka before…"

"Before she flies away. Oh yes. Four years we've been waiting for her to fly away. It's nice that you've finally come. Maybe it's a good omen."

I saw the man shift uncomfortably. The woman pursed her lips. "Juditka looks well," the woman said.

"We do our best."

"What news do you have from her parents?" the man asked.

"You must know. Or don't you? Oh yes, I forget. You brothers don't speak."

"Well, this is a nice welcome," the man said. "We came here in good faith. We'd like to get to know the child. She is family."

I could see the grownups talking through the open parlor door as I licked frosting from the cake. Family, the man said. Brothers. He must be my father's brother. Funny, I never heard my father mention a brother. This man didn't even look like my father, at least what I remembered of my father. My father had thick brown curly hair. This man had nearly none. My father had sharp eyes. This man could not see without thick glasses. My father was slim and strong, able to lift me high above his shoulders. This man was flabby in the middle. Life had been good to him. But there was also something familiar about him, something kind. Maybe it was his round face, maybe it was his smile, or the fact that he brought me cake!

"Families speak to each other," Zoli Bácsi went on. "I don't like my mother very much. She drives me nuts. Still, I go to see her every once in a while."

"Zoli, you know it's complicated between us."

"Yes. It's complicated. Everything is complicated."

"So, what have you heard?"

"Not much. They say there is someone in America, I don't know, a politician, who has taken an interest in the kid. He is trying to help, I think. Nagy Szilárd is working on it. He's been to Budapest a few times. People say the political winds are changing. Nixon went to China. That might help. Who knows? I do the best I can, but you can see my leg. I'm not in the best of health."

"Well, we are here now," said the woman. "We were hoping we could take Juditka to Pécs for a few days, get to know her a little, make sure she knows who we are . . . her other family."

My aunt was washing dishes in the kitchen. I took my plate and handed it to her to wash. "Do you know them?" I whispered.

"Not very well," she said, taking the plate from me and dropping it in hot water. "I've only met them once before."

"Is he my father's brother?"

"Yes."

"Why haven't they come before?"

"That's a good question. They live far away, I guess. Maybe they are busy," she said without looking at me as she scrubbed a heavy skillet.

"Everyone is busy."

I went back to the parlor, but the man and woman were already getting up to leave.

"Thank you, Zoli Bácsi," said the man. "We appreciate this." He shook my uncle's hand.

"Just make sure you drive her back. I can't afford a train ticket from Pécs."

"We will have her back in a few days," said the woman.

"Juditka, we have wonderful news," said the man, turning to me as he stepped down from the parlor. "You are coming to Pécs with us. We have so much we want to show you. The television tower, the university, and most especially, the bakery that made that cake! It looks like you enjoyed it."

I liked the cake, but I didn't like the lady's red lips or her fancy scarf and perfume. The man's shoes were too shiny, his pants too stiff. I'd probably mess up their fancy house. I didn't want to go, not after what happened in Veszprém. I wanted to stay at my grandmother's. This was my home now.

"*Gyere, Juditka,*" my grandmother called. "Let's pack you a bag."

"I know you don't want to go," she said after we closed the door to the bedroom. "But these people are your family."

"I don't want to leave you."

"They will show you nice things, nice places. Remember you said you wanted to know more about your family, your father's family?" She pulled a small suitcase out from under a bed and started packing it with clothes.

"But they are so . . ."

"Fancy . . . I know."

"I don't even have any nice clothes to wear."

"Yes you do. Here, take this little sweater Anyuka sent, and this skirt."

"But..."

"It's not the clothes that make someone special."

"I know . . . but. . ."

"Well then. Hold up your chin."

She walked me to their car and once again, I was hugging her goodbye. Funny how she felt so small. I had to bend down to hug her. I tried to wipe my shoes before stepping into the car, and got in the back seat. I turned around and waved goodbye to my grandmother as she grew smaller and smaller in the distance.

I sat nervously in the back seat, not sure what we'd talk about, what I'd say. We drove mostly in silence along the two-way roads heading toward Pécs, occasionally stuck behind a cart pulled by a mule.

"Did you know that your parents met in Pécs?" János Bácsi finally asked as we neared the city.

"No."

"They met at the university. Pécs has one of the oldest universities in the country. They were both studying to be doctors. They started right after the war."

"What war?"

"The Second World War. I guess you haven't learned about that in school yet. Anyway, they were both young."

I imagined them like the university students in Veszprém, carrying books and walking to and from beautiful stone buildings. "What were they like?"

"Your father was a handsome man," the lady said.

"Not as handsome as me," the man said, laughing.

"Well . . ."

"Ah-ha! Now we learn the truth."

"Don't worry. You are my one and only."

They laughed and made me laugh.

"Your father was shy," János Bácsi continued. "All he cared about were his studies. His head was always in a book."

"And my mother? What was she like?"

"She was studious too. But not like your father."

"How did they get married?"

"It wasn't love at first sight," Csilla Néni said. "Your dad didn't even look at the ladies in school. But later . . ."

"They met again in Mohács," János Bácsi interrupted. "They were both placed there as doctors."

"And by then, your mother had to fight off many other ladies for his attention," Csilla Néni added. "He was quite the ladies' man. Remember all those nurses, János?" she said, looking at my uncle. "I don't blame them. He was very handsome."

"Much better hair than me," my uncle said, laughing. "But he made the best choice in the end. Your mother is a beautiful lady, Juditka. Heart of gold."

"Where were they married?" I realized I had never seen a picture of my parents as newlyweds or a picture of their wedding.

"Budapest," János said. "Things were hard after the war. People didn't have a lot of money to make big weddings. They were married at the city hall."

"We should have gone," the lady said to her husband. "Someone should have gone, at least to take a picture."

"Yes. If we could only go back in time," he said, talking more to her than me.

As we neared Pécs, a strange thing caught my eye: a huge, rusting pipe rose from the ground like a giant serpent surrounding the city. It seemed to slither and wind itself around buildings, parks, and playgrounds.

"What is that?" I asked, staring at the monstrosity imprisoning the beautiful old city, its medieval steeples, its Turkish domes.

"That . . . Oh, it's steam heat," János Bácsi explained. "The pipe comes from outside the city and brings heat into all these apartments," he said, pointing to dozens of cement-block buildings, all in the same shade of dark gray. "Those all used to be little houses with straw roofs and room heaters, like your grandmother's. Today, the heat comes from a plant outside the city, where they turn coal into steam, then send it through the pipe into the apartments. No one needs to go out in the cold to shovel coal into heaters. They just turn a switch."

Seeing the monster, I decided maybe my grandmother's way might be better.

My aunt and uncle's house was perched on the side of a mountain. We parked the car uphill, then walked through a small gate. From the outside, their house seemed small, with just a single window to the street. The inside was something else.

"Let's get some light in here," Csilla Néni said as we walked through a dark hallway and into the main living area. She opened dark blue drapes, behind which was a huge floor-to-ceiling window overlooking the entire city, like a palace on a hill. Light came flooding in, revealing a beautifully furnished room with shelves for books, delicate porcelain figurines, a television and a comfortable couch.

Csilla Néni went to the kitchen to make dinner, leaving us in the living room.

"Come," János Bácsi said, "let me show you something."
We walked to the corner of the living room and he pointed to a
radio. "It's not just any radio," he said. "On this one, you can
get programs from England and America, even Israel." He
turned a dial. I could hear faint voices over the loud static in
languages I did not recognize.

"I know where America is."

"And you're going there. I know...One day soon, we hope.
Have you ever seen New York on a map?"

"No."

"Let me show you on the globe." He walked over to a
table on which stood a round object you could spin with a
finger, seemingly lit from within. He pointed to a green shape
on the edge of a blue one. "That's New York. That' where
you're going." Hungary appeared as a tiny dog-shaped land
colored in orange. America was across the wide expanse of the
Atlantic Ocean, a giant space, many times Hungary's size. For
the first time, I could see how far I'd be going, if I was going.

"Where is Israel?" I asked him since he mentioned it.

"Israel...hmmm, now let me see. How much do you know
about Israel?"

"I've never heard of it."

"It's right here," he said, turning the globe away from
America and pointing to a tiny spot. "It was once a country
called Palestine, but it is now our homeland, the homeland of
the Jews. That's why I listen to the radio . . . to hear news from
there."

"The Jews?"

"Yes. Jews."

"But I thought that was a . . ." I stopped. Instead I asked,
"What is that?"

"You don't know?"

"No. Zoli Bácsi said that word. But . . ."

"Oh. I see. He told you Jews were bad." He closed his eyes
and exhaled long and slow.

"He made it sound that way." I didn't want to say anything, or be impolite. I was his guest. But I was glad when he went on.

"It's like this, Juditka." He paused and sighed. "Jews are people, like everyone else. We go to school, we work, we have families. This country had many Jewish people before the war. In Mohács, where you grew up, there were so many. The Rosenthals, the Blums, the Kleins ... But some people, too many, don't like us so ... "

"Like Zoli Bácsi?"

"Maybe."

"But why?"

"That's hard to explain. We pray, but we don't go to a church. We believe in God, but not the same way your aunt does. We eat some of the same foods, but not all. Some people don't like that we choose to be different. There was a time when it became dangerous to be a Jew in Hungary and in other places. They wanted to get rid of us. All those people in Mohács, they are mostly gone now."

I didn't know what to say. I had so many questions, but I was too afraid to ask.

"But there was a time ..." he continued, "when it was a nice life. Back in Mohács, your grandfather owned a big store. He sold suits, and coats, and shoes. We had a nice house, two nice houses, and the store. Your grandmother kept a beautiful home. Your grandfather went to shul. On Friday nights, we lit candles. Our mother cooked chicken and baked challah and poppy seed strudel. Have you ever had that? Oy, it's delicious! Good times. But then the war came and well . . ."

"What war? The second one?"

"Yes, the one you haven't learned about in school yet."

"What happened?"

"It's a long and sad story, Juditka. How about we save it for after supper."

Csilla Néni came in from the kitchen with an apron around her pretty dress. "János, what are you telling this child?"

"Nothing, just old stories."

"Well, forget the old stories. Juditka, come to the kitchen. Supper is ready. You must be starving."

I didn't want to eat. I wanted more stories. This was the first time an adult took the time to talk to me about real things, important things, things that mattered. But we went into the kitchen anyway, where Csilla Néni had set the table for supper. We ate in the small kitchen, awkwardly passing the salt and pepper. Csilla Néni asked me about my school and friends and if I received any letters from America. I told her about going to Budapest and calling my mother on the telephone. She told me I was lucky because phones were hard to come by and someone must have worked hard to allow a phone call all the way across the sea.

After supper, we went back to the living room. I was looking at a bookshelf with photographs in frames. "Look at this one." János Bácsi held up an old photo of a family around a table covered in white lace. There were two older people, a woman in a black dress with fierce eyes and thick black hair, and a man with a proud smile on his face. Three young men stood to their left—all in suits and ties, each with a white handkerchief in the left pocket. One had eyes deep in thought, a younger one stared straight ahead as if asking a question, the oldest one stood tall and proud in the center of the photo.

"Is this your family growing up?" I asked.

"You guessed right!" He smiled as if I'd just passed a history test. "That's me in the center. Look at that head of hair! That's your father—always deep in thought. And that's your grandmother."

They looked rich, nothing like my aunt and uncle in the village, but with eyes that were kind and faces that were somehow familiar.

"Who is the other boy?"

"That is our brother. Tibor."

"But that's *my* brother's name."

"Your brother was named after your father's brother; my brother."

"Where is he now?"

"He's gone, like the rest of the family."

I was confused. Gone? Like my parents? Where? America? Is that why my father wanted to go there? To find his parents and brother?

¤ ¤ ¤

Csilla Néni called; it was time for bed. Like my grandmother and most everyone else, she didn't seem to like these old stories. But János Bácsi was different. He wasn't scary like Zoli Bácsi, or even like my father. He smiled easily. He could have talked all night. Csilla Néni led me to a room of my own and a big comfortable bed to sleep in. But I could barely sleep that night. If my uncle János was a Jew, and my father was a Jew, what did that make me? But he said some people didn't like Jews. Would my grandmother stop loving me if she found out? Would the people in my school? Is this a secret? Should I tell? Or will no one want to play with me anymore? I liked my uncle János. I liked the way he talked, the way he listened to the radio, the way he explained everything with patience. I liked his warm house, filled with photographs and books, and useful objects like the globe and a radio with channels coming from America and Israel. You could learn a lot living in a house like that.

"Csilla Néni," I asked my aunt the next morning while she was making the bed, "Are you a Jew, like János Bácsi?"

"No, Juditka," she shook head, as she smoothed the bed covers. "I'm not Jewish. Neither is your mother. Your uncle and your father . . . they went through a lot in that war. When it was all over, they changed a lot about their lives. They didn't think it was safe . . . to be Jewish."

"Not safe?"

"No, not safe at all. There were many people then, and now, who are prejudiced, here and elsewhere. They find reasons to hate just because they see others as being different, whether it's because of their religion, the color of their skin, or their race."

"But you don't think that way?"

"Me? I love your uncle more than anything in the world."

"And my mother?"

"She was the same. She adores your father."

"What about Zoli Bácsi or my grandmother?"

"I don't know about your grandmother, but Zoli Bácsi. Well, people like him are the reason your father and uncle changed their names."

"Changed their names?"

"Oh no. I think no one told you that either. Yes. Your father's name was once Berger. Berger Lászlo. Your uncle's name was Berger János."

"Did that make them safer? Changing their name?"

"Maybe a little. I suppose it showed some people that your father and uncle were trying to be more Hungarian, less Jewish. But me and your mother . . . it never mattered to us."

I could hardly touch breakfast. My mind was racing. . . Why would someone hate another human being just because they are a different religion? Or skin color? Then I thought of Ilona—all the times we we made fun of her because she was a half-Gypsy. The times Juliska Néni told me it was wrong to play with our Gypsy neighbors. The time I refused to enter our neighbor's house and then got sick. What if all this time, I wasn't Boros Judit, but Berger Judit? How would people have treated me?

¤ ¤ ¤

That day, they showed me around the whole city, pointing out the television tower on the tallest hill, the university, the espresso shops selling fancy coffee and cakes. While János Bácsi went into a bakery, Csilla Néni and I window-shopped. I'd never seen so many shops, one after the next. In one window, I spotted a delicate green porcelain statue.

"I've seen those," I said.

"That's Zsolnay porcelain. Their factory is here in Pécs. Your parents had a few nice pieces in their apartment."

"Did you visit us there?"

"A few times. Not as often as we should have. Your uncle and your father didn't talk much."

"Why?" I couldn't imagine not talking to your own brother if you had the chance.

"They had their differences, I suppose. After the war, it wasn't easy for either of them."

There was that war again. "What differences?"

"It doesn't seem important anymore. It wasn't important then either. Your father wanted to go to school to become a doctor. János Bácsi wanted them to go into business together. It was a strange thing. I never understood it. After the war, all they had was each other. You'd think they would be so happy to see each other after all that happened. Instead, they fought and argued all the time. But listen to me go on. Let's see what's happening with that cake."

We got home; our feet tired from all the walking. Csilla Néni started supper. János Bácsi and I sat down on the living room sofa. He turned on the radio; violins hummed, indicating it was time for the evening meal. He smiled and started singing to the tune. "*Egy ablaknál . . . álj meg czigany . . .*" He sang slowly, following the easy rhythm of the song. His eyes grew moist, like he was going to cry.

"Your father loved this song. I think it was his favorite. Sometimes, it even made him cry. Me too."

I pictured the young man in the song standing before a window, playing his fiddle softly until the beautiful girl cried. And I could imagine how my father would have cried, his eyes a little wet, his face a little sad. "Can you tell me more stories like you told yesterday? What happened in that war? The second one?"

As we finished off the cake from the bakery, he told me how my grandfather fought in another war, the First World War. He received a medal, an Iron Cross, for being a hero. He told me that my grandfather's dream was seeing all his sons in the clothing business; János would scout the world for the latest fashions, my father would be the tailor, or maybe, if they got lucky, hire other tailors, and run a factory. Tibor, the youngest, would run the shops. But my father refused to be a tailor, János said. He begged his father to let him go to gymnasium and study. His father was angry. But in the end, he relented. My father got to go; he learned Latin, Greek, German, literature, and science. He lived in a house with two girls who played violin. About a year after he started, he came home to Mohács with bad news. He said Jewish people were getting picked off the streets and sent away. He didn't know where. But it was no longer safe to stay.

"He begged our father to leave," János said. "'Let's go to Palestine and make a new home. A Jewish home.'"

"You mean Israel?" I asked.

"Yes. Israel today."

"And . . ."

"He slapped him across the face. 'You are a Hungarian, first and foremost,' he said. 'Never ever forget that.'"

"And . . ."

"Well, we never got to Palestine, that's for sure," he sighed, leaning back in his chair, as if knowing, even now, that such leaning was a luxury. "We stayed in Mohács. Our father said he didn't risk his life for that Iron Cross only to leave Hungary to go to some godforsaken place in the desert to plant trees."

He told me how the Germans attacked one country after another. The war finally came to Hungary and still they stayed. "It was an awful time."

"Did they die?"

"Yes."

"Even your little brother?"

"Even him."

"Was he a soldier? Is that how he died?"

"No. He was just thirteen."

"And the others?"

"Them too."

"That's why I only have one grandmother?" János Bácsi was a little startled by my question but he understood.

"Yes," he finally said. "That's why. It was wartime. Many people died."

"Where are they buried?"

I knew that people in our village were buried in the cemetery behind the church. There was a graveyard there with many mounds, some with fresh flowers. My grandmother told me her husband, my grandfather, was buried in such a cemetery not far from our village. One day she promised to take me to visit his grave. There is a stone there, she told me, with his name carved on it. Maybe we could visit my father's parents and brother and see their names carved on stone too.

"They are buried in a place far away," János said. "A small town called Auschwitz."

Twenty-One

A Nighttime Visitor

When my uncle János took me back home, Zoli Bácsi was gone. His room was empty, the air inside the house lighter. My grandmother told me he had to be taken to the hospital. He had been coughing nonstop since I left, she said, and when he tried to get up, he couldn't walk.

"Will he be back soon?"

"Yes. In a few weeks we hope."

"Can we see him?"

"No," she said. "They don't let children in the hospital."

The house felt quiet and lonely. Ildikó was now attending a trade school far from home and living there. She was learning to paint nails. She said she could make good money doing that for the tourists in the summertime. And she loved it. She came home on Sundays with beautiful colors and designs painted on her own nails. I thought she should try making my grandmother's nails look nicer since they were long, and hardened with black dirt under them. But my grandmother didn't want Ildikó to do that. And maybe she was right. My grandmother would not have been the same with fancy painted nails. Not even Katus Néni wanted her nails done. Maybe when Zoli Bácsi was back, she said, when she could stop worrying.

There was much I wanted to tell my grandmother about my visit to my uncle János, about the things I learned about his family, about my grandfather the merchant and his wife Irén, and about the war. But she never asked about the visit. And she didn't seem interested. Neither did Katus Néni. But that didn't surprise me. What did surprise me was how preoccupied they were with Zoli Bácsi being in the hospital. I would have thought they'd be relieved not to have him yelling for them all day and would welcome the peace and quiet. But they weren't relieved. Katus Néni puttered around the house in her housedress, looking for things to do. But the house stayed clean. She didn't even have to cook much; the three of us were happy to eat cream of wheat for supper. When she finally sat down, it was to her rosary to pray.

"What do you pray for, Katus Néni?" I asked her.

"I am praying for Zoli Bácsi to get better so he could come home," she said. I thought maybe she'd pray for the hospital to keep him.

"Is he very sick?"

"Yes. They say he might . . . well, never mind."

"What?"

"I didn't want to scare you, but maybe I should tell you, so when you see him . . ."

"What?"

She put her rosary down. "The doctors say they might have to amputate his leg."

"What does that mean?"

"They might have to cut some of his leg off."

I gasped. Cut off, as with scissors or a saw? I could not imagine how the doctors would do this, let alone what Zoli Bácsi would look like without a leg.

"He will need a wheelchair," my aunt went on, talking more to herself than me, as if she was trying to understand what this change would mean for her, the practicalities, like how they'd fit a wheelchair into Zoli Bácsi's bathroom, with the big tub and table already taking up all the space, or how she would lift him from the wheelchair onto his big floppy mattress on top of the bathtub.

She seemed lost in worry, but the thought of a wheelchair brightened me up. I imagined that one less leg might make Zoli Bácsi more likable, and less scary. "Maybe I can help push him around," I said, "like a baby in a baby carriage."

¤ ¤ ¤

Zoli Bácsi was home a few weeks later. I found him back in his bathroom, sitting in his usual chair, sipping a bowl of soup. He was even thinner, his gray hair longer, his face unshaved, his eyes tired. His clothes hung on him as if from a skeleton. He still had both his legs and he was in a bad mood.

My aunt took away his cigarettes, telling him it was for his own good, and he was mad. He yelled for my grandmother to help him out of bed and into bed, out of his chair and back in. He yelled for my aunt to make him soup and make him tea and make him pudding and make him a sandwich. He hollered for my grandmother to make his room hotter and make his room cooler, to take the bedpan out and bring the bedpan back. He was miserable and made everyone else feel the same.

After a week, my grandmother was exhausted. Never sick for even a day in her life, she caught a cold and had to spend a whole day in bed. After school, I made her tea, turning on the stove by myself, letting the kettle come to a boil and pouring the tea into a cup for her. I added five spoons of sugar because I knew she liked her tea sweet and brought it to her to sip in bed.

"*Aranyos kislány*," she said, sitting up between coughs. "What a good girl."

"I would bring chocolate, but I couldn't find any," I told her.

"It's all right," she said, smiling a big toothless grin.

"I hope you get better soon, Mamika. Who will take care of Zoli Bácsi?"

"I'll tell you, Juditka, I am tired of taking care of Zoli Bácsi."

But she was back on her feet a few days later, fetching water from the well, trucking coal from the shed, emptying the bedpans, opening the windows and closing them, bending down despite her crooked back to help Zoli Bácsi get up and sit back down.

"Thank God you're better," my aunt said. "I could not do this alone."

Every day Zoli Bácsi yelled and cursed, demanding that Katus Néni give him back his tobacco. He whacked his cigarette holder on his table and called her all kinds of names. He carried on for two weeks until she could take it no more and gave him back his stinky weed.

I decided that if they were going to cut off Zoli Bácsi's leg, there was no way I would push his wheelchair like a baby carriage.

¤ ¤ ¤

December arrived and with it my tenth birthday. The day passed like any other. My name day passed without mention too. Another Christmas came, and my cousins came home. Zoli Bácsi brightened. He seemed happy to see them. They brought news of the outside world—the latest music and styles. Piroska was now a full-fledged art teacher. Árpád and Zoli talked about water testing and bridge construction. Ildikó chattered on about all the special designs she was learning to paint on nails. She had her own money and a place to live and was talking about opening her own shop one day. She even had a boyfriend.

"Did Anyuka send a letter?" I asked my grandmother that night. It was my fifth Christmas at my grandmother's and in all that time, she'd never missed a Christmas letter. Even if the letters were short, or late, there was always at least the letter itself.

"I bet the mail is just late," she said.

I left my cousins to talk about The Beatles and The Rolling Stones and Hungarian bands that tried to sound like them. I went to bed early. A few days later, we took down the Christmas tree and tossed the empty candy wrappers in the trash. Árpád chopped up the tree and put it in the woodshed. My cousins said goodbye.

What was left of the family, the four of us, settled back to another cold winter by the lake. There was no letter the next week, or the week after, or after that. Occasionally, when my uncle did not wear her to the bone, my grandmother would whisper in my ear about skyscrapers, wide boulevards, big cars, and shiny shop windows with pretty shoes and sweaters. But I stopped thinking about America, about my family. They were faded old photographs, their faces fuzzy in my mind. I could no longer remember the feel of my mother's skin, her smell. Life was endless multiplication tables and my uncle's hollering. From time to time, my grandmother's pockets still produced a magical chocolate bar, but it was rare.

Laura and I walked home together from school. Sometimes we played at her house before I continued the journey home. Her house was small but warm. There were no greasy smells or squawking chickens and no uncle yelling all the time. The radio played music. Her mom said it was Mozart. We played house and pretended to send Laura's dolls to school and teach them to read and multiply. We were nice to them like Mrs. Novák would have been. Laura said she was going to be a teacher, so it was good to practice. I told her I would be a doctor, like my mom. We set up a baby clinic and I pretended to listen to our dolls' coughs. We told the dolls to open their mouths and say ahh.

We made plans for the summer and beyond. We decided we would go on a boat to the Badacsony one day and eat in a real restaurant. She'd come with me to Pécs to visit my uncle's house. We would climb the hill to the TV tower and we'd eat cake in a coffee house. We would go to Budapest and climb the steps to the Fisherman's Bastion and cross the bridge from Buda to Pest. We'd go to Veszprém to visit my godparents and maybe even go to the university there. We didn't talk about America or the skyscrapers or the shops on the boulevards.

By the time I got home, it was dark. My grandmother waited for me under the dangling electric bulb. I got ready for bed. I watched the news with my aunt, and hoped she would not notice as I watched the movie on the channel from Vienna. The news one night showed a man with a pointy nose in a nice suit shaking hands with a man in China. I asked my aunt what it was about. She said it was the president of America meeting with the leader of China. That seemed like a nice thing. The president smiled.

"Maybe it's the start of something good," my aunt said. "They say Nixon may go to the Soviet Union next."

Zoli Bácsi said the people on the news were all idiots. So I didn't pay much attention. What good could possibly come of a handshake?

The movie that night gave me nightmares. It was about a boy who walked into a refrigerator, but the door closed on him and he couldn't get out. He ate all the food that was in there, then slowly started to freeze. He was trapped. There was no way out. I closed my eyes. I didn't want to see how this movie ended.

¤ ¤ ¤

On one especially windy night in January, I was sitting at my makeshift homework table in the kitchen, practicing my multiplication tables. The sevens were the hardest. Twos, and fives, and tens made sense. But there was no logic to sevens. So I memorized. Five times seven is thirty-five, six times seven is forty-two, seven times seven is forty-nine, eight times seven is . . . eight times seven . . . What is it? I always forgot that one. I walked over to the ceramic stove to warm my hands. It had been bitter cold all that day. The wind shook our schoolhouse all morning long and sleet bounced from rooftops as I trudged home. The wind was now rattling the windows of our house, drowning out the radio from my uncle's room. Csutak whimpered in his doghouse. My aunt put on a second sweater; my grandmother found her coat and put it on. Zoli Bácsi yelled for a third blanket to cover his dying legs.

Eight times seven . . . eight times seven is fifty-six. That's it. Nine times seven, that's easy: sixty-three, the year I was born. Ten times seven is seventy. Done! I was ready for the test. I put away my school supplies and finished my supper, licking the last bit of sugar from the bottom of the bowl of cream of wheat. My aunt filled the tin basin with ice-cold water from the well. Outside, the trees shivered. Rap rap rap went the branch against a frozen window. I splashed the water on my face and dreamed of the hot water pouring from the silver spout at my godmother's. I dipped a towel in the water and washed under my arms. Rap tap tap went the tree again.

"Don't forget the Nivea," my grandmother called from my uncle's room as she helped ready him for bed. My whole left arm was covered with a splotchy-red and flaky rash that itched. The more I scratched, the more it itched. I got into pajamas. Rap tap tap went the branch again, louder and more insistent. My grandmother came into the kitchen. "What's all that noise?" she asked.

"It's the tree," my aunt said. "The wind's been howling all day. It's going to be another expensive year for heat."

Rap rap tap tap went the window again. My grandmother looked at it. "That's not the wind," she said. "There's someone at the door." She shuffled to open it. A gust of wind slammed it against the porch wall. "Szilárd!" my grandmother said, taken aback. "What are you doing here at this hour?"

Szilárd's coat was drenched. The heat from the house fogged his glasses.

"Mamika, finally," he exhaled hard, sounding like he'd raced here all the way from Veszprém. "I thought you'd never open this door. I've been knocking forever. Does your doorbell not work?" He took off his glasses and wiped them with his sleeve.

"Probably not. But we hardly ever need it. Come in quick. The devil is lurking out there tonight."

He stepped into the hallway. Katus Néni took his coat and hung it to dry. "We were just about going to bed," she said. "What brings you here so late, and on such a horrible night?"

"You won't believe this, Mamika. Katus Néni . . . Juditka, where is she?" he was still breathing heavily.

"She's getting ready to go to sleep. Why? What's going on?" Katus Néni said.

"Szilárd, sit down. You are going to give yourself a heart attack. Let me get you some tea."

"No. No tea. I mean, please, you don't need to go through the trouble, Mamika. Then he smiled, a huge wide grin. "I got it," he said. "I got the papers."

"You mean . . . *Jaj Istenem*. My God." My grandmother clutched her heart.

"It's true," he said, holding up the documents. "I came as fast as I could—all the way from Budapest. I just jumped in the car —Mamika, go get her! You need to tell her."

"No, Szilárd. You should tell her. This was your hard work . . . Juditka!" she called.

Twenty-Two

Time to Pack

The noise brought Zoli Bácsi limping from his bathroom, his cane clomping against the linoleum floor.

"Zoli, you better sit down," said Katus Néni. "Szilárd has some news."

"So I figured," he said, pulling a chair up to the hallway heater and lowering himself down with a sigh. "I think I can guess."

"It took a lot of trips," Szilárd said. "Five trips at least to Budapest and each time those heartless bastards . . . well, it doesn't matter now. I've got the documents—stamped and official." He held up a stack of papers; Zoli Bácsi took them, put on his reading glasses, and inspected them.

"What do you know?" he finally said. He looked at Szilárd, then looked at me. "It looks like you're finally leaving us, kid."

Szilárd showed me the documents but it was too thick with tiny words. All I could make out was my name on a line among a bunch of other words. I knew I was supposed to be happy, maybe jump up and down, but I didn't know what to think or do. I thought of the globe on János Bácsi's bookshelf. Until then, the furthest I had traveled was Budapest and that took a couple of hours by car. How different that city was from everything I had known. And that was still within our country's dog-shaped orange territory. I thought of how far the ocean was from Hungary, how far New York was from there. The skyscrapers weren't a fun fantasy game anymore. They were real, terrifyingly real. If Budapest was so different, if Pécs and Veszprém were unlike anything in my little village, what would it be like to live among those giant, monstrous buildings?

I didn't say anything. I smiled. But behind that smile lay a heavy feeling like a lie.

"Szilárd, I don't know how to thank you," my grandmother said.

"I'm glad I was able to help. I tell you this. I wasn't very hopeful."

"So what was it in the end? What made them change their minds?"

"Who knows? Times are changing—hopefully for the better. But that politician from America was helpful in the end. Piroska contacted his office. It was he who reached out to the consul in Washington, who then got things rolling in Budapest. I think he shamed the Hungarians into letting her go. Maybe they figured that keeping a family separated was bad politics. In any case, this is a happy day, right Juditka?"

I smiled again.

"Now, here is the tricky part," he said, turning back to my grandmother. "Juditka actually has to leave the country by February 15th, so we don't have much time and there's a lot to do. I've been in touch with Piroska and László. We spoke by phone earlier today. So they know the date and everything."

I looked up. Did he say February 15th? That was three weeks away. Twenty-one days!

My grandmother had the same idea. "Why that hardly gives us any time!" she said. "There is so much to do. I must withdraw her from school and take her shopping. She'll need some better clothes to travel on a plane to America. And she'll need to see the doctor and the . . ."

"Don't worry, Mamika," Szilárd said. "She just needs to get on the plane and we'll take care of that. Zsuzsa and I will drive her to Budapest."

"Yes but . . ."

"You have done enough for her, Mamika. But there is something else you need to know," Szilárd added. "Juditka will be giving up her Hungarian citizenship as part of this deal—for good."

"That hardly seems like a high price," Zoli Bácsi said.

"It's something she needs to know," Szsilárd added. "Juditka, you understand?"

I didn't. But I did have some idea what it would mean to lose the only life I'd known, the only friends I had, the place that had somehow become my home for the last five years. But that was apparently not something we would talk about. Since I came to live with my grandmother, we had hoped and prayed that one day I might be leaving to rejoin my family. What I didn't know was how much leaving would hurt. I swallowed and smiled and told him yes, I understood.

"Well, I better get home and let you all get some sleep. Exciting days are ahead of us."

"Juditka," my grandmother said, "don't you have something to say to your godfather before he leaves?"

I left my grandmother's side and gave him a hug. "*Köszönöm, Keresztapu*," I said. He reached down and hugged me back. "I'll see you in a few weeks . . . Oh, and I almost forgot," he said calling behind him as he walked out the door. "Twenty kilograms is all she can take."

My godfather left into the dark and howling wind. Zoli Bácsi turned to hobble back to his room, but my grandmother stopped him. "Zoli," she said. "Thank you—for signing the papers."

"Eh," he said. "Teenagers are expensive—and irritating. Her father can worry about it now."

I tossed and turned in bed that night thinking about what it would be like to live with the lady whose hair was no longer brown but red, the lady smiling in front of the big color television set. If I couldn't think of what to say to her on the telephone, what would I talk about with her every day? What would I say to the man smiling in front of the Bronx Zoo, to the man with the mustache who I barely recognized? I left my bed and got into my grandmother's. When she got into bed later on with her black housedress still on, she didn't tell me to move. We just lay there, curled up together tightly against the freezing night, against what changes would come.

¤ ¤ ¤

There was much to do and little time. My grandmother decided I needed new clothes, new shoes, and most immediately, a visit to the dentist. My baby teeth had pretty much all been replaced by adult teeth and all seemed fine until a few months ago, when I stopped being able to chew food on the right side of my mouth.

I switched to the left, but the pain on the right only grew worse. My grandmother said we should look into it before I went to America. I'd never met a dentist before. I didn't know there was such a thing. He had a nice clean office where several people waited, holding wet rags to their mouths; some were moaning. When it was my turn, he sat me in a big chair and told me to open my mouth.

"So, you are the little girl who is going to America?" he asked.

"Aha," I nodded.

"Your grandmother says your parents are in New York."

"Aha."

"Well, let's see what we have here." He tapped on my tooth with a silver spoon. I winced in pain. "Hmm," he said loud and slow. "Do you eat much candy, Juditka?"

"Aha." I nodded for the third time. If I could have talked, I would have told him how wonderful my grandmother's candies tasted at bedtime and how much I loved the chocolate bars from her magic pockets.

"Do you brush your teeth?"

I didn't say anything. I looked to my grandmother for an answer but she just looked at the ground. I did remember Enikő's toothbrush and how she taught me to use it. But I never had one at my grandmother's house. I shook my head no.

"All right. You can close your mouth . . . You say she is going to America in three weeks?" he said, turning to my grandmother.

"Yes. It's happening so fast. We have so much to do I can barely think."

"Well, this is what I think, Mamika. I think they have good dentists and dental instruments in America. Some of those permanent teeth will need to be removed. They are rotten beyond repair. But I think they should do it there—in America."

"I see," my grandmother said, growing more worried as we got up to leave.

"Oh, Mamika . . ." the dentist added. "Don't give her candy before bed anymore."

She nodded. We thanked the dentist and walked out. On the way home, I held her hand. I was ten years old and taller than she was. Her apricot hands felt soft and warm. "I liked the candy, Mamika," I told her. "And the chocolates too."

Next, I needed a new outfit for the airplane. My grandmother said she wanted me dressed nicely for the trip. So we got on the train. Instead of the orphanage, we went to a real store. My grandmother told the clerk to find me red stockings, red shoes, and a red hat—all to match the red coat that my mother had sent from America the previous winter.

"But Mamika, I'm going to look like Little Red Riding Hood!" I frowned. I wanted to look grown-up and stylish, not like a story-book character.

"You've changed a lot," she said. "How will your family recognize you at the airport?"

"All red?" the clerk at the counter said. She had her hair pinned in a gray bun and wore a blue canvas jacket like our school uniforms. "She must be getting ready to be a Young Pioneer."

"In a way," my grandmother said.

¤ ¤ ¤

News of my leaving spread quickly through the village. Neighbors and friends dropped in. "How did this happen?" they wanted to know. "What did you have to do?"

"It was not easy," Zoli Bácsi told them. "We had to write a lot of letters." My grandmother rolled her eyes.

Mrs. Novák stopped by. "So Zoli Bácsi did the right thing in the end?"

"He signed the papers, yes."

"Maybe under those wheezy lungs of his, there is a heart after all."

"Maybe a tiny one," my grandmother said, rolling her eyes again.

"And you, Mamika. How are you holding up?"

"It won't be easy," she said. "It never is."

"This will be hardest for you." She bent down and hugged her stooped figure and held her for a few minutes.

"Thank you."

"Juditka," she said, turning to me, her eyes shining with tears. "Promise to be a good student, a good girl. Don't forget us and write us from time to time."

☒ ☒ ☒

Ildikó came home to say goodbye. She looked so beautiful with her long brown hair, her eyebrows in perfect arcs, her eyelids painted shimmery blue, her long nails perfectly polished. She held a Hungarian-English dictionary. "This is for you," she said. "I think it will come in handy, especially since you're traveling alone."

I thought a lot about what it would be like to leave home and live in a new place with people I hardly knew. The one thing I never thought about was how I'd speak. In all this time, I didn't learn a word of English.

"Wanna learn a few words now?" Ildikó said, holding out the book. "It might help you to know at least a few." She was taking German lessons at her new school so she could speak more easily with the tourists who'd be her clients in the summer. German was not that different from English, she said, so she knew a few words. We sat down on the bed and opened the book. "The first word you should know is hello." She opened the book to the H section and showed me the word.

"Like we say on the telephone? That's easy. *Halo,*" I said.

"It's a little different. Try again. Hello, with an e not a."

"Hello," I repeated, stressing the e.

"Great. Now say, 'How are you?' It means *hogy vagy.*"

"Why is that important to know?"

"It's an American custom. You don't just say hello to greet people. You say, 'Hello, how are you?'"

"What if they start telling me how they are and I won't understand them?"

"They won't. It's just a greeting."

"That seems silly."

"Yeah. But I've heard it's how they do it," she shrugged.

¤ ¤ ¤

In school, my friends wanted me to teach them English. "How do you say *köszönöm?*" Laura asked.

"Thank you," I said, remembering Ildiko's lessons. "First you have to make this sound . . . th," I showed her the way Ildikó taught me. "No, no. You need to press your tongue against your teeth like this. Thhh."

"How do you say *repülő?*" Péter wanted to know.

"I know that one. Airplane."

We were too old to pretend we were piloting silver jets and driving Fords across the schoolyard. Instead, we huddled in a corner of the classroom and talked about the buildings that touch the sky.

"They are building two in New York that will be the tallest in the world," I told my friends. "Each will have 110 floors and a restaurant that revolves so you can see the whole city!"

"You are lucky," Péter said.

"Maybe I'll come in a few years and we'll get married," András said.

"Wouldn't you like that?" I blushed.

I walked home with Laura on my last day of school. "How you do say *szia?*" she asked when we parted.

"Goodbye." I said. Or you can say, 'See ya.'" We laughed and hugged for a long time.

"Better write me," she said.

"I promise."

¤ ¤ ¤

My godfather made one last visit to our village before our final departure. He brought more than a briefcase of documents this time. He was carrying a big box. Inside were two rolled up oil paintings, several books, a porcelain tea set, and the biggest item of all: a two-foot sculpture of a woman wearing a fancy dress. Her head, with hair parted in the middle and set in old-fashioned curls, peeked out of the box. He found me sitting on the floor of the heated bedroom surrounded by clothes, books, toys, dolls—all the things I was trying to stuff in the one suitcase I'd be allowed to take. He shook his head. "We might have to rethink this, Juditka," he said, placing his box down next to me.

"I was able to talk to your parents again by phone," he said. "These are some of the things they left behind when they left. When you were little. They couldn't take anything with them back then so they want *you* to take these things—to America."

"Why couldn't they?"

"Why couldn't they what?"

"Take things with them?"

"Well, one day you will learn the whole story, Juditka, but they were just going on a vacation then. At least that's what they told everyone. You don't take paintings and sculptures with you when you're going on a vacation."

I thought back to that time. It all seemed so blurry in my memory already, the vacation to Vienna. How long we waited for them to come home.

"Why these things? Why a tea set? Don't they have everything in America?" It seemed a curious thing to carry across the ocean.

"That's true," my godfather said. "But these things are special. They are hard to replace and hard to find new."

My grandmother came in the room and looked at the box on the floor. "*Jaj, Szilárd!*" she said, her hand over her mouth, a worried look on her face. "How are we going to fit all this? That statue alone weighs five kilograms! And we'll have to wrap it up well, which will add another two."

Szilárd shrugged. "It's the *Déri Né*, Mamika. It was at Zsuzsa's father's house. They were able to save a few special items after the police raided the apartment in Mohács."

I recognized the statue. It was a singer made of the special Hungarian Herend porcelain; it sat on the piano in our home in Mohács on a white lace doily. She had a delicate blushing face, tight ringlets of porcelain hair, and a wide ruffled skirt. She held a guitar in her buttercup hands, and her painted lips were parted mid-song. She was a famous singer, I remember my mother once telling me, an opera singer with a beautiful voice.

I stared at the woman, the paintings, the books, the tea set with delicate painted butterflies. There was so much I wanted to take: my clothes, *Grimm's Fairy Tales*, *One Thousand and One Nights*, Zsuzsi Baba. How in the world could I fit five years into one suitcase? And now this?

Szilárd read my mind.

"Juditka," he said, wiping his glasses with his shirtsleeve, and sitting down on the floor next to me. "Don't worry about these clothes. You will have much nicer ones in America. Your parents will take you shopping, and they will buy you everything new, including a new doll." He took Zsuzsi Baba, with her dirty face and hands, and set her aside on the floor. "But do take your books. They don't have these in America, at least not in Hungarian. And take these others." He handed me a stack of books: József Attila, Ady Endre, Petőfi Sándor, Madács Imre. "You can't buy these in America. They are part of what makes our country special." Then he turned to my grandmother. "Mamika, let's get these packed in there somehow. It will make Laci and Piroska happy."

My grandmother got Katus Néni to bring in some newspaper and the two of them began to carefully wrap the statue, the books, and the teacups, sheltering each delicate piece to withstand the journey.

As my suitcase filled up with all the things my parents wanted me to bring to America, I began to worry. What if they turned me back at the airport because I overpacked? What if I lose all this stuff? What if the statue breaks? Or the teacups shatter? Will my father call me a stupid child and send me back to Hungary? What if all they ever wanted was this stuff?

I walked away and let them finish packing. I picked up Zsuzsi Baba, and took her behind the house to the summer room I shared with Ildikó. It was cold in there. I could see my own breath. I found a clean rag and rubbed Zsuzsi Baba's cheeks. I scrubbed until I could see the pink in her cheeks and the red in her lips. I cleaned her ears, her neck, and her hands until they were almost the peach color of her tummy. I found her old navy-blue dress with the while collar and put it on her. I'd lost her shoes long ago, so she had to go barefoot, but I untangled her hair and tied it with a red bow. I kissed her cheek and set her on the bed. If I had been little, I would have told her not to worry, that my grandmother would take good care of her. But I was too old for dolls now. So, I left her there propped against the pillow with her bare legs sticking out, and went back to my aunt and grandmother to finish packing.

¤ ¤ ¤

"Let's weigh it," Szilárd said. Katus Néni left to find a scale. Szilárd placed the bag on it. It came in at just under twenty kilograms. But we weighed it three times to make sure. "Perfect," Szilárd finally pronounced. That made all of us feel a little better.

"All right, then. I will be back tomorrow to pick you up, Juditka. Then it's off to the big city, and then America."

¤ ¤ ¤

Trying to fall asleep, I listened to the oak tree and my grandmother's whispers from the kitchen. It would be my last night in this leaky old house with its peeling paint and frayed electrical wires, its cracked walls and muddy yard, its plum trees and willow trees, its well and coal shed, its wildflowers and strawberries. Would I ever see the Balaton's blue waters again? The sailboats? My grandmother's old hands?

When she finally came into our room, I got out of my bed and curled up next to her. I wanted nothing more than to stay there forever, to breathe the smell of her—of musty bread and apricot brandy. I wanted to nestle into her downy hair, to crawl into the pockets of her dress.

"Mamika," I whispered. "Come with me to America. We will have a nice house with heat and water and a big bed to sleep in."

"I am too old, Juditka," she sighed.

"I can take care of you. Anyuka too."

"You have to go to school," she said. "Learn English. Make friends. And your mother needs to work. But I will dream of you, and you can dream of me. We'll be together in our dreams."

"No, Mamika. Not our dreams. In real life." I sat up in the bed. It was cold and dark in the room. Katus Néni was snoring already. "Come with me, really. You'll never have to empty Zoli Bácsi's stinky bedpan."

"I am so old, Juditka. I can't get used to a place that's so different anymore. My place is here." I felt her hand on my forehead as she brushed the hair from my face. "But you, you're young. You have your whole life ahead of you."

"I can't do it without you."

"Yes you can."

"We can get on the phone with Anyuka tomorrow and ask her to tell that man that we both have to go. He can help us. Szilárd can make the call."

"Juditka, you know I can't."

"They will let you go. Just like they let me go."

"You know that's not so easy."

"If you don't come, I won't go."

"You will go," she said. "You will have such a beautiful life . . ." She sighed deeply and closed her eyes. "Now go to sleep, Juditka. I am tired and tomorrow's a big day."

I couldn't sleep. If she couldn't come with me, then I wasn't going either. I would get up before dawn, and run away. I'd climb the oak tree and hide in the tree house. I'd run into the field behind the house and follow the train tracks far away. I'd crawl into the woodshed and hide inside my cardboard box; I'd run to Laura's house and hide in her outhouse. Then after my godfather left, I'd come out and come back home. I could stay with my grandmother forever. And if Zoli Bácsi didn't want us, we could find a little house all our own, and live there together like Laura and her mother. We could get a radio and play Mozart. I could read books to her at night. I was big now. I could help her with all her chores. I'd go to school and get good grades and be a doctor like my mother and take care of her forever.

With my plan figured out, I finally fell asleep. But by the time I woke up, it was bright and sunny out, and my grandmother was waiting for me with hot cream of wheat on my little worktable in the hallway. The room was warm. My aunt was up and busy in the kitchen, putting dishes away. Even Zoli Bácsi was awake in his bathroom, reading the newspaper with the radio on. It was too late to hide.

I sat down at my table, but pushed away the steaming bowl. I didn't want to eat. I tried to say something, but the words twisted in my mouth and refused to come out right. I could barely breathe. A giant lump gripped my throat. I swallowed hard. I felt pain, like someone squeezing my throat hard. My hand ached. My pinky finger felt like it was going to fall off.

"I can't go, Mamika," I blurted out. "I won't go without you." She was dragging my suitcase from the bedroom, but now left it by the front door and sat on the steps leading to the parlor. Her long black dress covered her sneakers with holes in them.

"You know I can't, Juditka. We talked about this yesterday."

"I'll run away, then. I'll hide."

"Now why would you do something like that? After all the waiting . . ."

"I don't know. But I'm not going without you."

"Juditka . . ."

"I'm not going," I shouted. "I'll kill myself. I'll take a knife and . . ."

"Juditka!" she said sharply, raising her voice like the time I threw my mother's boots across the floor. I took a deep breath, but my heart raced and felt like it would burst.

"You have to come with me, Mamika," I tried pleading again. "I can't go without you. I just can't."

She sat there without a word as I collapsed heaving into her lap, crying so hard I drenched her black dress. She put her arms around me and held me close until I could breathe normally again.

"Juditka," she finally said. "You have so many good things waiting for you. A whole new life. A good life. You have no idea yet, but I know."

Outside, the bare arms of the birch tree reached for the February sky. The clouds moved on. The wind settled down. "You are going to your mother. She is waiting for you. Your whole family is."

Twenty-Three

America

The flight attendant aboard the Malév plane hung a sign around my neck. "Boros Judit" it said in big black letters. I didn't need a sign to know my name, but I guessed she did. She wore a red-green-and-white kerchief around her neck, our country's colors, and her hair was pinned back in a bun. She had the stern look of one of my kindergarten teachers as she walked me down the narrow aisle and pointed to my seat.

"Sit here," she said, "and don't get up until I tell you." I didn't need her to tell me that either. I was too scared to move a muscle, especially once the plane started to lift off into the winter sky. I sat rigid in my seat, afraid that even the slightest movement left or right would cause the plane to go crashing down. I looked out the window and saw my country grow dim as we flew higher and higher into the clouds. I looked for the Balaton and its volcanic mountains, and wondered what my grandmother was doing at this moment. Was she fetching coal from the shed? Getting supper ready for my uncle? How small she felt in my arms when we finally said goodbye. She wiped the tears from her eyes but they wouldn't stop coming. "When you see your mother," she said, "tell her we love and miss her."

"I will," I managed to stammer. "I will write you every day, Mamika. I will send you pictures and presents and I will come back. I promise."

My godfather arrived earlier that day to pick me up and take me to the airport in Budapest. My godmother and Enikő were both there. After the bag was weighed one more time and the documents were checked again for signatures, the whole family went outside to see me off. Even a few neighbors stopped by.

"Lucky girl," one said.

"Give your mother a kiss for us," said my aunt, wiping her eyes with a corner of her apron.

"Send us some blue jeans," Ildikó said, kissing me on each cheek. "Better yet, I'll come visit you and we can go shopping for them in New York."

From the back window of the car, I watched them grow smaller as the car pulled away from Vilma Utca 50. "Don't cry Juditka," said Enikő, holding on to my Barbie. I gave it to her to keep. "Maybe you'll be back one day. Or we can come see you."

I was terrified the next day when we arrived at the Budapest airport, which was surrounded by a fence and guarded by men in green uniforms armed with guns. One of them stood guard at the entrance. Szilárd rolled down his window.

"Papers please," the guard said.

Szilárd took out the stamped visa with my picture on it. "We are here to drop off the child," he said. "She is going to America." He smiled. My godfather seemed to take some pleasure in saying those words.

The guard smirked, then turned his attention to Enikő and me in the back seat. "Which one?"

"The one dressed in red," Szilárd said, pointing to me. I was wearing the airport outfit my grandmother assembled for me: red shoes, red stockings, red dress, red coat, and a small carry-on red suitcase Zsuzsa had given me that morning—

also red. As the guard with the gun looked me up and down, I started to get hot under all that red.

The soldier looked at the documents, looked at me, looked at the documents again, then waved us on. "All right," he said. "You may go."

Inside, there were more soldiers. We dragged my suitcase to the counter, where more soldiers greeted us.

"Papers please," one of them repeated.

Szilárd handed this one the papers too. The man scrutinized each document carefully, then motioned to another soldier to come over. "Put the bag on the scale please," said the man. My godfather lifted my suitcase and put it on the counter. We had weighed it five more times to make sure it was not a gram over twenty kilograms. After everything we went through, after five years of waiting, he didn't want anyone to have an excuse to stop me from getting on that airplane to America, he told me.

But as Szilárd hoisted the suitcase on to the counter, I was worried. Would they have a problem with the things inside the suitcase? By the looks on my godfather's face, there was reason to worry.

"We're going to have to inspect it," said the man behind the counter. A soldier took the suitcase and began walking toward a large, windowless room. "Follow me," he said.

We did as he said, following the soldier into a room lit by harsh white neon lights, leaving my godmother and Enikő behind. Inside the room, we watched nervously as he and another man in uniform unpacked each and every item from the suitcase, unwrapping the Déri Né, the oil paintings, the books of poetry, and the delicate teacups, which my aunt spent a lot of time carefully folding in newsprint. One of the soldiers held up a pink-and-white teacup. "You'd think they could find teacups in America," he said, laughing.

Now I was really hot. I started sweating and my mouth went dry. What if there were rules against taking the porcelain lady or the paintings? Surely there was some rule. There was always a rule. As they examined each item, a small part of me was almost relieved. Maybe they won't let me go after all and I can just go back to my grandmother, my friends, my village. Go back and forget this new life with people I didn't even know. How easy it would be!

"Do you have papers for these?" one of the men finally said, turning to my godfather. "These could be considered . . . how should I put it . . . national treasure."

"Yes, of course. We have permission for everything in there," Szilárd said, relieved that the man with the gun asked a question to which he had a ready answer. He handed a bunch of papers to the man, who inspected these as well, reading each document carefully, slowly. Finally, he looked up.

"All right," the soldier said. "It seems to be in order. You can wrap this back up. She's good to go." He turned to me, slung the gun on his back and winked. "Good luck in America. I hear it's nice there."

Szilárd turned around to look at me. He smiled a huge smile and let out a long sigh. "It looks like we did it, Juditka."

Back in the main terminal, I hugged my godparents goodbye.

"Don't forget us," Szilárd said. "And write us sometime." I reached up to hug him around the neck and gave him two kisses.

"Take care of Barbie," I said to Enikő and gave her a hug.

My godmother was crying and laughing at the same time, wiping the tears from her eyes. "We are so happy for you, Juditka," she said. "Tell your mother we love her." I put two kisses on her wet cheeks and waved goodbye as I went through the gate leading to the plane.

¤ ¤ ¤

From up in the sky, the Balaton was nowhere to be found. All I could see were the fallow fields of the Hungarian plains. It took almost no time for the plane to slip above the clouds, and in a moment, Hungary was gone.

Before long the flight attendant was back. "We will be landing in Amsterdam soon," she said. "I will walk you into the airport. The flight attendant from the next plane will come and get you when it's time to board the next plane."

"The next plane?"

"Yes. We only go as far as Amsterdam."

"Oh."

"You just stay where I put you and there won't be any trouble."

I nodded. The last thing I wanted was trouble. But why didn't anyone mention that I'd be taking two planes?

When the Hungarian plane landed in Amsterdam, I followed the flight attendant, sticking close to her starched black skirt as she hurried off the plane and into the huge, noisy, light-filled terminal. There were signs with letters I recognized. But none of the words made any sense. "Sit down in this chair and don't move until the KLM flight attendant comes for you," she said. "Oh, and don't forget this." She handed me a manila envelope with the words "Passenger Traveling Alone." I could read it, but did not understand these words either. I sat in the blue plastic chair, gripping my little red suitcase. Around me, people hurried back and forth. Neon signs announced glowing shops selling handsome leather bags, shirts in a million colors, chocolates, and perfume. How nice it would be to be able to walk into one of those and bring a present to my mother, I thought. Or to look around the many little restaurants selling tea and cakes. Even in Budapest I never saw so much glitter and color, so much yummy food. But I was supposed to sit on the chair, and I did.

I sat and waited and waited and waited for what seemed like hours. In front of me I could see a huge sign with blue letters saying KLM. The attendant behind its counter was busy talking to other passengers. Where was the flight attendant who was supposed to come?

The overhead speaker screeched the names of cities, some of which I knew and some that I didn't. London, Paris, Vienna . . . I could not make out the rest of the words. I imagined what it would be like to get on a different plane like we did in the school playground and simply fly to Paris or London to see the London Bridge or the Eiffel Tower.

I sat and waited more. My stomach growled and now I had to go to the bathroom. Was there even a bathroom here? I looked around. What would it look like? Off in a corner I saw a blue door with a lady on it. Next to it was the same door with the picture of a man. I could just run in there, I thought, but then the flight attendant might come and miss me, and leave without me, and the plane would leave without me and then all this waiting, these five years, would have been for nothing. I'd be left here under a sign that read *Schiphol Nederlandse*. I had no money, only a manila envelope. Out of boredom, I opened the envelope. There was small paper booklet in Hungarian, my birth certificate, testifying that I was a whole person with two parents born in Mohács to Dr. Boros Lászlo and Dr. Fördös Piroska. There was a letter marked KLM in the corner with words in English I could not read and my godfather's name and signature. And there was a booklet, a visa with my picture. It was not the picture that was taken in my little red fish dress the summer that my parents left. It was a school picture from the fourth grade. Little did I know that the picture would end up here, on this stamped document. I put it all back and smoothed the cover to make it seem like it was unopened, and kept waiting.

The loudspeaker screeched again. New York, New York, it squawked this time, followed by words I didn't recognize. That's me, I thought. I'm New York. Where is the flight attendant? Will she never come? The plane was leaving but I was instructed to stay and not move so I didn't move. I didn't know where to go, or whom to see. I stayed glued to the plastic chair, desperate for a bathroom and petrified that I'd be left behind forever—this time with no money, no food, no grandmother—with nothing but a name tag around my neck. I felt like I was going to cry and pee my pants at the same time.

After almost two hours, a smiling young woman with a perky hat finally found me. "Judit!" she said, as if she'd been running and was out of breath. She said a lot of other words too, but I didn't understand any of them. She gestured for me to follow and I did, relieved for permission to leave the plastic chair. We hurried through the crowds and a long dark tunnel that ended at the entrance to an enormous airplane with three columns of plush seats. All the other passengers were already on board. I was the last one. She smiled, pointed to a seat, and handed me a metal pin shaped like wings. She pinned it on my red jacket and buckled the seatbelt. "I'll be back," she said, and left.

I sat back in the comfortable blue chair and played with the buttons to make the chair go backward and forward, twisting the dial to allow the plastic tray to fall with a plop. I put it back, closed my eyes, and tried to relax as we waited for the plane to take off. This would be the plane to cross the ocean, I thought. How it would do that, by magic or science, I didn't know. Nor did I want to. It was easier to just pretend we were flying in the schoolyard. Soon though, we were up in the sky and above a vast body of water that must have been the ocean. And from here, I knew, there was no going back. All that was ahead was a strange new land and people whom I no longer knew.

"Would you like some crayons?" The young woman was back holding a kit filled with beautiful colorful crayons and a coloring book. I'd never seen anything like it. The booklet was filled with children traveling on planes to distant cities, and I could color them however I wished. She smiled and put the

251

coloring book on my tray and added to it other things, like a piece of cardboard covered in gray film that you could draw on with a plastic pen, and then erase. Magic Slate, it said on the top.

"Thank you," I said, pressing my tongue against my teeth, trying to remember how Ildikó taught me to say the words, my first English words. She took the red marker and showed me how it worked. "You can draw anything you want on the slate, and then erase it," she said, "like this." She drew a pretty tulip and a sun. She then lifted the gray film, and the drawing was gone, like magic. I smiled up at her face. She had a sparkling smile, big green eyes, pink cheeks and smooth black hair under her cheerful blue cap. How fun it would be to be to have her job, I thought. You get to dress up all pretty, put on makeup to make your lips shine like that, and travel to all kinds of fun places.

I played with the crayons then remembered I still hadn't gone to the bathroom. I looked around for the flight attendant, but she was gone. Around me were strangers who spoke in languages I couldn't understand. I didn't know how to ask them for help. But I couldn't wait any more. I unbuckled the seat and ventured to the back of the plane in search of a bathroom. I found a door with the image of a toilet. I pushed the door open. What magic this was! Somehow, they fit every convenience into this tiny space, down to a soft white tissue paper dispenser. If KLM only knew what we would have done for such tissues in our village school. They even figured out how to make a toilet flush in the sky! I sat down on the tiny white contraption and looked around at all the buttons. I wanted to try everything. I turned on the sink and mixed hot water with cold; I tried the soap dispenser and worked up a lather. I bathed my hands in the warm water. I took the tissue paper and filled up my pockets with it, just in case. I looked in the mirror. Before me I saw a girl I barely recognized. Did I really look like that? My red clothes had somehow tinted my entire face. My cheeks, my nose, even my eyes seemed red. I worried if this too would cause a problem. I put the thought out of my head and turned to leave the enchanted bathroom.

I pushed down on the doorknob to leave, but nothing happened. I pushed again, harder this time. Still nothing. I stood back, trying to study the situation. It was a small door, metal. Maybe I had to push ever harder. I shoved it hard with my shoulder. Nothing. My heart raced. I looked at the knob again. It was round, different than doorknobs in Hungary. How did it work? I tried prying it up and down again, then pushed it to the left and to the right. Panicked, I began to knock on the door. But no one came. Where was that friendly flight attendant with the perky hat? I imagined the plane crossing the Atlantic Ocean and landing in New York while I was stuck in the bathroom. I imagined it taking off again to its next destination. Maybe it would fly to Brazil, where they would finally find me, and not knowing what else to do, stick me in a home for abandoned children. I banged on the door even harder. I would have yelled, but didn't know what words to yell. I wished my cousin had taught me the word for help.

Suddenly, after what felt like a long time, the door fell open and I tumbled into the plane's kitchen. Relieved, I found my seat and tried to calm down. I'd have a lot to learn in America, I thought, starting with how to open a door.

The flight attendant came over to offer me some dinner. She handed me a tray of food covered in foil.

"*Köszönöm*," I told her, forgetting the word for thank you.

"You're welcome," she said sweetly. She even spoke Hungarian?

I couldn't wait to see what was inside the tidy box. I was famished. But when she pulled back the foil, the smell of meat and green beans almost made me gag.

"It's just airplane food," the lady across the aisle said, speaking in Hungarian. "It's always bad. The food in America is much better."

She was older, but looked elegant with brown hair and pearls. She wore a soft blue cardigan and had several interesting rings on her fingers.

"Are you traveling alone?" she asked.

"*Igen*," I said. Yes.

"Where are your parents?"

"In America," I said, straightening in my seat a little. It felt good to say those words; like getting a good grade on a test.

"Oh? They let you travel alone?"

"It's my first time going there. I mean, they live there already, but *I've* never been there."

"Wow. That sounds like a story. How long have your parents lived in America?"

I had to think for a minute. How long was it? "Five years," I finally said.

"Oh my goodness! That's a long time. Is this the first time you are seeing them in all those years?"

"Yes." I wasn't sure if it was alright to tell her these things, or how much more I could or should say. I took a bite of the meat and took a sip of the bubbly dark water that the flight attendant left next to the food tray.

"That's Coca-Cola," the woman said. "Tastes good, doesn't it?"

I made a sour face.

"Everything will be very new for you," she said. "Don't worry. You will figure it all out."

The flight attendant came back down the aisle to collect the small trays, and threw them in garbage bags. I thought about holding onto the plastic fork and knife. They'd make fun toys if I ever had an American doll. But I changed my mind when I saw the lady throw hers in the trash.

The lights were turned low and people around me reclined their seats and prepared to go to sleep. The plane was dark now, and I looked out the window at the empty darkening sky. A few stars flickered from far away. I closed my eyes and thought of my grandmother sleeping in her bed, the full moon shining brightly on the rooftop of the yellow house. She'd be waking soon, getting ready to light the fire in the stove or pull water from the well or empty my uncle's bedpan. Maybe her burden would be a little lighter today.

Hours must have passed by the time I woke up. The sky outside was still dark, but the plane was now so brightly lit that it felt like the middle of the day. Someone was talking to all the passengers. Where the voice came from, I didn't know, and though I had no idea what he said, it felt like the person was telling us to prepare to land. The lady next to me began to pack her things. Others were doing the same. I put the coloring book, the crayons, and the Magic Slate in the little red carry-on suitcase my godmother had given me, clasped it shut, and put my red coat around my shoulders, just like the lady next to me. I felt the plane descend, but instead of slowing, it felt like we were suddenly going much faster than before. Freezing raindrops hit the window, making popping sounds. Outside all I could see were black clouds and fog, and I wondered how the pilot would find the airport. I grabbed the armrest and held on as the plane shook, wobbled, dipped, then flew up again. My face must have turned white because the lady was smiling again. "It's normal; don't worry," she said. "We'll be on the ground in a minute. Just close your eyes."

She must have been right, because no one else was panicking like me. They all sat in their seats cool and unruffled. Only I was terrified, my heart pounding as loud as the engine outside the window. In a moment the plane hit the ground with a loud thud, and the passengers erupted in applause. The lady smiled. "See, nothing to worry about."

Everyone stood up to gather the things they stored in the overhead compartments. The lady put on her coat and wrapped a warm shawl around her neck. "Your parents will be so happy to see you," she smiled. "Good luck."

Not sure if I should follow her or the others, I remained in my seat and waited for the flight attendant to come back. I worried that she'd forgotten about me again, but she didn't. There she was, with her perky blue hat and silk scarf and a pile of documents in her hand. "Ready?" she said. "Let's go find your family."

¤ ¤ ¤

I followed her off the plane and into what looked like a windowless corridor. A blast of cold air whipped through my coat as I clutched my little red suitcase and made my way down the jet bridge into the airport terminal. Nothing could have prepared me for what was on the other side.

We exited into a huge, brightly lit white room filled with more people than I'd seen in my entire life. They were pushing and shoving, lugging heavy suitcases, and babbling in a hundred different tongues. They were white and brown with blonde hair and red hair and black hair, big and little, skinny and fat. I couldn't help but stare. I'd never seen so many kinds of people. Signs in what must have been English pointed this way and that. We followed one with a picture of a suitcase. A herd of people was doing the same. Before long, we reached our destination: a machine like a serpent spitting out luggage, then in quick order, swallowing them up again. I figured out what to do, and grabbed my suitcase from the mouth of the beast. I wasn't going to let that snake take all the things we packed.

From this chaos, lines started forming again and the flight attendant motioned for me to get in one of them alongside her. "We have to go through customs next," she said.

The lines led to uniformed men inside cages, dozens of them. They had no guns, but looked just as scary as the soldiers at the Budapest airport. They looked stern with bushy eyebrows and distrustful eyes. What would they think of me? Would they find me wanting and stamp my papers rejected?

We inched our way slowly to the head of the line and handed one of the guards my documents. He examined the black-and-white photo on my visa closely, then looked at me and my red jacket, hat, shoes, and bag. I was trembling inside those red shoes. I looked at the guard nervously, avoiding his big brown eyes, and suddenly felt so stupid dressed up like Little Red Riding Hood. Then, just as I thought the man was going to reject me for looking so silly, he smiled at me. "Someone is meant to notice you," he said. Then with a loud thunk, he put his stamp on my visa. "Welcome to America."

My companion smiled. "There," she said, "that wasn't bad at all." She squeezed my hand and led me into an adjoining room. This too was brightly lit and cavernous, but without all the people. In fact, it was almost empty. A group here and there was waiting. A man found a woman with three children and they hugged. Enormous banners hung from the ceiling with words I did not understand. We walked in what seemed like circles. "They must be here somewhere," the flight attendant said, surveying the large room. A worried look replaced her cheery smile.

I tightened my grip around her hand. I didn't want her to let go. I was getting hot under my red coat and hat and sweating through the tight red shirt my grandmother made me wear. My throat hurt, my nose was running, and I had the worst stomachache. I wiped my nose on my red jacket sleeve, leaving a stain. Maybe we won't find them, I thought. Then I could say at least I tried, and then turn right around, get back on the next plane bound for Amsterdam, or London or Budapest and go home. My grandmother would be waiting for me. She'd give me a chocolate bar, and let me sleep next to her. I'd go back to the village school, and tell my friends about the plane ride across the Atlantic Ocean. I'd tell them about the tiny bathroom and the soft tissues and the toilet that flushes in the sky. I'd tell them about the tiny plastic trays of food and the crayons and the Magic Slate. We could pretend to fly around the schoolyard or drive our fancy cars.

Then from far away I heard a man's voice. It was Hungarian, crisp and clear and very deep. "*Látom! Ott van! Ott van a Judit!* I see her. There! There she is." I followed the sound with my eyes and there, about twenty feet away, I saw for the first time in five years, my family. They were huddled in a circle, an island in the sea of white in the vast room, small and alone. My brother was first to spot me, and I saw him break away from their circle and start walking toward us. I recognized his big bushy hair and mustache from the photo taken at the Bronx Zoo. He was tall, commanding, and confident as he motioned to my mother and father to follow him. He brushed the top of my head when he reached me and turned to the flight attendant to shake her hand. "Thank you" he said. "Thank you very much."

My father came up behind him, laughing and crying. Only he looked unchanged from five years ago, wearing a suit jacket over a collared shirt and tie, still handsome with his dark, curly hair, neatly brushed back. "*Na, Judit,*" he said. "*Mijen nagy lány lettél?* What a big girl you've become." He squeezed me, holding me so close I could feel his scratchy chin against my face, and smell his breath on my neck. His smell awoke an old memory that now flooded my senses: aftershave mixed with garlic, onion, maybe even sausage.

It was a smell that could only be my father and no one else, a thing I knew like I knew my own breath or the beating of my own heart. He kissed me on both cheeks, then bit my nose so hard, his teeth left marks. I didn't know how to respond, or what to say. I just rubbed my nose.

"I think we've found the right people," the flight attendant smiled.

Finally, there she was, my mother, small and frail, in a brown wool coat, waiting at my father's heels, her eyes wet and shining. I could see how she had changed: her hair was different, as I had seen in pictures she'd sent, reddish instead of chestnut brown. She seemed older too, and tired. "Juditka," she cried, circling me inside her arms gently. "I can't believe it. I can't believe it's you," she kept saying over and over. I was as tall as she. Her hands were smaller than mine and delicate, like the porcelain teacups in my suitcase; she smelled like the Nivea my grandmother rubbed on my dry skin back home.

I smiled nervously but could not think of a thing to say. We stayed there in that big empty room for a few more minutes as the overhead speakers blared, as the neon lights buzzed, as people in a hurry came and went dragging big suitcases, the five of us, including the flight attendant, crying, laughing, and hugging. "Well, I think I better get going," the young woman finally said. "You all seem pretty good to me." She left the documents with my brother and headed back toward customs.

My father turned to my brother. "We better start heading back. The parking lot is going to cost more than $5. Take her bag, Tibi. Let's go." He took hold of my hand then, and started pulling me toward the exit signs. "Wait until you see the new car," he said, "It's huge. And the highways and the tall buildings. You're not in Balaton Mária Fürdő anymore."

We went through a set of spinning doors; the blast of cold air on the other side made me gasp. My red coat was unzipped, and much too thin for this weather. I pulled it tight around me with one hand while trying to hold on to my father, who was now walking fast and pulling me along. Tibor was carrying my suitcase, hurrying to keep up. I looked back to see my mother limping and falling further and further behind. My father didn't seem to notice. He was talking a mile a minute, but I couldn't hear a word above the roar of the jet planes, the cars, the taxis honking in line, and the police officers shouting. I wanted to wait for her and hold her hand. But I couldn't seem to free myself from my father's grip.

It was nighttime, but the sky was lit by buzzing bright white lights from above. Everything seemed a dull gray: the buildings, the sidewalk, the roads, the cars covered in gray film, the snow. Where were the stars? After some time, we found the car in a building filled with thousands of others. Our schoolyard games came true! Here were more cars than I thought existed in the world. Somehow my father knew how to find ours. And he was right; our car was the biggest car I'd ever seen—a huge green machine with big comfy seats in the front and back, a dashboard lit up with three big dials and a radio. A shiny chrome plate on the back said Pontiac LeMans. My father fumbled for the keys in his pocket and let us all inside. He got behind the giant steering wheel. Tibor sat next to him in the front, and my mother and I got in the back.

"*Viggyáz, Laci,*" my mother said to my father as he backed out of the parking spot way too quickly, nearly hitting an oncoming car. "Be careful."

"I see it, I see it," he said, stepping on the brake, pulling forward and reversing again. I didn't know how he got that huge car to do what he wanted. It was as big as a boat.

Within moments, we were out of the building and on a busy highway surrounded by hundreds of other cars and huge, noisy trucks. It was all so fast, and scary. All I could see were the bright red lights ahead of us and glaring yellow lights coming at us. My father was pumping the gas pedal with his right foot and braking at the same time with his left. The car lurched ahead fitfully, making me dizzy. Oncoming cars flashed their lights at us; those passing us honked as we bounced along the highway in the green boat, but he didn't care. He just kept pumping away at the pedals and talking about the things we would see and do. "We go to City Island next week and you'll see the ocean. Then we go to the zoo and maybe see the Rockettes in Times Square." I didn't understand anything he was saying. I was exhilarated and terrified, like the time he lifted me high above his head at the Balaton and plunged me into the murky water before scooping me back up. Like the time he pushed my swing so high, like the time he lifted me to put an angel on the Christmas tree, then almost dropped me to the floor. I gripped the seat and tried to hold on for what dizzying adventures, what ups and downs would await with this man, my father, and the family I needed to get to know all over again.

"I hope she has the Herendi," I heard my father say to my brother.

"And some books," Tibor said.

"Did Mamika help you pack your bag?" my father asked me, his eyes flashing in the rearview mirror.

"Yes, she and Katus Néni packed them," I said, awkwardly to the back of his head. "The statue and the teacups too."

"It will be a miracle if they made it," Tibor said. "Those baggage handlers can be pretty rough on luggage." Then, turning to me, he said, "Do you remember if they wrapped it with tape?"

"I don't know," I said, worried now that all those precious things they wanted would be broken to bits.

"We'll know soon enough," my father said. "As soon as this traffic starts moving. I must be back on the highway early tomorrow to get back to the hospital . . . See Juditka, it's all work here in America. No time to rest. But maybe on Sunday, we go to Gimbel's, and we buy you a nice new coat, and we can go to the Howard Johnson's after. Wait 'till you see what big ice cream they make."

"She could use a new coat," my mother said. "Here, Juditka, wipe your nose with this." She pulled a soft white tissue from her pocketbook. It felt comforting against my chapped red skin.

"She looks sick," Tibor said, turning to my father.

My father looked at me again through the rearview mirror. "Aah, she'll be all right in a day or two. It's just a cold."

"But she looks so thin," Tibor added. "Did they not feed her anything over there?"

"Maybe a year's salary was not enough for food."

I thought back to my grandmother's magic pockets, to the chocolate bars she somehow found for me, to the fresh crescent rolls and chocolate milk for breakfast, to the cream of wheat sweetened with sugar and cocoa for supper. I thought back to Katus Néni's delicious meals on special days. It was not fancy but it was certainly enough. I may have been skinny, but I never went hungry. I wanted to tell them that really, they took good care of me. Despite the cold rooms with never enough coal to heat them, the muddy front yard, the frayed electrical wires, the never-ending work that kept my aunt and grandmother so busy, and Zoli Bácsi's constant hollering, they did the best they could. I was all right.

Sitting on the train heading to my grandmother's village all those years ago, I was so scared, not knowing what would happen, why we were going back there, where my parents were, what kept them from coming home.

Sitting now in the car that was like a boat on a roaring river that my father called the Major Deegan Expressway, I knew there'd be so much new to learn. I had some answers but there was also much more I wanted to know. I wondered about the people in the car, my family, why they left me, why they wanted so badly to come to America. But I also knew that whatever would come next, I'd be ready. My grandmother said a beautiful life was waiting. As the boat rocked and swerved, I held on to that.

Tibor turned around to look at me. "Not to worry, Juditka. "There is so much food in America, people literally throw out half of what they buy. This is an amazing country, you will see. They have thirty-one flavors at the ice cream store!"

In the front seat, Tibor and my father continued to talk about work and a place called Jersey City, about chemistry tests, and college applications, about Nixon and Vietnam and the traffic on the Major Deegan and the George Washington. Finally, the car slowed down and we got off the highway.

"Welcome to the Bronx," a sign said.

I looked out again to see if I could see any glittering shop windows or buildings that touched the sky. But all I could see was a store with a sign flashing red letters saying John's Bargain Store, and and a huge billboard hanging from what looked like a train station above a busy street. On it was a fearless woman with brilliant brown skin. KOOL, the giant letters announced.

In the back seat, my mother moved closer to me, and placed her hand on mine. "You must be hungry after such a long trip," she said quietly. Then from her small gray pocketbook she took out a big bright orange and began peeling the skin. The juice trickled down her fingers, as she broke off a bite-sized piece, taking care to peel the bitter white part from the sweetness that lay inside. She handed me the slice.

"Here," she said. "Try it."

EPILOGUE

I tasted the orange and many other new things in the years to come, both sweet and bitter. I learned that besides my godparents in Hungary, one man was responsible for my emigration: Jonathan Bingham, a congressman from the Bronx, who reached out to the Hungarian embassy, determined to reunite our family. A few weeks after arriving in America, I carefully rehearsed two sentences in English, so I could thank him properly on the local news.

I settled into life with parents and a brother who had become strangers, and public school in the Bronx where children played on asphalt behind an iron fence. I learned to speak English quickly and like all immigrant children, adapted. I made friends—Cuban, Korean, Puerto Rican and Jewish. I even learned to love peanut butter and fried fish sticks. Our home in the Bronx did not quite touch the sky, though it did rise six floors above the Major Deegan Expressway. And when we opened our windows in the spring, the scent from the Stella D'oro cookie factory was heavenly.

Over time, I came to know my parents as they were, here in this new place. My mother sat with me every night, teaching me English from a yellow illustrated children's dictionary. Her patience was endless. My father was gone all week, just like in Hungary, but returned every Saturday bearing smoked meat and rye bread. He drove us in his big green Pontiac to Gimbels Department store in New Jersey, where there was no tax on underwear, and to Howard Johnson's up the parkway, for an ice cream sundae so enormous, I cried when I could not eat it all. He took me to Manhattan to see The Rockettes, and to Vermont to taste maple syrup. He was so full of life and energy; it could scarcely be contained. This, I eventually came to realize, is why New York was his perfect place.

Tibor and I had grown up in such different worlds, we could never be real siblings again. He was more like a second father, teaching me how to ride a bicycle, taking me to Disney World, but like my father, never asking me what I wanted or how I felt about anything. He never got those things from our father, either. In some ways, he had it worse than me. Tibor witnessed a much harder side of our immigration story: he saw my mother cry in Rome when she watched little girls go to school, and again in New York, after the Hungarian officials told her to forget ever seeing me. He endured my father's messianic highs, leading them out of Hungary like Moses, and his abysmal lows, once almost jumping from their sixth-story window.

The painful days did not end when I arrived at John F. Kennedy Airport in February of 1974. My parents struggled to find jobs and keep jobs, to fit into a society that did not welcome them, and to cope with a past that was almost unfathomable. Unlike my Uncle János, my father was loathe to talk about his past or the Holocaust. I'd eventually learn those stories from others, including my mother, whose boundless love for him was always evident, though for the rest of his life, he'd walk ahead of her and never treated her as an equal.

We never talked about our separation. It was a secret locked away in a jar that no one dared open.

My mother and I returned to Hungary to visit my grandmother twice before she died in 1987. I towered above her and I hugged her tight. She had not changed at all, but I had, so much so that seeing her stooped in her black dress made me feel ashamed. Here I was, a teenager from America wearing bell bottom jeans; she'd been left behind in that drafty house with my uncle and aunt. But they too had changed. Both of Zoli Bácsi's legs had been amputated. He no longer scared me. In fact, all I could feel for him was pity. My aunt had withered into an even smaller version of herself. She still barely spoke.

About my coming to America, my grandmother was right. I did ultimately have a beautiful life, filled with more love than I could have ever imagined or hoped for. I graduated from college and went to work as a journalist, writing stories for newspapers in a second language that had become like a comfortable pair of jeans. I met a young poet with longish hair who taught me that love could be easy. We eventually made a family. And that's when I realized how hard a choice my parents made. Looking at Katie's precious face, feeling Leah's tiny fingers, listening to Joe's wise questions, I knew that it was a choice I could never make. I could barely leave them in a day care center for a few hours, let alone across the ocean, not knowing if I'd ever see them again.

Intellectually, I knew why my parents made the choice they did. Once I learned my father's history—the murder of his parents, his grandmother, and his little brother in Auschwitz, and his own unlikely survival—it was understandable why he would give up so much to escape. To this day, Hungary has failed to confront its collaboration with the Nazis, and its part in the confiscation of property and the murder of more than half a million Jews. It's a small country that lives in perpetual fear, while anti-Semitism and discrimination against Roma, refugees, and others who don't "fit the mold" persists. I look back on all the ways we were taught this racism against Jews and the Roma in the school yard and at home. It took me years to unlearn it. In America, my father was able to speak his mind, to make money and to spend money, to vote or not to vote, to observe his faith—or not. It was up to him, not some party *apparatchik*. And I am grateful for their choice and the life it has allowed me to build for my family and children.

What I had trouble understanding was the question of the heart. How do you leave behind your child, not knowing whether you'd ever see them again? But I was too afraid to confront my father, perhaps because I feared the answer: that maybe he loved his freedom, or the idea of it, more than he loved me.

I finally did ask my mother. She and I had grown close over the years. One of the happiest days of my life was when she moved in with my family. Surrounded by grandchildren who adored and loved her, she finally allowed herself to talk freely of the past. She left me, she told me, because she loved my father so very much, she could not imagine a life without him. She was afraid, she said, that he would one day say the wrong thing, and the Hungarian government would lock him away for good. She feared that he would be forcibly confined to a mental institution, where he would languish and die, broken and alone. She never said it was the wrong decision. Only that she could make no other. She chose her husband over her child. "I was a coward," she said, crying.

She did not ask me to forgive her. Nor was forgiveness needed. She did what she felt was right at the time out of love for him.

And ultimately, we all found an abundance of it.

ACKNOWLEDGEMENTS

As in all projects like this, there are many people to thank. First, as always, is Peter Temes, who always believed in me and this project, and supported and encouraged me at every step. I am also grateful to Roberta Temes, who read more versions of this manuscript than I can remember, and refused to allow me to give up. To my brother Tim Boros, thank you for sharing your own stories and understanding the importance of this one. To my children, thank you for your curiosity, questions, and appreciation of our past. Infinite thanks also go to Elizabeth Cohen, whose guidance was invaluable, Samme Chittum for her sharp edits, and Linda Morrison for shaping the final manuscript. I am deeply grateful to Nancy Nimoy for turning an old photograph of me into a work of art for the front cover, and Ron Starbuck of Saint Julian Press for stepping into the world of memoir publishing with this work. I am eternally grateful to you all.

NOTES

1. Epigraph: Adrienne Rich, "A Ball Is for Throwing,"
   POETRY, 1957, Volume XC Number 5, Page 303.

ABOUT THE AUTHOR

Judy Temes is a teacher, writer, and journalist whose work has been published in *Crain's New York Business, The Boston Globe, The Patriot Ledger,* and other publications. She lives in Seattle, WA.

Visit her author page at https://judytemes.wixsite.com/judy-temes

Typefaces Used:

TYPEFACE: GARAMOND – Garamond
¤ ¤ ¤   WINGDINGS – Wingdings

CPSIA information can be obtained
at www.ICGtesting.com
Printed in the USA
BVHW071200230621
610212BV00003B/138